The Enlightenment

Debate over the meaning of 'Enlightenment' began in the eighteenth century and still continues to this day. This period saw the opening of arguments on the nature of man, truth, the place of God, and the international circulation of ideas, people and gold, but did the Enlightenment mean the same for men and women, for rich and poor, for Europeans and non-Europeans? In the third edition of her acclaimed book, Dorinda Outram addresses these and other questions about the Enlightenment as controversy increases about its place at the foundation of modernity. She studies it as a global phenomenon, setting the period against broader social changes. This new edition offers a new chapter on political economy, a completely revised further reading section, and a new feature on electronic sources to stimulate primary research. This accessible overview will be essential reading for students of eighteenth-century history, philosophy and the history of ideas.

DORINDA OUTRAM is Clark Professor of History at the University of Rochester. Her previous publications include *Georges Cuvier: Science and Authority in Post-Revolutionary France* (1982), *Uneasy Careers and Intimate Lives: Women in Science, 1789–1979* (1987) and *The Body and the French Revolution: Sex, Class and Political Culture* (1989).

NEW APPROACHES TO EUROPEAN HISTORY

New Approaches to European History is an important textbook series, which provides concise but authoritative surveys of major themes and problems in European history since the Renaissance. Written at a level and length accessible to advanced school students and undergraduates, each book in the series addresses topics or themes that students of European history encounter daily: the series embraces both some of the more 'traditional' subjects of study and those cultural and social issues to which increasing numbers of school and college courses are devoted. A particular effort is made to consider the wider international implications of the subject under scrutiny. To aid the student reader, scholarly apparatus and annotation is light, but each work has full supplementary bibliographies and notes for further reading: where appropriate, chronologies, maps, diagrams, and other illustrative material are also provided.

For a complete list of titles published in the series, please see:

www.cambridge.org/newapproaches

The Enlightenment

Third Edition

Dorinda Outram
University of Rochester

CAMBRIDGE
UNIVERSITY PRESS

University Printing House, Cambridge CB2 8BS, United Kingdom

Published in the United States of America by Cambridge University Press, New York

Cambridge University Press is part of the University of Cambridge.

Itfurthers the University's mission by disseminating knowledge in the pursuit of education, learning and research at the highest international levels of excellence.

www.cambridge.org
Information on this title: www.cambridge.org/9781107636576

First published 1995
Reprinted 9 times
Second edition 2005
Eighth printing 2011
Third edition 2013
Reprinted 2013

Printed in the United Kingdom by the CPI Group Ltd, Croydon CR0 4YY

A catalogue record for this publication is available from the British Library

Library of Congress Cataloguing in Publication data
Outram, Dorinda.
The Enlightenment / Dorinda Outram. – 3rd ed.
p. cm. – (New approaches to European history)
Includes bibliographical references and index.
ISBN 978-1-107-02739-8 (hardback) – ISBN 978-1-107-63657-6 (pbk.)
1. Enlightenment. 2. Europe – Intellectual life – 18th century. I. Title.
B802.O98 2012
001.1094′09033 – dc23 2012027119

ISBN 978-1-107-02739-8 Hardback
ISBN 978-1-107-63657-6 Paperback

For Dr L

Contents

Illustrations

Chronology

1686	German Pietist August Francke opens Bible study at Leipzig; Charles, Duke of Lorraine, takes Buda from the Turks
1687	Isaac Newton, *Philosophiae Naturalis Principia Mathematica*
1688	William of Orange ousts James II as king of England
1689	John Locke, *Letters on Toleration*
1690	John Locke, *An Essay Concerning Human Understanding*
1691	New East India Company formed in London
1693	John Locke, *Thoughts Concerning Education*
1694	Founding of Bank of England. Birth of Voltaire
1695	John Locke, *The Reasonableness of Christianity*
1697	Peter the Great travels to Prussia, Holland, England and Vienna to study European technology and thought
1702	Asiento Guinea Company founded for slave trade between Africa and America
1704	Isaac Newton, *Optics*
1707	Political and legal union between England and Scotland. Linnaeus born
1709	First Copyright Act in Britain
1713	Abbé de St Pierre, *Projet pour la paix perpétuelle.* Peace of Utrecht closes War of Spanish Succession
1715	Louis XIV of France dies; succeeded by his great-grandson Louis XV, under Regency of the duc d'Orléans
1716	First company of English actors appears in North America at Williamsburg, Virginia
1717	Inoculation against smallpox introduced into England from Turkey by Lady Mary Wortley Montagu. First Freemasons' Lodge established in London
1718	Yale University founded at New Haven, Connecticut; New Orleans founded
1719	Daniel Defoe, *Robinson Crusoe*

1721	Montesquieu, *Lettres Persanes*; J. S. Bach, Brandenburg Concertos. Regular postal service between London and New England
1722	Daniel Defoe, *Moll Flanders*
1723	Ludovico Antonio Muratori publishes *Rerum italicarum scriptores*, 28 vols. of medieval documents. End of Regency in France. Bach, St John Passion
1724	Professorships of modern history founded at Oxford and Cambridge. Paris Bourse (Stock Exchange) opens
1725	Foundation of Petersburg Academy of Sciences; of Prague Opera House. Vico, *Principles of a New Science*
1726	Jonathan Swift, *Gulliver's Travels*. Voltaire arrives in England
1727	American Philosophical Society founded in Philadelphia. Isaac Newton dies
1728	Ephraim Chambers (ed.), *Cyclopaedia or An Universal Dictionary of Arts and Sciences*
1729	J. S. Bach, St Matthew Passion; Newton's *Principia* translated into English
1730	John and Charles Wesley found Methodism at Oxford
1731	Abbé Prévost, *Manon Lescaut*; Voltaire, *History of Charles XII*. Franklin founds subscription library at Philadelphia
1732	Covent Garden Opera House founded in London
1733	War of the Polish Succession opens. Alexander Pope, *Essay on Man*
1734	University of Göttingen founded; Koran translated into English by George Sale
1735	Francesco Algorotti, *Il newtonismo per le dame*; Carl Linnaeus, *Systema Naturae*
1738	Papal Bull *In eminenti* condemns Freemasonry. Excavations begin at Herculaneum. Voltaire, *Eléments de la philosophie de Newton*
1739	David Hume, *A Treatise of Human Nature*
1740	Frederick II becomes king of Prussia and founds Berlin Academy of Sciences. Maria Theresa becomes Empress of Austria. Frederick seizes Silesia, opening War of the Austrian Succession. Samuel Richardson, *Pamela*. George Anson begins circumnavigation of globe
1741	Handel composes *Messiah*
1746	Condillac, *Essai sur l'origine des connaissances humaines*
1747	La Mettrie, *L'homme machine*

1748 End of War of Austrian Succession; Marie-Thérèse Geoffrin opens *salon*; Samuel Richardson, *Clarissa*; David Hume, *Philosophical Essay Concerning Human Understanding*; Montesquieu, *De l'esprit des lois*

1750 Rousseau, *Discours sur les sciences et les arts*; Jewish sect of Hassidism founded

1751 First volume of Diderot and d'Alembert's *Encyclopédie*; David Hume, *Enquiry Concerning the Principles of Morals*; Voltaire, *Le Siècle de Louis XIV*; Pope Benedict XIV condemns Freemasonry

1752 First condemnation of the *Encyclopédie*

1754 David Hume, *History of Great Britain*; Diderot, *Pensées sur l'interprétation de la nature*; Rousseau, *L'inégalité parmi les hommes: discours*

1755 Earthquake in Lisbon; Samuel Johnson, *Dictionary of the English Language*

1756 Beginning of Seven Years' War

1758 Claude Adrien Helvétius, *De L'Esprit*; Rousseau, *Lettre à D'Alembert sur les spectacles*; Quesnay, *Tableau Economique*

1759 Second condemnation of the *Encyclopédie*; Jesuits expelled from Portugal; Voltaire, *Candide*; Charles III succeeds as king of Spain; Samuel Johnson, *Rasselas*; Adam Smith, *Theory of Moral Sentiments*; British Museum opens in London, at Montague House; Wolfe takes Quebec from the French

1760 George III becomes king of Great Britain

1761 Rousseau, *La Nouvelle Héloïse*

1762 Catherine II becomes Empress of Russia; Diderot, *Le Neveu de Rameau*; Rousseau, *Du Contrat social, Emile*; Calas trial

1763 Peace of Paris ends Seven Years' War. Voltaire, *Treatise on Toleration*

1764 Jesuits suppressed in France. *Salons* founded in Paris by Mme Necker and Julie de Lespinasse. Cesare Becarria, *Dei Delitti e dei Pene*; Voltaire, *Philosophical Dictionary*; J. J. Winckelmann, *History of Ancient Art*

1765 Joseph II becomes co-regent with his mother Maria Theresa; Turgot, *Réflexions sur la formation et la distribution des richesses*

1766 Adam Ferguson, *Essay on the History of Civil Society*; Bougainville begins voyage to Pacific

1767 Rousseau in England. Jesuits expelled from Spain and Naples. Laurence Sterne completes *Tristram Shandy*. Joseph Priestley, *The History and Present State of Electricity*

1768 Purchase of Corsica by France from Genoa; Quesnay, *Physiocratie*. James Cook's first voyage to the Pacific
1769 William Robertson, *History of Charles V*; Diderot writes *Le Rêve d'Alembert*
1770 Court doctor von Struensee becomes Chief Minister in Denmark. Cook lands at Botany Bay, Australia. Raynal, *Histoire . . . des Deux Indes*; d'Holbach, *Système de la Nature*
1771 French *Parlements* exiled. Rising tension between them and monarchy. First edition of *Encyclopaedia Britannica*. William Robertson, *History of America*; Arkwright produces first spinning mill; Luigi Galvani discovers electrical nature of nervous impulses; Lavoisier establishes composition of air
1772 Fall of Danish reformer Struensee; First Partition of Poland; James Cook's second circumnavigation begins
1773 Boston Tea Party. Pope Clement XIV dissolves Jesuit order
1774 Louis XV of France dies, succeeded by Louis XVI. Goethe, *The Sorrows of Young Werther*. Turgot becomes minister
1775 American War of Independence begins. Peasant revolt in Bohemia against serfdom; Beaumarchais, *The Barber of Seville*; 'Guerre des farines' in Paris and Northern France
1776 Declaration of Independence by American rebels, mainly drafted by Thomas Jefferson. Turgot forced out of government; Edward Gibbon, *Decline and Fall of the Roman Empire* (–1788); Adam Smith, *An Inquiry into the Nature and Causes of the Wealth of Nations*. James Cook begins third voyage into the Pacific
1778 James Cook discovers Hawaii. Deaths of Voltaire and Rousseau; Buffon, *Les époques de la nature*
1779 James Cook murdered. Serfdom suppressed in France and its colonies. David Hume, *Dialogues of Natural Religion* (posthumous publication)
1780 Empress Maria Theresa dies; Joseph II succeeds as sole ruler. Filangieri, *Science of Legislation*. Abolition of judicial torture in France
1781 Kant, *Critique of Pure Reason*; Rousseau, *Confessions*, published; Mendelssohn, *On the Civil Amelioration of the Condition of the Jews*
1782 Laclos, *Les Liaisons dangéreuses*
1783 American colonies win independence from Britain. Mendelssohn, *Jerusalem*, plea for religious toleration
1784 Bengal Asiatic Society founded by William Jones
1785 William Paley, *Principles of Moral and Political Philosophy*

1786 Death of Frederick II. Mozart, *Marriage of Figaro*
1787 Rising political tension in France. Meeting of the first Assembly of Notables. Lavoisier reforms chemical language with *Méthode de nomenclature chimique*. Mozart, *Don Giovanni*
1788 Elections for the Estates-General in France. Kant, *Critique of Practical Reason*. Pierre Simon de la Place, *Laws of the Planetary System*
1789 Estates General meets (May). Mutiny on the *Bounty*
1790 Joseph II dies. Edmund Burke, *Reflections on the Revolution in France*
1791 Thomas Paine, *The Rights of Man*
1792 Mary Wollstonecraft, *Vindication of the Rights of Women*. France at war with Austria and Prussia
1793 Second Partition of Poland. Condorcet, *Esquisse d'un tableau historique des progrès de l'esprit humain*

1 What is Enlightenment?

> The time will come when the sun will shine only on free men who have no master but their reason.
>
> (Condorcet)

The Enlightenment has been defined in many different ways. Even in the eighteenth century, contemporaries were well aware that when an Italian called this movement of ideas *Illuminismo*, he meant something other than the word *Lumières* which would have been used by a friend in France, or the *Aufklärung* current in the German states. With such diversity, it was no wonder that the Berlin pastor Johann Friedrich Zollner (1753–1824) in an article in the December 1783 number of the *Berlinische Monatsschrift* should have asked 'What is Enlightenment? This question is nearly as important as the question What is truth? This question must be answered before anyone can begin to enlighten themselves. And yet I have never seen it answered anywhere!' This question, hidden away in a footnote to an article on matrimonial law by an obscure pastor, was one of the most fruitful ever asked. Essays in answer to it began to be submitted to the *Monatsschrift* by leading thinkers. For the Jewish philosopher Moses Mendelssohn (1729–86), who published an essay in the September number in 1784, 'Enlightenment' referred to an as yet uncompleted process of education in the use of reason, which should be open to all. Mendelssohn therefore supported the movement for 'popular philosophy' which sought to spread Enlightenment ideas among lower social classes. Other competitors, such as Schiller, Herder, Wieland, Hamann, Riem and Lessing, some of the great names of the German Enlightenment, put forward quite different ideas, often, as did Schiller, emphasising aesthetics as defining the Enlightenment. These essays can be read as a compendium of the diverse meanings which by the end of the century had come to be attached to the word 'Enlightenment'.

The Prussian philosopher Immanuel Kant also participated in the competition. Kant wrote, in a now famous, though often misinterpreted essay, in the December 1784 number of the *Monatsschrift*, about the apparently paradoxical ways that Enlightenment should operate in the world. Kant believed that the use of reason should be as far developed as possible. Yet, he was well aware that the unbounded development of reason, if carried too far with unlimited questioning or redefining of current meanings, could dissolve social, religious and political order into chaos. On the other hand, Kant could also see the Enlightenment far more positively. Enlightenment is also, in a much quoted phrase, 'man's release from his self-incurred immaturity' through the use of reason without guidance from others. The ancient motto, '*Sapere aude!*' (Dare to know!), was, as Kant proclaimed early in his essay, the motto of the Enlightenment.

Yet the knowledge gained by such daring might not all be the same. Kant produced so many different interpretations of the Enlightenment in his essay that contemporaries sometimes regarded it as a satire on the meanings and uses of Enlightenment in the Prussian kingdom, whose king Frederick II replicated in his own person all the contradictory meanings of Enlightenment present in Kant's essay. Frederick regarded himself as 'enlightened', as even being himself a philosopher. He took personal care of the Berlin Academy of Sciences, yet was also interested in maintaining power over public opinion and religious controversy. As Kant remarked, reflecting this ambiguity: 'The public use of man's reason must always be free, and it alone can bring about Enlightenment among men; the private use of reason may be quite often seriously restricted.' In what he calls the public sphere, a place where people are free from the obligations of their calling, subjects are free to write or speak critically. In what he calls the private sphere, subjects have an actual duty to restrain the expression of wayward political judgement, in the interests of upholding the ruler's will and lessening the likelihood of the outbreak of chaos. The curate must not criticise the bishop, the soldier his superior officer, even if their commands seem absurd.

Kant thus poses, in different words, the same problem which appeared in Mendelssohn's essay: what happens if men think without limits? Does such thought necessarily have a positive outcome? Kant makes clear his irritation with those who saw Enlightenment as an uncomplicated progress towards the achievement of rational social and political change. For him it was clearly full of dangers, problems and contradictions. It was thus, even for contemporaries, very difficult to define 'Enlightenment'. For men like Immanuel Kant, though many others would have disagreed, Enlightenment seemed to present itself more as a series of processes and problems, rather than as a list of intellectual projects which could be resolved quickly and neatly.

It is helpful to follow Kant's lead, and to think about the Enlightenment as a series of interlocking, and sometimes warring problems and debates. These were problems and debates which affected how the Enlightenment worked not only in Europe, but also in the rest of the world. These are perceptions which will be incorporated into this book. This presentation of the Enlightenment sees this movement as a group of capsules or flash-points where intellectual projects changed society and government on a world-wide basis.

However, this is a new interpretation. Until quite recently, it was normal to understand the Enlightenment as ultimately a unitary phenomenon, as if there was an entity called *the* Enlightenment. This version of Enlightenment saw it as a desire for human affairs to be guided by rationality, rather than faith, superstition or revelation, a world view based on science, and not tradition. In this interpretation Enlightenment, in spite of its universal aspirations, was largely something which happened in France. French attitudes were taken as typical. Yet the hostility of thinkers like Voltaire and Diderot towards the Catholic Church was quite different from the profound interest in theological questions shown by such German thinkers as Christian Wolff and Leibniz. The questioning of royal and ecclesiastical power, which was so common in the French Enlightenment thinkers such as Diderot or Voltaire, found little echo in Germany before the 1790s, where a full-scale science of administration called *Cameralwissenschaft*, based on natural law and the interest of the common good, had already been developed.

It was also typical of this approach that the Enlightenment was presented as bounded by philosophy. The leading pre-war synthesis of the Enlightenment, Ernst Cassirer's 1932 *The Philosophy of the Enlightenment*, defined it as a period bounded by the lives of two philosophers: Gottfried Wilhelm Leibniz and Immanuel Kant. To be so bounded by movements in philosophy also implied that the Enlightenment was a-political. Interpretations today are very different, making Enlightenment very much nearer general history, and more concerned with the manifestations of Enlightenment beyond the works of leading thinkers in western Europe and especially France.

Cassirer's views on the Enlightenment were to a large extent reproduced in the leading synthesis of the post-war period. Peter Gay's two volumes, *The Rise of Modern Paganism* and *The Science of Freedom*, indicate his definitions of the Enlightenment. Like Cassirer, he defines the Enlightenment as a unity, and defines its chronology in terms of the lives of the great thinkers. For Gay, the first period of the Enlightenment was that of Voltaire, the second that of Denis Diderot, d'Alembert and Jean-Jacques Rousseau; the late Enlightenment is defined as the lifetimes of

Lessing and Kant. Gay defines the programme of the Enlightenment as one of hostility to religion, and as the search for freedom and progress, achieved by a critical use of reason to change man's relationship with himself and society. He sees the Enlightenment as a liberal reform programme, and dwells less on writers such as Rousseau, whose works cannot be easily fitted to this mould.

However, Gay also is one of the first to link the American colonies of England, and the later American Republic, to the Enlightenment. He discusses the American inventor, statesman and printer Benjamin Franklin, and the third President of the United States, Thomas Jefferson, and argues that the Declaration of Independence of 4 July 1776, and in particular its commitment to 'Life, Liberty and the Pursuit of Happiness', were the fulfilment of Enlightenment programmes. Gay's account thus recognises that the Enlightenment had found a place outside western Europe.

Gay's synthesis dominated the 1960s. By the next decade, however, new strands of analysis were coming to the fore, which emphasised a much more complete picture of the Enlightenment outside Europe. H. F. May's 1976 *The Enlightenment in America* was the first full modern treatment of this theme, and was followed by A. Owen Aldridge's work on the Enlightenment in the Spanish American colonies, his 1971 *The Ibero-American Enlightenment*. Both books made it impossible any longer to see the Enlightenment as a unified phenomenon, or one which was unaffected by geographical location. Aldridge in particular pointed to the difficulties of applying standard ideas of the Enlightenment to colonial societies living on European models and yet surrounded by largely incommensurable indigenous cultures.

Increasingly since the 1970s, historians have expanded the geographical area which they have been willing to see as affected by the Enlightenment. The Italian historian Franco Venturi sees Enlightenment as a force in Italy, Greece, the Balkans, Poland, Hungary and Russia, on the so-called periphery of Europe. Venturi's 1979 work, *Settecento riformatore*, and his *Utopia and Reform* of 1971, emphasised the transmission of ideas through newspapers, pamphlets, letters, books and political events which at the same time fed off and contributed to the western world of ideas. In fact, Venturi argued that it was precisely in these 'peripheral' areas where the stresses and strains within the Enlightenment could best be analysed.

By the 1970s it was also clear that historians were becoming far more interested in the social basis of the Enlightenment, in the problem of how ideas were transmitted, used and responded to by society. There was a recognition that more knowledge was needed of the now obscure and forgotten writers who in fact had been more widely read than had works by the great names. As Robert Darnton pointed out, the majority of books in the eighteenth century had not been produced by great minds, but by now forgotten professional writers, who wrote for the market anything from pornography to children's books, to handbooks for the traveller, to textbooks on Roman history. These commercial writers, far from regarding themselves as lofty public educators or scholars advancing knowledge, wrote simply in order to be able to afford to eat. It was but a small step to enquire into the economics of the Enlightenment, the creation of markets and the strategies of sales. Darnton investigated this using the case history of the *Encyclopédie* edited by Diderot and d'Alembert, in his 1979 *The Business of Enlightenment*. All this testifies to a new willingness to place the Enlightenment in comparative contexts. There is nowadays a multiplicity of paths into the Enlightenment.

The Enlightenment has, however, been unique amongst historical periods in the way it has been captured and put to use by philosophers wishing to substantiate their writings about the present, and to define modernity itself. Such different philosophers as Max Horkheimer and Theodor Adorno, Jürgen Habermas and Michel Foucault, have used the Enlightenment as a jumping-off place to comment on the present. Rather surprisingly, their work, although produced to gain a leverage on the present rather than to gain an accurate picture of the past, has become an icon for many historians of the period, perhaps glad to have presented to them a convenient paradigm of their period, validated by the renown (as philosophers) of intellectual great names.

In 1947, Horkheimer and Adorno published their *Dialectic of Enlightenment*. Writing in the immediate aftermath of World War II and the Holocaust, the authors examined 'why mankind, instead of entering into a truly human condition, is sinking into a new kind of barbarism'. This happened, in their view, because of the paradoxical nature of the Enlightenment. As they write in the Introduction to the *Dialectic*:

> The Enlightenment had always aimed at liberating men from fear and establishing their sovereignty. Yet the fully enlightened earth radiates disaster triumphant. The program of the Enlightenment was the disenchantment of the world: the dissociation of myths and the substitution of knowledge for fancy.

Man gained control over nature, and then over other human beings, by controlling them 'rationally' through the use of technology. This means that nature is no longer seen as the location of mysterious powers and forces. Enlightenment in this view is ultimately totalitarian in the sense that it abandons the quest for meaning and simply attempts to exert power over nature and the world. The Enlightenment relies on 'rationality', reasoning which is free from superstition, mythology, fear and revelation, which is often based on mathematical 'truth', which calibrates ends to means, which is therefore technological, and expects solutions to problems which are objectively correct.

But it is notorious that human beings often fail to arrive at rational solutions. Having given up non-rational ways of explanation like mythology or revelation, the only way to resolve such differences was by the use of force. At the heart of the Enlightenment lurks political terror. Horkheimer and Adorno thus argued that the Enlightenment had left no legacy which could resist the technologically assured man-made mass death of the Holocaust. Gas ovens relied upon modern chemistry, the calibration of food to individual in labour camps was minutely developed. Trains, one of the technological triumphs of the century, brought hundreds of thousands to extermination camps, on minutely calibrated timetables and fuel. Human beings were treated as mere objects to be administered, and then consumed by a 'rational' technological system at its starkest expression.

Another important interpretation of the Enlightenment is far more positive. The German philosopher Jürgen Habermas adopted many of the insights of Horkheimer and Adorno into the way in which the Enlightenment consumed culture, turned culture into a commodity, and turned knowledge into information. These are themes which are pursued in Chapter 2. For Habermas, however, other potentials of the Enlightenment still made its ideas worth pursuing. Habermas followed Kant's perception that far from being an epoch which was closed and over, the Enlightenment had still to be brought to completion. The Enlightenment, he argued, contained the potential for emancipating individuals from restrictive particularism in order to be able to act, not as 'Germans' embattled by adherence to a particular national and cultural ethos, but rather as human beings engaged in a common search with other human beings for universal values such as freedom, justice and objectivity. Habermas thus also opposed even thinkers of the Enlightenment itself, such as Johann Gottfried Herder (1744–1803) who had decried attempts to override feelings of local identity based on culture, religion and language.

Habermas also saw the Enlightenment as the creator of what he called the 'public realm'. This meant that a 'public opinion' could arise and start to question privileged traditional forces. Habermas' public realm is a space, very like Kant's 'private realm', where men could escape from their role as subjects and gain autonomy in the exercise and exchange of their own opinions and ideas. Very differently from Horkheimer's and

Adorno's accounts, Habermas reinterpreted the culture of the Enlightenment as a world where knowledge retained its capacity to liberate through criticism, even while remaining a commodity. He was also demonstrating the possibility of historical analysis filled with moral meaning for the present.

Habermas' work converged with that of the influential philosopher Michel Foucault, who had himself published philosophical interpretations of historical eras, such as his book *Discipline and Punish* on the growth of institutions of confinement for criminals and other groups, or *Madness and Civilisation*, about differing definitions of madness and the growth of asylums. Like Habermas, Foucault saw Kant's essay as the major definition of the Enlightenment. Abandoning earlier positions in which he had argued that there was no continuity between Enlightenment and the modern world, Foucault took up Kant's view that the Enlightenment was not complete, and used Kant's essay as the starting point for a new understanding of the idea of the critical use of reason in the public realm as an agent for change. Both thinkers agreed on the importance of the Enlightenment as a yardstick by which to assess the present. All these debates may be approached in Paul Rabinow's 1984 collection of essays, *The Foucault Reader*.

Enough has now been said to show that the Enlightenment has been interpreted in many different ways. The Enlightenment is very unusual in the extent to which its historical study has been influenced by analyses originating in philosophical enquiry. Foucault, Habermas, Horkheimer and Adorno, not to mention Kant and Hegel, have not only shaped ideas about the structure of Enlightenment thought; they have also written with the conviction that the Enlightenment is not a closed historical period, but one which, whether for good or ill, is still at work in the present. As we have seen, recent writing on the Enlightenment by professional historians has opened up new areas of enquiry, especially in the social history of ideas, rather than maintaining the former concentration on the works of a canon of great thinkers. We are now far more aware of the many different Enlightenments, whether national or regional, Catholic or Protestant, of Europeans and of indigenous peoples. This diversity mirrors the inability of eighteenth-century people themselves to make any single definition of Enlightenment.

This chapter has maybe implied that, in the end, the term 'the Enlightenment' has ceased to have much meaning. A more positive reaction might be to think of the Enlightenment not as an expression which has failed to encompass a complex historical reality, but rather as a capsule containing sets of debates which appear to be characteristic of the way in which ideas and opinions interacted with society and politics.

Yet, in spite of all the ways in which Enlightenment interpretation has changed over the past decades, Enlightenment scholars have yet to come to grips with the issues of the relationship between the Enlightenment and the creation of a global world. By globalisation is meant here the study of the history of the factors which, with accelerating speed since the Enlightenment, have come together to make the world a single system. Such factors might include the large-scale movements of people, especially through the organised slave trade; the formation of interconnected markets in commodities and in capital; the world-wide circulation of certain commodities, such as tea, furs, cotton, whale oil and gold; the expansion of merchant fleets to transport these commodities; the state financing of geographical exploration which demonstrated how oceans and continents were linked; the emergence of transcontinental European empires very often administered on standardised bureaucratic models, and the emergence of multinational trading companies, such as the Hudson's Bay Company, the British East India Company, and its Dutch equivalent, the VOC.

Globalisation was a world drama. This was the time in which European ideas, beliefs and institutions began to be spread into the rest of the world. Cross-cultural contact became an increasingly common experience, and one which for the Europeans often crossed social as well as cultural barriers. Sailors working in the merchant fleet or in the royal navies, East India Company soldiers, the artisan missionaries sent out by the Moravian church from Siberia to the West Indies, clerks employed by the trading companies, trappers working for the Hudson's Bay Company, represent only a small sample of working-class people who, just as much as naval or scientific elites, made the global world.

How have historians of the Enlightenment dealt with this global story? The answer is that few indeed have tried to integrate the creation of a unified world with the structures of Enlightenment thought. Many general historians are working on the problem of increasing global contacts, but again, few relate it to Enlightenment ideas, or the problems raised by globalisation. This is the more surprising in that some Enlightenment thinkers were already working out what a world history would look like. Schiller, Herder, and lesser figures like the Göttingen Professor Schlüter all wrote world histories, in Schlüter's case for both adults and children. These were also important because the genre of world history had existed before, but was written as an account of God's will working itself out in the world of men. Now, world history was being reworked as the global history of men.

One of the most convincing recent demonstrations of the link between Enlightenment and the globalisation of the Enlightenment has come from the historian Jorge Canizares-Esguerra. His work concentrates on eighteenth-century Mexico and the ways in which historians of European descent tried to work out the meanings of the histories written by indigenous peoples before and after the Spanish conquest. This task was of great importance not just for scholars on both sides of the Atlantic working on this problem and trying to set rules of historical interpretation, but also because this was a time when colonial elites were beginning to detach themselves from Spain. One part of this cultural detachment, part of the long run-up to the wars of independence of the 1820s, was to construct a history which emphasised not the dependence of the colonists on the Crown, but how scientific, professional men and colonial administrators, as well as indigenous elites, had constructed a world which was hardly in need of the Crown government in Madrid, but had entered the international community. The working out of the rules of evidence for history, the techniques of documentary interpretation and the interpretation of pictorial evidence, were also debated at this time in Europe, and thus incorporated the Mexican historians in important debates three thousand miles away.

Three thousand miles would be a small measurement in the scale of Richard Groves' 1995 *Green Imperialism*. Groves looks at the eighteenth-century international link between standardised institutions, like botanical gardens, acclimatisation stations and geodesic stations. He for example demonstrates that debates about the causes of deforestation took place world-wide between professional botanists and agronomists, as a matter for urgent decision-making. Botany and ecology became part of empire-building and the management for resources of states. Botanical decisions were also inevitably bound up in the growth of the large-scale empires of the eighteenth century.

Enlightenment had many meanings. In order to understand how it could affect so many levels of society and politics, and be present not just in Europe, but throughout most other parts of the world touched by European influence, we turn in the next chapter to explore the new social and economic background to the production and marketing of ideas in this period.

2 Coffee houses and consumers: the social context of Enlightenment

> In opulent or commercial society, besides, to think or reason comes to be, like every other employment, a particular business, which is carried on by a very few people, who furnish the public with all the thought and reason possessed by the vast multitudes that labour. Only a very small part of any ordinary person's knowledge has been the product of personal observation or reflection. All the rest has been purchased, in the same manner as his shoes or his stockings, from those whose business it is to make up and prepare for the market that particular species of goods.
>
> (Adam Smith)[1]

Introduction

Recent historical research has focussed overwhelmingly on the social context in which Enlightenment ideas were produced, received and marketed. Historians such as Robert Darnton have produced a wealth of new information on the readers, the writers and the entrepreneurial publishers of the increasingly large number of books, newspapers and pamphlets sold in this period.[2] Historians such as Roger Chartier and Robert Muchembled have examined the penetration of Enlightenment ideas from the elite to the lower social classes, from 'high' to 'low' culture.[3] Others have focussed on the spread of literacy, and the changing nature

1 W. R. Scott, *Adam Smith as Student and Professor* (Glasgow, 1937), 344–5, from draft for the Wealth of Nations composed in 1769.

2 R. Darnton, *The Great Cat Massacre and other Episodes in French Cultural History* (New York, 1984); 'The High Enlightenment and the Low-Life of Literature in Pre-Revolutionary France', *Past and Present*, 51 (1971), 81–115; *The Business of Enlightenment: A Publishing History of the Encyclopédie 1775–1800* (Cambridge, MA, 1979); *The Literary Underground of the Old Regime* (Cambridge, MA, 1982); *Mesmerism and the End of the Enlightenment in France* (Cambridge, MA, 1968).

3 Roger Chartier, *Cultural History: Between Practices and Representations* (Ithaca, NY, 1988); Robert Muchembled, *Popular Culture and Elite Culture in France, 1400–1750* (London, 1985) translated from his *Culture populaire et culture des élites dans la France moderne* (Paris, 1978).

of the experience of reading.[4] The importance of visual representations – pictures, engravings, stage-sets, statues in public places – in the transmission of ideas, alongside the written word, has been closely examined by historians such as Thomas Crow.[5] Many writers have also pointed to the establishment, all over Europe, of new institutions and organisations where ideas could be explored and discussed. Some of these institutions, like masonic lodges, learned academies and societies, were formal affairs, whose membership was carefully controlled.[6] Others, such as public lectures, coffee houses, lending libraries, art exhibitions, operatic and theatrical performances, were nearly all commercial operations, open to all who could pay, and thus provided ways in which many different social strata could be exposed to the same ideas.[7] These different media and social institutions focussed on the diffusion and interchange of ideas and together formed what Jürgen Habermas has described as the 'new public sphere' of the eighteenth century.[8] Later in this chapter we will be examining Habermas' ideas more closely and asking what impact, if any, the social setting of ideas produced on the nature of ideas themselves in the Enlightenment.

That social setting, however, was also the result of very large social and political changes in Europe and in the rest of the world. In most areas, especially in western Europe and North America, the eighteenth century was a time of economic expansion, increasing urbanisation, rising population and improving communications in comparison to the stagnation of the previous century. In some areas of north-west Europe agricultural production also rose significantly. Parts of Britain, the Netherlands and northern Italy entered what historians have decided to call 'the Industrial Revolution'. Production of many goods by artisans in relatively small

4 R. A. Houston, *Literacy in Early Modern Europe* (London, 1988); R. Darnton, 'First Steps towards a History of Reading', *Australian Journal of French Studies,* 23 (1986), 5–30.

5 Thomas Crow, *Painters and Public Life in Eighteenth-Century Paris* (New Haven, CT, and London, 1985).

6 D. Roche, *Le siècle des lumières en Province: Académies et académiciens provinciaux, 1680–1789* (2 vols.; Paris and The Hague, 1978); M. C. Jacob, *The Radical Enlightenment: Pantheists, Freemasons and Republicans* (London, 1981); N. Hans, 'UNESCO of the Eighteenth Century: La Loge des Neuf Soeurs and its Venerable Master Benjamin Franklin', *Proceedings of the American Philosophical Society,* 97 (1953), 513–24; G. Gayot, *La franc-maçonnerie française. Textes et pratiques, XVIIIe–XIXe siècles* (Paris, 1980).

7 By 1760, Vienna alone had at least sixty coffee houses. London and Amsterdam had many more; Crow, *Painters and Public Life,* 104–34; J. Lough, *Paris Theatre Audiences in the Seventeenth and Eighteenth Centuries* (Oxford: Oxford University Press, 1957); R. M. Isherwood, 'Entertainment in the Parisian Fairs of the Eighteenth Century', *Journal of Modern History,* 63 (1981), 24–47.

8 J. Habermas, *The Structural Transformation of the Public Sphere: An Enquiry into a Category of Bourgeois Society* (Cambridge, MA, 1989), trans. by T. Burger from *Strukturwandel der Öffentlichkeit* (Darmstadt, 1962).

workshops often under trade guild regulation was replaced for many commodities by production in large factories. Many more objects could be produced in the factories because of increased use of machines to perform tasks hitherto the preserve of skilled human labour. Through 'division of labour' every production process was broken down into its smallest components and the skilled craftsman making an entire object from start to finish was to some extent replaced by unskilled labour which was capable of only one small part of that process. This change, whatever its social consequences, enabled greater quantities of consumer goods to be made at lower prices; rising population and better communications enabled these goods to find purchasers and thus boosted manufacturing profits.[9] The increasing volume of goods made and sold included many consumer items such as books, pamphlets, newspapers, pictures, all of which were media for the transmission of ideas and attitudes.[10] Trade in such cultural media between European countries was aided by the increasing practice of translation and also by the fact that in most countries, with the exception of Britain, social elites were trained in the use of French, which in this period almost completely replaced Latin as an international language. It is this increasing trade in cultural media which makes it possible to understand those violent impacts between new ideas and old traditions which Franco Venturi identified as one of the most important ways in which Enlightenment thinking was formed in Europe.[11]

Nor was this trade in cultural media confined to Europe. By the eighteenth century many European states possessed colonial Empires in the Americas, the Caribbean, India and what is now Indonesia. To these colonies, ideas arrived in the trading ships sent out from Europe. Nor was this a one-way traffic, either in commodities or in ideas. Colonial products such as tea, coffee and sugar were vital to the coffee and tea-houses of Europe, where customers met to drink, talk and read the newspapers or the latest books; just as importantly the colonial experience of indigenous cultures was to send back shocks into the Enlightenment in Europe. In the end, the global exchange of ideas, like all market exchanges, broke down barriers between cultural systems, religious divides, gender differences and geographical areas. It promoted a

[9] P. Mathias, *The First Industrial Revolution*, 2nd edn (London, 1983); M. Berg, *The Age of Manufactures: Industry, Innovation and Work in Britain, 1700–1820* (London, 1985).

[10] N. McKendrick, John Brewer and J. H. Plumb, *The Birth of a Consumer Society: The Commercialisation of Eighteenth-Century England* (London, 1982); T. H. Breen, '"Baubles of Britain": The American and Consumer Revolutions of the Eighteenth-Century', *Past and Present*, 19 (1988), 73–104; G. Barber, 'Books from the Old World and for the New: the British International Trade in Books in the Eighteenth-Century', *Studies on Voltaire and the Eighteenth Century*, 151 (1976), 185–224; Darnton, *The Business of Enlightenment*.

[11] See Chapter 1.

new kind of equality between the 'consumers' of culture, all who could pay for the same book or picture. It also contributed to the increasing homogenisation of the world manifested in the breakdown of indigenous cultural systems and the beginning of the world-wide imposition of the cultural systems generated by Europeans which we became familiar with in the twentieth century. This process of cultural homogenisation continued apace, in spite of the numerous criticisms to which it was subjected at the end of the Enlightenment.[12] In spite of the emergence of forms of cultural nationalism within some European states by the 1790s, European culture when it came into contact with that of indigenous peoples still had the same effect of causing the collapse of indigenous cultural systems.

In spite of the importance of the visual media and performing arts as vehicles of ideas in this period, it is clear that the printed word occupied a unique position in the transmission of ideas. Books and pamphlets could be easily sold in large numbers, were relatively portable, and could cross language, cultural and geographical boundaries more easily. It is thus important to find out about how and to what extent the printed word was received in the eighteenth century. Historians of literacy, however, have faced notorious problems in estimating how widespread was the ability to read or write. Few historical sources bear directly on this problem and historians have often disputed the very meaning of 'literacy' itself: does it mean fluent reading and writing skills or can its incidence really be indicated, as some have argued, by the numbers of those able to sign their names to surviving formal legal documents?[13] There are additional complications to any such estimates when we realise the great differences in the teaching of reading and writing between our own day and school practice in the eighteenth century. Robert Darnton has pointed out that in Catholic Europe most people were taught to read only to enable them to follow the Latin of the Mass and never gained any fluency in reading the vernacular. Numbers of those affected by elementary schooling are thus not indicators of literacy as we would understand it.[14]

Most of the data that historians use to estimate literacy levels are thus indirect indications, often stemming from social elites. All the indirect indications that we have, however, do point to an increase in the numbers

12 See Chapter 5.

13 Houston, *Literacy*; François Furet and Jacques Ozouf (eds.), *Reading and Writing: Literacy in France from Calvin to Jules Ferry* (Cambridge, 1982); trans. from *Lire et écrire: L'alphabétisation des français de Calvin à Jules Ferry* (Paris, 1977), contentions that literacy is inherently critical, opening the way to the mobilisation of mass challenge to the existing order, are themselves critically examined in J. Markoff, 'Literacy and Revolt', *American Journal of Sociology*, 92 (1986), 323–49.

14 Darnton, 'First Steps Towards a History of Reading'.

of books, newspapers, journals and pamphlets printed and purchased in this period: and while, strictly speaking, this increase does not prove that a greater number of persons in Europe could read and write fluently, it is a finding certainly congruent with that conclusion. Records of book fairs, for example, show an increasing number of titles being printed. So do the records of the literary censorships established by many governments, especially in Austria and France.[15] Increasing numbers of libraries were opened to the public, some on a commercial basis, some, like the Royal Library in Paris, being hitherto private institutions. Analysis of wills left by private individuals more frequently mentions books among the deceased's possessions, even at quite low social levels.[16] All these indications are fragmentary and it is often hard to make comparisons between different parts of Europe at the same time. Nonetheless, all the indirect indicators point in the same direction: that familiarity with the printed word was spreading throughout society.

Some historians have also argued that the experience of reading itself changed quite dramatically in this period. The German historian Rolf Engelsing has gone so far as to argue that a 'reading revolution' took place by the end of the eighteenth century. Until about 1750, he argues, people read 'intensively'. They possessed only a few books, such as a Bible, devotional works or an almanac; in the English-speaking world, Bunyan's *Pilgrim's Progress* was a typical work found among the books of poorer households. These books were read over and over again, sometimes in silence by their owners, but were just as often read aloud to an audience of family and friends. In this way even illiterates gained exposure to the printed word. By the late eighteenth century, Engelsing argues, people were tending to read 'extensively', by which he means reading many printed works once only and then passing quickly on to others. Engelsing also believes that 'extensive' reading was accompanied by an increasing tendency for reading to be done alone, for it to become a solitary, introspective habit, rather than a social one.[17] Insofar as this

[15] In 1764, the Leipzig book-fair catalogue included 5,000 titles of newly published books; by 1800 the number had risen to 12,000: Paul Raabe, 'Buchproduktion und Lesepublikum in Deutschland 1770–1780', *Philobiblon*, 21 (1977), 2–16. Similar trends are discernible in France: Robert Estivals, *La statistique bibliographique de la France sous la monarchie au XVIIIe siècle* (Paris and The Hague, 1965); and in colonial North America: G. T. Tanselle, 'Some Statistics on American Printing, 1764–1783', in B. Bailyn and W. B. Hench (eds), *The Press and the American Revolution* (Boston, MA, 1981), 315–64.

[16] Darnton, 'Towards a History of Reading', 10–12; Daniel Roche, *Le Peuple de Paris: Essai sur la culture populaire au XVIIIe siècle* (Paris, 1981), 204–41; Rudolf Schenda, *Volk ohne Buch. Studien zur Socialgeschichte der populären Lesestoffe, 1700–1910* (Frankfurt-am-Main, 1970), 461–7.

[17] Rolf Engelsing, 'Die Perioden der Lesergeschichte in der Neuzeit. Das statische Ausmass und die Soziokulturelle Bedeutung der Lektüre', *Archiv für Geschichte des Buchwesens*, 10

change penetrated the lower social classes, it made it more difficult for illiterates to have access to the ideas and attitudes carried by the printed word. This is an attractively simple picture, seemingly well able to explain the origins of our own reading habits today, which are certainly predominantly 'extensive', private and silent. It is also an argument supported by the American historian David Hall, who has described a similar transformation in the reading habits of New Englanders between 1600 and 1850. By the late eighteenth century, New England communities seemed likewise to have abandoned their reliance on a limited repertoire of devotional works and were almost swamped with new genres – novels, newspapers, children's books, travel and natural history – each ravenously absorbed and then discarded for the next.[18] However, it is possible that Engelsing's and Hall's depiction of changes in reading habits is too schematic and based only on small samples of their chosen region. It is also easy to point to much evidence of 'intensive' reading surviving even among the social elites, for example in the many autobiographies which mention obsessional *re*-reading of certain works, and especially of the great best-sellers, such as Samuel Richardson's *Pamela* (1740) and *Clarissa* (1747–8), Jean Jacques Rousseau's *Julie ou la Nouvelle Héloïse* (1761) or Johann Wolfgang von Goethe's *Sorrows of Young Werther* (1774).[19] But while there are certainly many indications that the picture is more complex than some historians have maintained, it still does seem that the late eighteenth century in particular, especially for the upper social classes, was a turning point, a time when more reading material of a more varied character was eagerly seized upon by a broader reading public than ever before.

No doubt this development was encouraged because physical access to printed materials also became easier in many different ways. The growth of cheap commercial lending libraries allowed many to read 'extensively' who did not possess the financial resources sufficient to build up a large private collection of books. Coffee houses offered newspapers and journals and some of the latest books for the use of customers, for the price of a cup of coffee. Booksellers' shops sometimes also offered light refreshments and a small circulating library for the use of patrons.

(1969), cols. 944–1002; *Der Bürger als Leser: Lesergeschichte in Deutschland, 1500–1800* (Stuttgart, 1974).

[18] David Hall, 'The Uses of Literacy in New England, 1600–1850', in W. L. Joyce (ed.), *Printing and Society in Early America*, 1–47.

[19] This so-called 'Lesewut' or 'reading fever' is treated in Kurt Rothmann, *Erläuterungen und Dokumente: Johann Wolfgang Goethe: Die Leiden des jungen Werthers* (Stuttgart, 1974); R. Darnton, 'Readers Respond to Rousseau: the Fabrication of Romantic Sensitivity', in *The Great Cat Massacre*, 215–56.

The very existence of such institutions was dependent on the regular trade in colonial products, on a rising population and the increasing numbers of people living in towns.

They also made possible the penetration of ideas expressed in print to both genders and to social strata well outside the elites. This increasing phenomenon was helped by the change in the very nature of the books published. The switch from publishing in Latin to publishing in living languages helped many to read, particularly women, who lacked the necessary classical schooling to read fluently in Latin. Devotional and theological works seem to have lost their pre-eminent position as reading material. By the late eighteenth century, borrowing in German, English and North American libraries had fallen into strikingly similar patterns. Over 70 per cent of books borrowed fell into the category of novels; 10 per cent for history, biography and travel; less than 1 per cent for religious works.[20] In other words, this period saw the rise of the novel, directly at the expense of theology, as the major vehicle in which readers encountered ideas and attitudes. It is thus not surprising that many Enlightenment novels are as concerned with conveying factual information and discussing controversial points of view as they are in weaving an imaginative narrative structure.[21]

All these changes in reading were necessarily accompanied by profound changes in the social position of writers and publishers. Writers of all countries were often collectively described as belonging to an idealised 'Republic of Letters'. In 1780, the editor of the literary survey the *Histoire de la République des Lettres en France* described the 'Republic of Letters' as existing:

> In the midst of all the governments that decide the fate of men; in the bosom of so many states, the majority of them despotic . . . there exists a certain realm which holds sway only over the mind . . . that we honour with the name Republic, because it preserves a measure of independence, and because it is almost its essence to be free. It is the realm of talent and of thought.

Members of this Republic, he went on, 'form a species by their merit, and gain a reputation as brilliant as that of the great powers of the earth'.[22]

[20] D. Roche, *Les républicains des lettres: Gens de culture et lumières au XVIIIe siècle* (Paris, 1988). Albert Ward, *Book Production, Fiction and the German Reading Public, 1740–1800* (Oxford, 1974); the classic work is still Daniel Mornet, 'Les enseignements des bibliothèques privées (1750–1780)', *Revue d'histoire littéraire de la France*, 17 (1910), 449–96.

[21] Ian Watt, *The Rise of the Novel* (London, 1957); Michael McKeon, *The Origins of the English Novel, 1660–1740* (Baltimore, MD, and London, 1987).

[22] Quoted in L. Daston, 'The Ideal and Reality of the Republic of Letters in the Enlightenment', *Science in Context*, 4 (1991), 367–86 (367–8); from Anon., *Histoire de la République*

By 1780, these ideas had become commonplace. The idea that writers as knowledge and opinion shapers formed a sort of power which was as formidable as that of organised governments, the idea of equality between all those involved in the Republic of Letters, the values of cosmopolitanism, the idea that knowledge and its producers acted across political boundaries, were all very much to the fore in the Enlightenment.

How far did such ideas correspond to reality? How accurately did they describe the lives and social situations of those who wrote the books, the increased circulation of which fuelled the Enlightenment? This is a topic which has attracted much attention in recent decades and the results of historical research in this field have done much to undermine the older picture of the Enlightenment as the work of a small group of great thinkers. Historians have pointed out that the books most widely read in the Enlightenment were often written by men and women whose names are never mentioned in the canon of great Enlightenment thinkers.[23] These authors were professional writers for a commercial market in the written word, turning out to order books and pamphlets on subjects ranging from political scandal to pornography, to newspaper articles, book reviews, children's books, novels, theatrical scripts and opera libretti, to retellings of medieval romances for the rural audiences of cheap publishers, to popular science and travel books. It was these writers, rather than the elite such as Diderot and Voltaire, who produced the bulk of what was actually read in the Enlightenment. Called collectively 'Grub Street' by Robert Darnton, its very existence demonstrated a great change in the position of writers.[24] Most writers of previous centuries had gained the greater part of their incomes from commissions from personal patrons often drawn from the church, the royal courts or the aristocracy, who often regarded artists and writers in their employment as little more than skilled craftsmen. Such relationships had often involved a high degree of personal and political dependency and social subservience. By the eighteenth century such relationships were very far from over and many, like the musicians Mozart and Haydn, for example, led lives which contained large elements both of personal patronage and of writing for a large commercial audience.[25] But in spite of this incomplete transition,

des Lettres en France (Paris, 1780), 5–6. See also S. Neumeister and C. Wiedemann (eds.), *Res Publica Litteraria: Die Institutionen der Gelehrsamkeit in der frühen Neuzeit* (Wiesbaden, 1987).

23 Daniel Mornet, 'Les enseignements des bibliothèques privées'.

24 Darnton, 'The High Enlightenment'; *The Literary Underground of the Old Régime.*

25 Wolfgang Amadeus Mozart (1756–91) was at various points under the patronage of the Prince-Bishop of Salzburg until 1781, but also wrote his operas for general performance; Joseph Haydn (1732–1809) spent much of his life under the patronage of the Esterhazy

it was still widely felt that a very different social situation was in the process of creation for the producers of ideas and cultural objects and perhaps especially for writers. In the 1740s, for example, the mathematician and thinker Jean d'Alembert (1717–83) was arguing passionately for the independence of men of letters from personal patronage.[26] Such independence was necessary, he argued, if objective, impartial opinions were to be produced and also to maintain reasonable equality between members of the Republic of Letters. By the 1750s, Denis Diderot (1713–84) could point to the real existence of such a group of men of letters, which alone, he remarked, made possible the appearance of large collaborative ventures such as the *Encyclopédie* (or Encyclopedia of Arts and Sciences) which he was to publish between 1751 and 1772.[27]

However, the emergence of 'Grub Street', of a distinct community of writers independent from personal patronage, could not in practice guarantee the equality which was one of the ideals of the Republic of Letters. There was little in common in reputation between such well-known thinkers and writers as Diderot and d'Alembert, who consorted with monarchs and aristocrats, in spite of their lowly social origins, and obscure hacks turning out pot-boilers in basements and attics. In terms of income, too, there was little comparison between the wealth obtained by some writers such as Voltaire and the precarious existences which Robert Darnton has chronicled for 'Grub Street'. Nor was the Republic of Letters so united in its attitudes towards the powers that be as its idealised description implied. In a controversial article, Darnton has depicted the members of 'Grub Street' as envenomed with envy of the status of the small literary elite, manifesting their alienation from the literary establishment by forceful criticism, which Darnton identifies as one factor leading to the break-up of the Old Regime in France and the opening of a revolutionary situation at the close of the century.[28] Whether or not this latter contention is true, it is certain that attacks from 'Grub

family in Hungary, but also wrote for the open 'market' in music during prolonged stays in London.

26 Jean d'Alembert, 'Essai sur la société des gens de lettres et des grands, sur la réputation, sur les mécènes, et les récompenses littéraires', in *Mélanges de littéraire, d'histoire et de philosophie* (Amsterdam, 1759).

27 The *Encyclopédie* has been used by Robert Darnton as a test-case for the commercialised diffusion of the ideas of the Enlightenment in *The Business of Enlightenment*. Diderot noted the importance of a large literary community for the preparation of the *Encyclopédie*: 'you will be obliged to have recourse (rather than to learned societies or famous individuals) to a large number of men of different sorts and conditions – men of genius to whom the gates of the academies are closed by reason of their low rank in the social scale': entry *Encyclopédie*, reprinted in K. M. Baker, *The Old Régime and the French Revolution* (Chicago and London, 1987), 71–89, esp. 74.

28 Darnton, 'The High Enlightenment'.

Street' on the *status quo* were bolder and more direct than much of what issued from the pen of the literary elites – who were often, as for example were Diderot and Voltaire, either paid or pensioned by reigning monarchs, such as the Empress Catherine of Russia or Frederick the Great of Prussia.[29]

There was a further way in which the Republic of Letters was divided: between men and women. Much of this division has its roots in aspects of Enlightenment thinking about gender which will be more fully discussed in Chapter 7. More specifically, while there were many women members of 'Grub Street' and even many women belonging to social elites who pursued ideas, such as Voltaire's own companion, the Marquise Emilie du Châtelet, there was at the same time a concerted attack by many male writers on the capacity of women in general to contribute to the store of ideas and discussions.[30] Often these attacks came down to the idea, forcefully stated in Rousseau's educational novel *Emile* (1762), that woman was a creature whose physical make-up ensured that she was ruled by emotion, rather than rationality, fitted by her biology to be only the mate and helper of men and dominated by her reproductive function.[31] Why was this attack on women's rationality, her very capacity to think, so strong a feature of the allegedly egalitarian Republic of Letters? In Rousseau's *Emile*, Sophie, the female protagonist who was presented as Emile's ideal mate, is so precisely because she is excluded by her femininity from the education which it is the book's entire purpose to define for Emile. The reasons for this are explored in much greater detail elsewhere in this book. But, in social terms, part of the problem may have come from the insecurity of the intellectual class itself. Still completing the transition from hired dependant of the great to autonomous intellectual producer, the Republic of Letters yet laid claim to be a political force in its own right, capable of building and moulding 'public opinion', in a way which obeyed, in theory, the dictates of reason, impartiality and humanity, and just as powerfully as could established governments. Because of this, the autonomy of knowledge producers was a crucial issue: how could they lay claims to be the legitimate builders of the opinions of the public, if they were not themselves independent and impartial? By definition, to

29 This range of responses to the *status quo* in government and society, from the supportive to the critical, will be examined in greater depth in Chapters 3, 4 and 10.

30 Jocelyn Harris, 'Sappho, Souls and the Salic Law of Wit', in A. C. Kors and P. J. Korshin, *Anticipations of the Enlightenment in England, France and Germany* (Philadelphia, 1988), 232–58.

31 Maurice M. Bloch and Jean H. Bloch, 'Women and the Dialectics of Nature in Eighteenth-Century French Thought', in C. P. MacCormack and M. Strathern (eds.), *Nature, Culture and Gender* (Cambridge, 1980), 25–41.

most eighteenth-century people, women could never be independent or autonomous, because of their family duties, or impartial, because of their emotional natures. The participation of women was thus seen as reducing the legitimacy of the Republic of Letters as a whole. Their equivocal position, as knowledge producers who were never truly accepted as part of the Republic of Letters, demonstrates how, in spite of its universalism, the Enlightenment itself often seemed to devote as much energy to designating entire social groups, such as women or peasants, as impervious to the voice of reason, as it did to constructing a better world for human beings.

In examining other crucial institutions in the spread of Enlightenment ideas, it is probably more accurate to see such institutions as effective ways of producing unity between elite groups in society, rather than reaching out to other, unprivileged social groups. In Britain, for example, extensive literacy and a large and wealthy professional and commercial middle class produced institutions which were aimed at the discussion of ideas, and whose membership of local elites also helped those elites to meet on common, neutral ground and forge firmer contacts with each other. Among such societies could be mentioned the Manchester Literary and Philosophical Society, founded in 1785 and still in existence, or the 'Lunar Society', a Birmingham-based group including the industrialist Josiah Wedgwood, the poet and doctor Erasmus Darwin, grandfather of the naturalist, and the inventor Richard Arkwright,[32] which well illustrates how a common interest in Enlightenment ideas could produce a new social institution able to fashion a new interplay between manufacturers, men of science and local intellectuals. All these groups meeting for discussion and experimentation were new forms of sociability centring on the exchange of ideas, social institutions where distinctions among different members were temporarily abandoned in the impartial search for truth and the pursuit of ideas.

This emphasis on equality was carried even further in another social institution, that of Freemasonry. Throughout Britain and Europe, Masonic lodges flourished, and saw the heavy involvement of aristocrats and even reigning princes such as Frederick the Great of Prussia, and Francis I of Austria, in the central European lodges. Their membership, which was supposed to be secret, vowed to cast aside social distinctions and unite their members with pledges to the practical fulfilment in society of key Enlightenment ideas such as rational benevolence. Masonic Lodges, some of which were open to women, became centres of debate where members tried to understand the world in ways which were often

[32] R. E. Schofield, *The Lunar Society of Birmingham* (Oxford, 1963).

tinged with mysticism and which sought the moral regeneration of society and individuals without reference to established religions. Mozart's opera, *The Magic Flute* (1791), with its extensive use of Masonic imagery, is the highest artistic expression of this ideal. In some parts of Europe, however, Masonry attracted hostility. It was condemned by the Catholic Church. In some German states, its programme of total social regeneration and its secrecy laid Masonry open to misinterpretation, as a challenge to the social and political *status quo*, especially as some Masons were also members of secret societies such as the Illuminati, which aimed to establish their members as a new ruling order. The movement frequently, therefore, met a hostile reception, especially as political tensions climbed towards the end of the century. In these contexts, Masonry illustrated the central dilemma of the Enlightenment: having created 'opinion' as a new political force, how far was it practicable or justifiable to use that force to produce social and political change?[33]

In France and Italy, different institutions were to the fore in promoting debate on Enlightenment ideas and bringing together old and new sections of the elite. Learned Academies were founded in many provincial towns in this period. These were formally organised bodies, often with constitutions laid down by royal charters and usually possessing their own premises and library. Membership was open to those who could pay a fee, which in practice meant the local elites: the aristocracy, the higher members of royal and ecclesiastical bureaucracies, the commercial elites, the wealthier members of professions such as medicine and the military. They existed to promote debate, to comment on papers on learned or topical subjects presented by their members, to encourage intellectual life by providing a library and, in the case of the wealthier institutions, to launch and finance prize essay competitions.[34] The prize essays, once reprinted, were capable of mobilising public opinion far beyond the confines of Academy membership, as witness the furious public debates which took place on the subject of capital punishment, after the prize

[33] Reinhard Koselleck, *Critique and Crisis: Enlightenment and the Pathogenesis of Modern Society* (Oxford, New York and Hamburg, 1988), translated from *Kritik und Krise. Eine Studie zur Pathogenese der bürgerlichen Welt* (Freiburg and Munich, 1959), 86–97.

[34] The provincial Academies in France have been studied in D. Roche, *Le siècle des lumières en province. Académies et académiciens provinciaux, 1680–1789* (2 vols., Paris and The Hague, 1978). Many other academies, such as the Royal Society of London and the Academy of Sciences in Paris, were more formally organised under direct royal control in the late seventeenth and eighteenth centuries: Roger Hahn, *Anatomy of a Scientific Institution: the Paris Academy of Sciences 1666–1803* (Berkeley, CA, 1971); James E. McClellan III, *Science Reorganised: Scientific Societies in the Eighteenth Century* (New York, 1985). Societies devoted to economic reform and development are discussed in the classic work of Robert J. Shafer, *The Economic Societies in the Spanish World, 1763–1821* (Syracuse, NY, 1958).

competition at the Academy of Metz in 1784, or on the social role of the Arts, after an equally renowned competition at Dijon in 1750.[35] Such institutions, as their historian Daniel Roche has remarked, performed not only valuable intellectual roles, but also helped in bringing together the social elites, both new and traditional, of each region and making them part of the new force of 'public opinion'.[36]

But in all this debate about the social institutions and social impact of the Enlightenment we have so far been concentrating on the experience of social elites: of those who were literate, who could afford to pay for membership of an Academy, club, or Masonic Lodge, or the purchase of a cup of coffee in a coffee shop, or the membership fee of a circulating library. Overwhelmingly, therefore, we have also been discussing an urban population. We now have to turn to the opposite side of the social divide. How far, and with what means, did Enlightenment ideas penetrate into social classes outside the elites and outside the towns; into the rural populations which in most European countries still made up the vast majority of the population? This is a topic which certainly exercised contemporaries.[37] It is also one which has attracted increasing attention from historians in recent years, as has every other aspect of the social history of the Enlightenment. This interest sprang into prominence beginning in 1975, with several studies of the *Bibliothèque Bleue*, the collection of small-sized, cheaply produced and crudely illustrated books produced for a semi-literate rural market by the Oudot firm of printers and publishers based in the French town of Troyes.[38] Sold in large numbers at country fairs and by cheap booksellers, these books included almanacs with farming advice and weather predictions, sensational biographies of

[35] The Metz competition was won by Pierre-Louis Lacretelle, 'Discours sur les peines infamantes, couronné à l'Académie de Metz, en 1784, et ensuite à l'Académie française, en 1785, comme l'ouvrage le plus utile de l'année', in P.-L. Lacretelle, *Oeuvres Diverses* (3 vols., Paris, an X, 1802), I, 171–329. The future French Revolutionary leader Robespierre was runner-up. The Dijon competition was won by Rousseau with a *Discours sur les Sciences et les Arts* which sparked immediate public debate, and fed directly into the public realm.

[36] For discussion of this concept in the Enlightenment see Habermas, *Structural Transformation*, 89–117. In French, the term was first used by Rousseau in his 1750 *Discours*: J. J. Rousseau, 'Discourse on the Sciences and Arts (First Discourse)', in R. D. and J. R. Masters (eds.), *The First and Second Discourses* (New York, 1964), 50. By the 1730s, the term was current in English meaning the articulation of personal rational reflection, through the public clash of argument. The term is first documented in English in 1781 by the *Oxford English Dictionary*.

[37] Many writers were concerned that their works should *not* reach the lower social classes; Diderot wrote to his publisher 'There are . . . some readers whom I don't want and never shall; I write only for those with whom I could talk at my ease' (quoted in J.-P. Belin, *La mouvement philosophique de 1748 à 1789* (Paris, 1913), 73).

[38] G. Bollème, *La Bibliothèque Bleue: littérature populaire en France aux XVIIe et XVIIIe siècles* (Paris, 1980); R. Mandrou, *De la culture populaire en France aux XVIIe et XVIIIe siècles. La bibliothèque bleue de Troyes* (Paris, 1964).

famous criminals, condensed versions of recent novels, devotional works and, in the great majority, retellings of medieval romances telling the deeds of Roland, the chevalier Bayard, or the four sons of Aymon. Literary historians have seen this literature as purely escapist, even as a way in which poor folk were deliberately deprived of access to Enlightenment debate. Others, such as Bollème, have seen the *Bibliothèque Bleue* as evolving towards increasing harmony with Enlightenment thinking. But to view the *Bibliothèque Bleue* in this way is to oversimplify the complexities of the relationships between what historians have sometimes called 'low' and 'high' culture: the culture of the mass of the population and the elites. Even setting aside the notorious problems which have surrounded the definition of the word 'culture', there is much evidence for an interpenetration of cultural reference points between social classes; at the same time as the *Bibliothèque Bleue*, for example, peddled retold medieval romance to its humble readership, such romances were also being sold to the upper-class readership of the *Bibliothèque Universelle des Romans*, initiating what literary historians have called a 'Gothic Revival'.[39] It should also not be forgotten that the largest single occupational group in most cities was composed of domestic servants, who often came from rural communities. Living in enforced intimacy with their employers, we can posit that their role in transmission between town and country, peasants and urban employers, was of considerable importance in breaking down any hard and fast divisions between 'high' and 'low' culture, or rural and urban worlds, and this role of transmission was enhanced by the expansion, in western Europe at least, of postal services which enabled even the minimally literate to communicate their experiences and ideas to each other.[40] This picture has been supported by the work of Roger Muchembled, who sees the end of the eighteenth century as a time of great cultural convergence. Muchembled pinpoints the lower-middle class in France in particular as an area where 'high' and 'low' cultures mingled.[41] Other historians of culture in this period, such as Roland Chartier, emphasise the very severe problems in the way

[39] The *Bibliothèque Universelle des Romans* was published between 1775 and 1789 and owed much to the medieval adaptations of the Comte de Tressan (1705–83).

[40] Beaumarchais's Figaro (the original of the Mozart opera character) could not have been the only gentleman's valet in the 1780s to be familiar with some of the latest ideas. In Philadelphia, shopkeepers and craftsmen were members of the American Society for Promoting and Propagating Useful Knowledge, the forerunner of the American Philosophical Society. Pictures were also a powerful means of conveying Enlightenment ideas. William Hogarth (1697–1764), the great British artist, for example designed his 1751 series of engravings *The Four Stages of Cruelty*, an eloquent attack on cruelty to animals, specifically for the working class. See R. Paulson, *Hogarth*, vol. II (New Haven, CT, and London, 1971), 109.

[41] Robert Muchembled, *Culture populaire et culture des élites dans la France moderne* (Paris, 1977).

of anyone who tries to get behind literary and artistic images of peasants and workers, to find what their real reading and thinking were. Chartier's studies seem to reveal a largely traditional world, in which a rural population remained relatively unaffected by the ideas of the Enlightenment.[42] A similar picture emerges from Robert Darnton's portrayal of the mind-set of urban apprentices in Paris.[43] Both these historians, in spite of many conflicts between them, in fact present a picture of the social penetration of Enlightenment thinking which is very close to a certain strand of opinion in the Enlightenment itself. Many Enlightenment reformers approached the rural population in a way which reminds us of the way missionaries in the following century would regard indigenous peoples. They saw peasants as beings living almost in a different world, incapable of understanding the Enlightenment and buried instead in incomprehensible folk superstitions, irrational traditions and religious loyalties.[44] To break down the peasants' resistance to Enlightenment was one of the major objectives of Enlightenment social reformers; but it was a task which, simultaneously, they often despaired of completing.[45] In the divergence between Darnton, Chartier and Muchembled, we probably simply have to conclude that the jury is still out: the vastness of the subject, the difficulty of international comparisons, the problematic distinctions involved in defining 'high' and 'low' culture, and the comparative scarcity and intractability of the evidence, mean that in all likelihood no resolution of this problem, as it is presently defined, is probable. All that we can conclude is that the very complexity of historical interpretation on this subject might well itself reflect a flexible and ambiguous reality of the social penetration of Enlightenment thinking. It should also remind us that ideas, reference points and attitudes did not simply 'trickle down' from the literary and intellectual elites to the deprived masses; movement may well have occurred in the opposite direction.

Conclusion

The Enlightenment was an era where dramatic shifts occurred in the production and accessibility of ideas and especially in the case of print

[42] Roger Chartier, 'Figures of the Other: Peasant Reading in the Age of the Enlightenment', in *Cultural History*, 151–71; and in *Dix-huitième siècle*, 18 (1986), 45–64.

[43] Darnton, *The Great Cat Massacre*, especially the title study.

[44] Harvey Mitchell, 'Rationality and Control in French Eighteenth-Century Medical Views of the Peasantry', *Comparative Studies in Society and History*, 21 (1979), 81–112; D. Outram, *The Body and the French Revolution* (New Haven, CT, and London, 1989), 41–67.

[45] See Chapter 3.

media. New social institutions were constructed based on the interchange of ideas, rather than to mark or display social and political rank. Knowledge and the ability to debate ideas in public began to be one of the ways of acquiring status for those born outside aristocratic elites. Simultaneously, a world-wide trade developed in consumer goods, including portable cultural products such as books, newspapers, pamphlets and reproductions of paintings. Increasingly, culture became 'commodified', a development explored in the philosophical analysis of Enlightenment by Horkheimer and Adorno, which has been previously referred to. The rendering accessible of information and debates to a wide audience became big business and was carried out not only by the elite of Enlightenment thinkers, but by an army of professional writers whose names are now largely forgotten. Visual representations and performance arts also carried ideas to wide audiences outside the social elites. All this led to the emergence of 'public opinion' as a force to be reckoned with. Indeed, a second major paradox of the Enlightenment is the way in which 'public opinion' as a critical political force was brought into being at the same time, and through many of the same social and economic mechanisms through which culture also became part of an international system of trading and exchange. Did commodification itself create the public realm? That too is a question on which the jury is still out.

Nonetheless, as Daniel Roche has pointed out, the growth of 'public opinion' also itself raised a third fundamental problem: that of defining the real elite. Was it that of birth or that of intellect? Questions of the control and spread of knowledge and ideas became part of the uneasy relationships between social classes; they also became part of the relationships between government and subjects.

3 Enlightenment and government: new departure or business as usual?

A properly constituted state must be exactly analogous to a machine, in which all the wheels and gears are precisely adjusted to one another, and the ruler must be the foreman, the mainspring, or the soul – if one may use the expression – who sets everything in motion.

(Johann von Justi)

Absolute monarchies are but one step away from despotism. Despotism and Enlightenment: let anyone who can try to reconcile these two. I can't.

(Franz Kratter (1787))

I go about, I learn, I see, I inform myself, and I make notes. That's more like being a student than a conqueror.

(Joseph II (1773))[1]

A major theme of this enquiry so far has been the relationship between knowledge, critical reflection and power. As we have seen, it was not only philosophers like Immanuel Kant who reflected on the lengths to which unlimited Enlightenment could be taken, before it began to disrupt, rather than illuminate, the structures of society. In this chapter we confront the issue in the most direct way. We examine the extent to which Enlightenment ideas were used by governments in this period, and what impact if any these ideas had not only on government policy, but also on the nature of government itself. We will see if debates on government intervention in the economy, and in church–state relations as well as much wider ranging controversy on what constituted legitimate government may have prepared the way for the wave of revolutionary movements which accompanied the Enlightenment and which was to culminate in the upheavals in France from 1789 onwards (Chapter 10).

[1] Johann von Justi, quoted in G. Parry, 'Enlightened Government and Its Critics in Eighteenth Century Germany', *Historical Journal*, 6 (1963), 182; Franz Kratter, *Philosophische und statistische Beobachtungen vorzüglich die Österreichischen Staaten betref-fend* (Frankfurt and Leipzig, 1787), 23–4; Joseph II quoted in D. E. D. Beales, *Joseph II* (Cambridge, 1987), I, 361.

We will also try to establish how Enlightenment ideas helped or hindered rulers in their search for international success, and internal stability and prosperity.

These are complex questions, not least because the constant flux affecting the exercise of power is not peculiar to the eighteenth century. Rulers have always striven to make their lands stable, secure, and prosperous. We may find it hard therefore to distinguish how the Enlightenment made a specific contribution. Historians in fact have expended much ink for over a century in trying to come to grips with the problem, although it is difficult to say that this historiographical legacy has in fact been successful in enhancing our understanding.

In the nineteenth century, German historians such as Wilhelm Roscher and Reinhold Koser began to use the label 'Enlightened Absolutism' to refer to a form of monarchy, heavily influenced by Enlightenment ideas, whose emergence they discerned particularly in the German states, and especially in the Prussia of Frederick II. Roscher argued that Enlightened Absolutism represented the final stage in the evolution of monarchy since the confessional conflicts of the sixteenth century. Efforts by monarchs in that period to anchor their authority in imposing confessional unity on their subjects had, Roscher argued, been replaced in their turn by those of monarchs such as Louis XIV who represented themselves as sole and absolute public representatives of their peoples. By the eighteenth century, Enlightened Absolutism would lead to the emergence of the idea of the ruler being the 'first servant of the state' in the words of Frederick II.[2]

This conceptualisation of the relationship between Enlightenment and monarchy, however, attracted very little attention in western Europe. After the First World War, new attempts were made to define this relationship. The International Commission on Historical Sciences, searching for a unifying theme for its membership, established an international research project on what it chose to label 'Enlightened Despotism'. Its 1937 report on this theme, and particularly the overview produced by the ICHS Secretary, Michel L'Héritier, produced a concept of the relationship between Enlightenment and government, largely conceived as the impact of French thinkers on monarchies, which was widely influential.[3]

After 1945, the concept of 'Enlightened Despotism' came increasingly under attack. Anachronism was one charge: no eighteenth-century ruler

[2] R. Koser, 'Die Epochen der Absoluten Monarchie in der Neueren Geschichte', *Historische Zeitschrift*, 61 (1889), 246–87.

[3] Michel L'Héritier, 'Le despotisme éclairé, de Frédéric II à la Révolution', *Bulletin of the International Committee of Historical Sciences*, 9 (1937), 181–225.

used the term to describe themselves. Ambiguously formulated by the French writer Mercier de la Rivière in his 1767 *L'ordre naturel et essentiel des sociétés politiques*, its use was very uncommon in the eighteenth century.[4] Whatever their claims to absolute ultimate authority, it was difficult to point to any eighteenth-century monarch who truly ruled despotically, that is without restraint by laws; let alone without challenge by elite groups and institutions. How, for example, could the history of the British monarchy, hedged around with Parliamentary restrictions as it was, be related to the concept of absolutism? What was the value of any term which could not stretch to the reality of government in what was a major state? There were others who pointed out that the ICHS definition encapsulated an interpretation of the Enlightenment itself which was fast being discarded. As we saw in Chapter 1, by the 1960s it was increasingly difficult to see the Enlightenment as in any way a unitary phenomenon, dominated by a few, mainly French, 'great thinkers'. 'Enlightenment' was increasingly seen as different from state to state, region to region, and thus it followed that the relationship between government and the crucible of concerns and debates that made up Enlightenment would also be different.

Another, and even more damaging criticism of the concept of 'Enlightened Despotism' or 'Absolutism' was that it offered no way to separate out what government actions were specifically due to Enlightenment concerns, and those which were rooted in much older ideologies such as neostoicism, or were responses dictated by the pure pursuit of advantage. By the 1970s, scepticism both about the value of the label 'Enlightened Despotism', and about the possibility of adequately investigating the relationship between Enlightenment and government to which it referred, was at an all time high, and seemingly with good reason. But, as usual in historical scholarship, at the very moment of its entrenchment, such scepticism itself came under attack. The sceptics, it was said, had confused an inadequate and misleading label with a more complex and interesting reality. Discarding the labels should not mean that no further interest be paid to the relationship between government, policies, debates and attitudes in the eighteenth century. Was it not, to say the least, unlikely that monarchs and their ministers could so effectively insulate themselves as to know nothing of the often heated debates about government and society raging outside their palaces and offices? If Enlightenment was of no concern to monarchs, why did so many, like Catherine of Russia,

[4] B. Behrens, 'Enlightened Despotism', *Historical Journal*, 18 (1975), 401–8; a less hostile view in her *Society, Government and the Enlightenment: The Experiences of Eighteenth-Century France and Prussia* (London, 1985).

or Frederick II of Prussia, bother to maintain lengthy correspondences, and long and often troublesome personal and financial relationships with figures such as Diderot and Voltaire?

Many of these perceptions crystallised due to the publication and translation of work by Franco Venturi. His publication of numerous texts by Italian economists, historians and political commentators, many of whom were also governmental advisors, showed beyond a doubt the importance of Enlightenment ideas in the making of governmental policies and attitudes.[5] After this, a flurry of reconceptualisations emerged. It was suggested, for example, that Enlightenment could be understood as a facilitator for 'modernisation'; though problems with understanding what was meant by 'modernisation' seemed at once to reflect the current quandaries of development economics, and to take the focus off the problem of understanding Enlightenment in a broader sense.[6]

A second point of view came from Marxism, then at the height of its intellectual and political influence in western Europe. The Marxist approach essentially saw Enlightenment as irrelevant to absolutism, assuming that the former was an ideology of the bourgeoisie, while monarchy existed to bolster the interests of the 'feudal' aristocracy. Thus, in the Marxist view, eighteenth-century monarchies were faced with the impossible task of trying to reconcile irreconcilable interests, feudalism and capitalism, aristocracy and bourgeoisie. Enlightenment acted merely as an 'ideological superstructure' which was used to gloss over the ensuing contradictions of values and interests.[7] There are, of course, many problems with this approach. It is difficult to apply to the many monarchies whose states, particularly in eastern and central Europe, contained no significant numbers of bourgeois; conversely, it is very open to doubt whether the aristocracy of many states, particularly in western Europe, could be helpfully described as 'feudal' by the eighteenth century. Nor is it easy to endorse the Marxist assumption that social groups are only receptive to or influenced by programmes directly related to their objective economic interests. This approach also, by definition, has little to

[5] Franco Venturi, *Settecento riformatore* (Turin 1969–); and his *Utopia and Reform in the Enlightenment* (Cambridge, 1971).

[6] E.g., A. M. Wilson, 'The *Philosophes* in the Light of Present Day Theories of Modernization', *Studies on Voltaire and the Eighteenth Century*, 48 (1967), 1893–1913; H. B. Applewhite and D. G. Levy, 'The Concept of Modernization and the French Enlightenment', *Studies on Voltaire and the Eighteenth Century*, 74 (1971), 53–96.

[7] For example, Perry Anderson, *Lineages of the Absolute State* (London, 1974); Albert Soboul, introduction to Philippe Goujard (ed.), *L'Encyclopédie ou Dictionnaire raisonné des Sciences, des Arts et des Métiers: Textes Choisis* (Paris, 1952, 1976, 1984); Horst Möller, 'Die Interpretation der Aufklärung in der Marxistisch–Leninistischen Geschichtsschreibung', *Zeitschrift für Historische Forschung*, 14 (1977), 438–72.

offer the many different republican states. Nor were 'aristocracy' and 'bourgeoisie' monolithic social groups, with completely unified attitudes towards 'Enlightenment'. To treat the Enlightenment as mere 'superstructure' is also to perpetuate (though for very different reasons) the distinction between deeds and thoughts, which was so central, paradoxically, to the older style of historiography of the Enlightenment.

Different again was the approach in Reinhard Koselleck's influential 1956 *Critique and Crisis*.[8] This work sees the relationship between Enlightenment and the state as being determined by reaction against the religious conflicts of the sixteenth and seventeenth centuries. Reformation ideology had enabled individuals and groups to legitimate unlimited critique of monarchies and rulers of different faiths, thus producing an era of pervasive and long-lasting disorder in Europe. In the eighteenth century, Koselleck argues, ordered government was re-established by the ideals of at least limited religious toleration – which stopped some governments from claiming to operate as ethical agents – and even more by the support given to the idea that 'critique', with all its disruptive consequences, should be confined to the private sphere. This is an idea which is still very strong, as we have already seen, in Kant's essay on Enlightenment (see Chapter 1).

Koselleck argues, somewhat controversially, that this situation can be traced back to the writings of the English political theorist Thomas Hobbes (1588–1679), who, in the aftermath of England's own Civil War, had argued for the subordination of the claims of individual morality, or 'critique', to the requirements of the necessity for a strong political order. This, however, Koselleck argues, left no clear place for the increasing levels of exchange of ideas and the rise of 'public opinion'. Public opinion and its informal institutions such as Masonic Lodges, or its conceptualisations such as the 'Republic of Letters', became substitutes for real politics, and judged monarchs and the politically active by 'utopian' rather than practical standards. Koselleck charges that these utopian judgements were 'hypocritical' in that they were taken from a position of irresponsibility and without adequate realisation of the impact of unrestricted 'critique' on the crisis of the old order by the end of the century.

Koselleck's book, even though published as long ago as 1956, has recently enjoyed a revival, manifested in its numerous recent translations. But it has also sustained many damaging cuts from critics, who

[8] Reinhard Koselleck, *Critique and Crisis: Enlightenment and the Pathogenesis of Modern Society* (Oxford, New York and Hamburg, 1988); originally published as *Kritik und Krise. Eine Studie zur Pathogenese der bürgerlichen Welt* (Munich, 1956).

have pointed out that this view of the relationship between Enlightenment and government is overwhelmingly driven by the author's wish to account for the Cold War, which had divided his own country. On a less grandiose level of explanation, it has also been questioned whether Hobbes was really representative of the seventeenth-century crisis of 'critique'; whether Enlightenment rulers really thought of themselves as ruling by *raison d'état* rather than by Christian values; a major ruler like Maria Theresa of Austria, for example, would hardly fit this bill. Was Enlightenment 'critique' really always undertaken in conditions of utopian hypocrisy and irresponsibility? This seems to be directly contradicted by the view of the Italian Enlightenment emerging so forcefully from the pen of Franco Venturi.

From this welter of controversy about the nature and meaning of 'Enlightened Despotism', or 'Enlightened Absolutism', emerges one major question: why have historians experienced, for so long, such a high level of difficulty in discussing this theme? Part of the problem for the eighteenth century undoubtedly arose from the way in which the Enlightenment was itself early characterised as an autonomous body of thought, floating free of situation and circumstance. Formulations of 'Enlightenment' as the ancestor of modern liberalism, such as that by Peter Gay, also produced unreal expectations for the actions of eighteenth-century monarchs, who were castigated if they failed to fulfil nineteenth- and twentieth-century 'liberal' criteria through refusing to abandon warfare, or refusing to restructure their societies and economies completely by abolishing such key institutions as serfdom. The task today is to find a way of thinking about the relations between Enlightenment and monarchy which is more dynamic, less anachronistic, and more sensitive to the pressure of regional and national patterns and situations.

Previous historiography thus seems to have hindered rather than helped our understanding of the relationship between government and Enlightenment. In any case we would encounter considerable difficulties in trying to approach this theme. Governments come in all shapes and sizes and face very different challenges. Large national states such as France were no less a part of Enlightenment Europe than were the merchant oligarchies of the Venetian and Genoese Republics. Giant multinational monarchies such as Austria and Russia co-existed with more than three hundred small German states. Clearly the challenges faced by large and small states, monarchies and republics, were very different, as were their previous histories and the local ideologies of what constituted good government. There is also the problem that all states in this period faced stresses which may have been heightened in the eighteenth century but which were still not different in kind from those faced by previous generations. The pressures of warfare and international competition, the problem of obtaining the cooperation of elites and ordinary people alike, the challenges of rising population and economic expansion, had all faced governments before.

In this sense eighteenth-century government was business as usual. It is also the case that many states, particularly in central Europe, already possessed a much older body of thinking about the nature, operation and legitimation of government, which remained powerful well into the Enlightenment. This body of thinking was called Cameralism. Cameralism was particularly powerful in the German-speaking areas of Europe, the Austrian monarchy and the German states, as well as in areas which often drew their governmental elites from Germany and Austria, areas such as Sweden, Denmark and Russia. So important was this body of thought that it might even be argued that one of the major divisions within Europe was not so much between Catholic and Protestant states, or large and small states but between states which used Cameralist thinking and those which did not.

France, so often seen as the heart of the Enlightenment, saw few of its leading intellectuals in office, or acting as close advisors to government. In spite of the growth of 'public opinion', power remained largely in the hands of the aristocracy, and the struggle to enter its ranks was fierce. Among the ruling class, there was little consensus on future directions for the monarchy, just as there was little consensus among the intellectuals. Few wished to challenge the existing order outright, but opinion was divided on whether the powers of the monarchy should be decreased (to avoid 'despotism'), or increased (to achieve reform, efficiency and greater equity, through restructurings of government, finance, and the army opposed by powerful entrenched interest groups). All this led to a lack of consistency in support for reforming ideas, and also prevented the adoption of efforts to create and teach a technical science of government on the model pursued in the German states. In spite of much support for Enlightenment, improvement and physiocracy among the Intendants, the single appointment of a genuine Enlightenment intellectual to high office in central government, the physiocrat Anne-Robert Turgot (1727–81), was a disaster. Weakened from the start by wavering court support, Turgot had to be removed from office when his insistence on establishing a free market in grain led to massive price rises, and the violent resistance by ordinary people, which historians have labelled the 'Guerre des Farines' of 1775. Other reforming ministers with strong connections to the Physiocrats were likewise briefly supported by the monarchy, then abandoned. In France 'Enlightenment', in the political sphere, often seemed to become merely grist to the mill of the competing court factions. It did not act as a unifying factor for the French upper class, even less so as in the 1770s conflict between the efforts of the King and his ministers to achieve reform, and the efforts of bodies like the Parlements to resist them in the name of the nation, became acute, and divided the French governing class.

Very different was the situation in the German states, and in the central government of the Habsburg lands. Here, a highly organised body of thought antedating the Enlightenment, called Cameralism, attempted to deal with the science of, and justification for, bureaucracy and monarchy. Cameralism emphasised the importance of a state's wealth, and emphasised the virtues of a strong government in obtaining this objective.[9] Cameralism also argued that rulers should attempt to regulate the lives of their subjects in detail to obtain the vital economic objectives of a strong, healthy, numerous, and loyal population. Cameralism was important, because however much it emphasised the importance of the strong state, it also included social regulation and *social* welfare among the characteristic and legitimate objectives of government, not just the *dynastic* and personal aims with which rulers often approached war and territorial acquisition. It was thus a set of beliefs about government which were well adapted to the German situation where many states were too small to afford their rulers any stage for dynastic posturing; it also worked well in the Habsburg lands, where the challenge of the 1740s – rising aggression between Austria and Prussia, which led to the global war known as the War of the Austrian Succession – made successive rulers well aware of the importance of control and development if they were to muster the necessary resources to compete with predatory rivals such as the Prussia of Frederick II.

The replication of Cameralist thinking was institutionally assured by the foundation of a wave of new universities and training schools in the German states whose curricula were primarily geared toward the training of an enlightened, Cameralist bureaucracy often under the close supervision of the monarchs themselves. This meant that, quite differently to the situation in France, university teachers often occupied major government positions, and the converse was also true.[10] All these factors helped to make sure that high-ranking bureaucrats became an international

[9] 'A prince, ordered by God to be leader and protector of a people, is justified in doing everything that the welfare of the state entrusted to him demands': Joseph von Sonnenfels, *Politische Abhandlungen* (Vienna, 1777), 254. A. W. Small, *The Cameralists* (Chicago, 1909), is still useful. See also K. Tribe, 'Cameralism and the Science of Government', *Journal of Modern History*, 56 (1984), 263–84.

[10] E.g., Johann von Justi occupied the positions of Professor of Cameralism at Vienna and Göttingen, as well as being Director of Mines for Prussia.

class, often moving from state to state. This itself helped to homogenise thinking about government, about the direction of reform programmes, and about social and economic intervention, across wide geographical areas.[11] This is why there was such relative homogeneity in government thinking across the areas affected by Cameralist thinking, which also spread into modernising states like Russia. This was not to say that relations between Cameralism and rulers were always smooth: thinkers such as Joseph von Sonnenfels sometimes produced ideas which were seen as pushing change too far. But it is still generally true that Cameralism acted, far more than did Enlightened attitudes in France, as a unifying factor between monarchs, their servants and their societies, and gave coherence to the governing elite itself.[12] Cameralism also had other impacts. While not anti-religious, it certainly placed great weight on a view of government, and hence monarchy itself, as a machine for producing action and decisions, rather than a location for sacred unifying symbolism. This is the importance of Justi's description, at the head of this chapter, of government as a machine – and machines are devices for turning work into output – and the monarch as only the supreme mechanic. Cameralism also saw the basis for the monarchy's responsibilities to its subjects as lying in natural law as much as in Christian dogma. Nature and economic life were both seen as open to 'management' and exploitation to meet the needs of the state, and justified by rationality. This is an important point, because it showed how in many ways Cameralism was congruent with central Enlightenment concerns such as the importance of 'rationality'. Such concerns also enabled governments to offer legitimation for intervention in society, a legitimation particularly important for those rulers whose territories, like those of the Austrian Habsburgs, included a multiplicity of local privileges and jurisdictions, capable of providing obstruction to the ruler.[13] Cameralism, for example, allowed the construction of a theoretical basis for proceeding with agrarian reform if necessary without the consent of the aristocracy, by reference to man's duty to control nature – thereby exhibiting rationality – and by the search for natural justice through uniform legal structures. The drive towards

[11] The impact of Cameralism on Russia is discussed in the classic study by Marc Raeff, *The Well-Ordered Police-State: Social and Institutional Change through Law in the Germanies and Russia 1600–1800* (New Haven, CT, 1983); 'The Well-Ordered Police State and the Development of Modernity in Seventeenth and Eighteenth-century Europe', *American Historical Review*, 80 (1975), 1221–43.

[12] See, for example, the arguments of Rudolf Vierhaus, *Deutschland im 18. Jahrhundert: Politische Verfassung, Soziales Gefüge, Geistige Bewegungen* (Göttingen, 1987).

[13] For examples of legitimations produced for specific policies of reform in the Habsburg lands, see E. Wangermann, 'The Austrian Enlightenment', in R. Porter and M. Teich (eds.), *The Enlightenment in National Context* (Cambridge, 1981), 127–40, esp. 134.

fuller exploitation of the resources of economy and nature could often only be achieved by imposing a uniform relationship to the monarchy on regions with very different legal definitions of their obligations to the crown.

It is probably a misconceived enterprise to try to untangle the specifically Enlightenment contribution to Cameralism. It is probably more fruitful to adopt a 'functionalist' approach, and try to establish *how* the holding of such ideas about government helped or hindered rulers in their search for international success and internal stability and prosperity. One could argue that legitimation for measures of social and economic reform, such as the reform of guild organisations to which the Austrian monarchy devoted much effort, gave governments wider choices in policy. Universalistic appeals to Enlightenment values such as humanitarianism potentially gave princes a legitimate way to disregard particularism and local rights by appealing to the elites' sense of belonging to an enlightened section of society. In other ways, Enlightenment ideas could also actually limit the options open to government particularly in often ruling out the use of greater force against the peasantry in the cause of agricultural reform.[14] If reform continued at a moderate pace, as was the case under Maria Theresa of Austria (1740–80), appeals to Enlightenment values could disguise, or make it more difficult for educated elites to oppose, the increasing efforts by governments to exploit natural and economic resources in their territories in ways which directly competed with the exploitation of those same resources by the aristocracy and church. In some contexts, able to point to a compelling combination of injunctions generated by Enlightenment universalistic ideals, as well as the danger posed by external threats, monarchs were more able to persuade privileged groups in society to accept changes which enhanced the state. Monarchs such as Frederick the Great were able to persuade their privileged orders to accept changes which enhanced the power of the state, by subsuming their own personal powers in that of the state apparatus. The privileged orders were inclined to accept the situation if they could see that the state was being run in their interests, as Prussia was, and Austria did not appear to be after 1780, and if the monarchy was particularly successful in warfare, as that of Prussia was and that of Austria was not. In doing so, in this particular way, monarchies were also often (though not always) able to decrease the 'transaction costs', or frictions in the machine of government. In this process, Cameralism succeeded in both

[14] John Komlos, 'Institutional Change under Pressure: Enlightened Government Policy in the Eighteenth-Century Habsburg Monarchy', *Journal of European Economic History*, 40 (1978), 234–51; Wangermann, 'The Austrian Enlightenment', 135–7.

providing continuity with the pre-Enlightenment period, and paving the way for Enlightenment objectives.

It is now time to look at the impact of specific bodies of thought on the operation of government. We also discuss in Chapter 9 the importance of religious thinking to rulers. Movements of religious reform such as Pietism allowed rulers such as Frederick William I of Prussia to legitimise programmes of church reform in the monarchy's interest. Even without the appearance of such reform movements within the churches there would still have been very considerable unity within Enlightenment thought about the necessity for church reform. Jansenist concerns about returning to the simplicities of the early church fitted well with the concerns of governments struggling to diminish the power of the Catholic Church within their own dominion, as is shown by the universal attack on the Jesuit order from 1759. Rulers like Joseph II attacked the church's hold over education by attempting to set up a system of secular schools, and by opening the University professoriate to laymen. Joseph, like his brother Peter Leopold, legislated against ecclesiastical practices which were seen as a drain on economic productivity: excessive numbers of monks and nuns, of saints' days holidays, excessive display in church services, interparochial processions that often became the occasion for competitive conspicuous consumption, not to mention scenes of wild disorder. Religious orders which did not perform socially useful functions such as teaching or nursing were forbidden to take in new recruits, and many religious houses were closed. In Tuscany, Peter Leopold used his Jansenist bishops to spearhead reductions in the power of the episcopate and the economic and social functions of the church. At the same time Joseph II began to increase toleration for non-Catholic groups. These religious measures were undertaken for a variety of motives. Motives ranged from the military (declining religious recruitment would increase the pool of recruits for the army), the economic (releasing church resources into more productive uses), the legal (enhancing the jurisdictional power of the monarchy at the expense of that of the church), the social (hoping to control disorderly behaviour associated with lavish and frequent church ceremonies) and last but not least by gaining control of education, of refocussing loyalty from Pope to monarch.

While Joseph II's methods were the most radical, most Catholic states adopted some version of this programme, showing a commitment to a quite uniform set of policies. At the same time there was also genuine commitment to a new religious value: that of toleration. While Frederick II experienced no serious opposition to his toleration policies, Joseph II had a thankless and politically damaging task in introducing toleration edicts in the Habsburg Monarchy. That Joseph persisted in his efforts to enhance toleration could only have been due to personal commitment. Toleration not only aroused hostility, it also hacked at the roots of the church–state relationship traditional to the Austrian Monarchy, and involved it implicitly in a radical redefinition of its own powers and legitimation, as we will see in Chapter 9. It is first in the campaign for toleration that we see possibly most clearly demonstrated both the commitment of some monarchs to a specifically Enlightenment idea, and the price that they paid for it.

Many attempts to reform the structures of the church had strong economic motivations. In many Catholic countries the church was a major landowner, if not the largest single landowner. Economists such as Pietro Verri in Milan or Francesco Galiani in Naples pointed out that the church's dominance of the land market retarded agricultural development and prevented the emergence of a dynamic land market which could adjust to the needs of a rapidly rising rural population and generate higher agricultural profits. This attack on the church's economic role was only one aspect of economic debate in the Enlightenment much of which had direct impact on government. For most governments, especially in western Europe the Enlightenment saw the abandonment of previous orthodoxies which have usually been described under the collective heading of Mercantilism; and which, in general, held that real wealth lay in manufactures and in the accumulation of precious metals and restrictions on trade with commercial competitors. In the eighteenth century, as the economy expanded, it became more widely accepted that economic resources also included people, industry and innovation, and that free trade was likely to benefit all by making a generally higher level of economic activity possible. These ideas were developed by a group in France often known as the Physiocrats, who saw the true basis of wealth as land and agriculture. They believed that wealth was dependent on free trade in agricultural products. Higher prices would lead to greater profits, profits would raise agricultural productivity, and greater abundance would be produced in the long run. Physiocrats, who included influential publicists such as Mercier de la Rivière, Quesnay, Mirabeau and Dupont de Nemours, advocated the end of government controls on grain, the abolition of internal customs barriers, and the end of monopolies in trade. For a brief period (1774–6) the physiocrat Anne-Robert Turgot was in control of French government finances, and lifted government controls on grain, as Peter Leopold in Tuscany was also to do in this period. The results were predictable in both cases: a rapid rise in the price of grain, followed by widespread riots by the poor. In Turgot's case, the aptly named Guerre des Farines of 1775 produced such disturbances that it was directly responsible for the abandonment of free trade in grain, and the minister's own fall from power.

In the long run, far more influential were the economic theories of Adam Smith, who published his *Inquiry into the Nature and Causes of the Wealth of Nations* in 1776. Smith was convinced, unlike the Physiocrats, of the importance of manufacturing industry. Smith emphasised the idea that what increased wealth was not agriculture or industry *per se*, but how labour was applied to human activity. Nature, or, alternatively, the operation of self-interest, would infallibly secure the deployment of labour where it was most productive. Smith's views were highly influential (see Chapter 4). But to put them into practice would have required that restrictive labour practices such as guild organisations should be weakened on the Continent to the extent that they already were in Britain. Governments which, like Austria for the 1740s, or France for the 1780s, tried to weaken guild organisation did so under heavy and effective fire from traditionalists. Nor did Smith's study of the division of labour really address the situation in eastern Europe, where industrialisation had barely begun, colonial trade, where it existed, was still carried out under heavy protectionist tariffs, and, above all, the majority of the labour force were unfree serfs. 'Enlightened' rulers such as Frederick II of Prussia, or Catherine of Russia, unlike Joseph II, did not actively seek to destroy serfdom. Joseph paid a very high price in terms of heavy resistance from aristocratic landlords in Hungary and Bohemia; Catherine and Frederick gained a generally harmonious relationship with their aristocratic elite from their abstention from the issue. In this area, as so often, the limits of Enlightenment were set by fear of social and political chaos.

It is thus easy to see that specific debates generated by the Enlightenment did have an effect on actual government policy. On a broader canvas, we can also say that Enlightenment did cause some fundamental questioning of the basis of monarchy, the most common form of government in eighteenth-century Europe. By the end of the century it is certainly possible even to discern a change in how monarchs thought of themselves. This is an important point to make, not simply by virtue of the radical challenge to monarchy in France after 1789, but also because in major and minor states alike, the implementation of Enlightenment policy, for all its rationality and universalism, was almost always still dependent on the physical survival, or the human will, of the monarch. At any moment, long-term reform plans could be overturned by death or whim. This was something which happened, for example, to Peter Leopold's policies in Tuscany, after his departure for Vienna in 1790. The ruler, his or her powers and his or her way of legitimating authority, was crucial for Enlightenment reforms. Maria Theresa's self-image as a Catholic monarch, for example, deriving legitimation from the church and from her membership of a community of believers, led her to adopt an attitude towards the issue of religious reform which was radically different from that of her son, Joseph II. By the end of the century, the religious legitimations of monarchical rule, the belief that monarchy in general, as well as each individual monarch, were chosen by God to rule as his lieutenants was becoming eroded, as were the elaborate court ceremonials evolved in the seventeenth century to emphasise the distance between monarchs and ordinary mortals. Louis XVI of France, Joseph II of Austria, and Frederick of Prussia all dispensed with much of this ceremony. As Joseph said, he became more like a student than a conqueror. While Louis XVI certainly retained a vision of monarchy as divinely sanctioned and legitimated by the Catholic church, it was precisely this which was to bring him into the conflict with widespread opinion within the regime which ruled France after 1789.

If kingship itself was becoming secularised, it was also losing its 'proprietary' character. Few believed, as had Louis XIV, that their territories were theirs in the same way that ordinary men possessed personal property. It is difficult to avoid the conclusion that this change was helped by the way in which the Enlightenment had begun to reflect on what legitimate government might be. Often, the answer they arrived at did not look very much like traditional absolutism. Locke, for example, had opened the century with his *Two Treatises on Government*, with an argument that what constituted legitimate government was not divine right, but a contract between government and subjects. As the century progressed, the idea that human beings were innately locations of 'rights' which could not be overriden by governments also started to become more powerful, even though the application of demands for 'rights' beyond the boundaries of race and gender (Chapters 6 and 7) were still seen as deeply problematic, and the notion of rights itself was thus not taken to its logical extension. All these tendencies led to monarchy being regarded in quite a different way. Enlightenment and the justification of 'despotism', the rule of one person without the restraint of legality or the subject's welfare, truly were incompatible. It was because of this that some Enlightenment princes, for example Peter Leopold in Tuscany, and Frederick II in Prussia, began to draft constitutions which would make manifest the nature of the contract between ruler and ruled and stabilise it beyond the lifetime of a particular monarch.

Enlightenment ideas, like all ideas, cannot simply be understood in a functional sense. Their impact cannot be understood if we regard them merely as tools which enabled rulers to do with new and better legitimation that which external threat and international competition pressed them to do in any case. They were not simply grist to the mills of Justi's machine state. They were not simply means to an end (and means often alter ends). They carried messages of their own. Through these messages, perceptions about the nature of monarchy itself were to change dramatically in some parts of Europe by the end of the century, both for subjects and for the monarchs themselves.

Part of this change came from tensions inherent in the relationship between monarchy itself and programmes of Enlightened reform. Because of the supreme executive power still held by most European rulers, the fate of programmes of reform was still dependent on the decisions of the ruler, who could withdraw support from policies at a moment's notice. The death of a ruler, or his departure to rule other realms, could throw entire reform programmes into doubt, as occurred for example in Tuscany, when its Grand-Duke Peter Leopold departed to Vienna in 1790 to succeed his brother Joseph II as Emperor of Austria. Monarchal will, and monarchal mortality thus posed deep problems for officials and sections of the elites committed to reform programmes which only had validity as long-term enterprises. At a conceptual level, the premises of rationality and uniformity on which many Enlightenment and Cameralist policies were based were at odds with the intrinsically personal nature of monarchal involvement.[15] Enlightenment also raised another problem: how far was 'critique', the use of rationality, to be allowed to proceed? Who was to be allowed to exercise this allegedly universal human trait, and to what extent? This is exactly the question raised by Kant's famous essay (see Chapter 1). Was not the untrammelled exercise of reason sure to perturb that very authority on which the practical implementation of Enlightenment depended?

Was there any way out of these dilemmas, short of the path of revolution, of the overturning of monarchy and its replacement by the rule of the (allegedly) virtuous and rational elite in the name of the sovereign people, as was to occur in France? By the 1780s, it was officials in the German states who were trying to find a peaceful way out of this dilemma. They were helped in their reformulation of monarchy by the increasing tendencies of monarchs themselves to discard the ceremonial and symbolic aspects of kingship which their ancestors had expended such energy in creating. Louis XVI of France turning to artisan trades in his spare moments (one can hardly imagine Louis XIV patiently

[15] J. Mack Walker, 'Rights and Functions: The Social Categories of Eighteenth-Century Jurists and Cameralists', *Journal of Modern History*, 40 (1978), 234–51; Wangermann, 'The Austrian Enlightenment', 135–7.

constructing watches and turning table legs) was only one among many, in an age which saw the disintegration of elaborate royal ceremonial and symbolism. Joseph II of Austria saw himself at moments as a bureaucrat compiling information, rather than as God's regent, as the opening quotation of this chapter shows. Frederick the Great encapsulated this process by describing himself as the 'First Servant of the State', a description which, while in no way diminishing the King's absolute position in the state, did place the focus squarely on the monarch as justifying his position in terms of deeds, rather than by providing a sacralised symbolic centre for the realm. Other voices, more radical, called for princes to give written constitutions to their states, which would stabilise the tension between princely will, and long-term reform programmes on universalistic, rational lines. The *Berliner Monatsschrift* asked in 1785, only two years after the Constitution of the new American State was introduced, for example, for a constitution which would make it impossible 'for his successors arbitrarily to alter the laws he had introduced'.[16] Elements in the Prussian bureaucracy also put forward the idea that in an absolutist state, it was they who stood in the place of a constitution, as it was they who assured the continuity of the state; and that their position should be protected by legal guarantees against arbitrary decrees by the monarchy. Many of these ideas were encapsulated in the *Allgemeines Landrecht*, the first unified law code for Prussia, debated under Frederick II and drawn up in 1794. At many points, the *Landrecht* deliberately sets the state, as a permanent organisation, above the mortal person of the monarch.

In conclusion: By the end of the century, most major states in Europe, as well as many minor ones, were committed to programmes of reform which often involved substantial modifications of interest groups, such as trade guilds, sovereign legal bodies, aristocratic representative institutions and legal jurisdiction over their tenants, and often the economic and jurisdictional interests of the Catholic Church. These programmes also involved steadily more intervention by the monarchies in the social life of their subjects, by such means as programmes of public hygiene, setting up of systems of elementary education, and economic regulation. These programmes were designed to produce a healthy educated population, capable of giving rational assent to monarchal measures. Many of these programmes were set in motion by the pressure on all states to reform, which came from the increased pressures of global competition. Many of them represented major change, and were legitimated by Enlightenment

[16] Quoted in F. Hartung, *Enlightened Despotism*, Historical Association Pamphlet (London, 1957), 29. This article first appeared in *Historische Zeitschrift*, 180 (1955).

ideas such as benevolence, and the duties of states to produce rational assent to policies through education.[17] None was aimed at producing major increases in social mobility, or basic transfers of power in society. These 'limits to reform' have often been discussed: the fact that Enlightenment rulers were reluctant to contemplate major and therefore risky social upheaval does not lessen their debt to the Enlightenment, few of whose thinkers ever contemplated this either. But, in the end, Enlightenment was able to raise major problems for monarchies, as well as being of major importance in reform. Its reform programmes pointed logically to a dissociation of the personal ends of the monarchy from the needs of the state, a situation which would have been anathema to an earlier phase of Absolutism typified by 'L'état c'est moi'. Enlightenment also assisted in the creation of important new factors, such as 'public opinion', which intervened in the process of social and political manipulation by monarchies. Enlightenment gave subjects new aspirations and new expectations from monarchs, expectations for change and reform which were useful if successfully mobilised by monarchs, but were difficult to control in regimes without sufficient institutional representation of the unprivileged. Once 'critique' began, it was difficult to stop. In the end, Enlightenment and 'despotism', or absolute monarchal power, were difficult to reconcile. It is a measure of the success of many monarchs, paradoxically, in using Enlightenment to diminish the frictions of the machine of state that the conflicts between Enlightenment and monarchy started to become intense only late in the century. Whether the resulting *impasse* actually 'caused' the French Revolution and its associated upheavals is discussed in the final chapter of this book.

[17] James Van Horn Melton, *Absolutism and the Eighteenth-Century Origins of Compulsory Schooling in Prussia and Austria* (Cambridge, 1988); Harvey Chisick, *The Limits of Reform in the Enlightenment* (Princeton, NJ, 1981).

4 Political economy: the science of the state and the market

Political economy, the science of production, buying and selling and their relationship with law, custom and government, and thus connected to the changes in government which we examined in the last chapter, was largely elaborated in the Enlightenment. The term was first used in French in Antoine de Montchrétien's 1615 *Traîté de l'économie politique*. It was not replaced by the term 'economics' in English until the 1890s. Many seventeenth-century writers worked in this field but it was in the Enlightenment that the subject came together far more strongly as a consistent academic discipline. It was formed by the confluence of several contemporary sciences of the economy in its relationship to government, such as Cameralism, physiocracy and mercantilism. It was also influenced by views of the political economy of distant civilisations, such as China. University chairs in political economy appear for the first time in the eighteenth century, the first being at Naples, held by Antonio Genovesi; in 1763 one was founded in Vienna, held by the Cameralist statesman Joseph von Sonnenfels, in 1769 for Beccaria in Milan, and in 1782 for Paradisi, the theorist of Italian decline, at Modena.[1] The field acquired a formalised mathematical language in the work of Pietro Verri in Milan, who argued for the status of political economy as a science wedded to objective laws.[2] Other conceptual advances in political economy also marked the Enlightenment: in France, the Physiocrat school of political economy developed macro-economic models for the first time, in François Quesnay's 1758 *Tableau économique*, while the Scots thinker Adam Smith developed the first full-scale description of mercantilism in an industrialising society.

All these developments took place in a world whose economy was rapidly changing. First of all came the economic and demographic

[1] Sophus A. Reinert, 'Lessons on the Rise and Fall of Great Powers: Conquest, Commerce and Decline in Eighteenth-Century Italy', *American Historical Review*, 115 (2010), 1395–1425.

[2] Till Wahnbaeck, *Luxury and Public Happiness: Political Economy in the Italian Enlightenment* (Oxford, 2004), 176.

take-off of the mid eighteenth century, as compared to the stagnation of the seventeenth. Rising population and an inelastic agricultural production led to frequent regional dearths in France and outright famines in other parts of Europe such as Bohemia and Austrian Silesia in 1770–1. It was widely seen as the business of government to guard the people against famine and dearth, and the French Physiocrats, as we will see, were strongly concerned with agricultural productivity and the regulation of trade. The Atlantic colonial empires also all saw an increase in volumes of trade and capital devoted to their products. The end of the century saw the beginnings of industrialisation in Britain, France, the Netherlands and northern Italy. The pressures of international competition and modernisation (see Chapter 3) led governments to take an increasing role in the economy in order to maximise their resources. All these factors made contemporaries increasingly aware of getting and spending, taxing and producing. Their response to these problems forms the body of this chapter, which will proceed by way of case studies of the British mercantilists and French thinkers, such as the Physiocrats.

So united were the Physiocrats, men like François Quesnay, Victor Riqueti de Mirabeau, and Dupont de Nemours, that contemporaries labelled them a 'sect'. They assumed that the economy was subject to certain objective laws discoverable by human reason. Major works by the Physiocrats include Victor Riqueti de Mirabeau's *L'ami des hommes ou traîté de la population* (1756) and his *Théorie de l'impôt* of 1766, and his 1763, with Quesnay, *La philosophie rurale*. In the *Encyclopédie* the articles 'Fermiers' and 'Grains' in volumes VI and VII, 1756 and 1757, are by Quesnay, whose 1758 *Tableau économique* has already been mentioned. This work should be read as an idealised version of the French economy, which makes the assumption of the exclusive productivity of agriculture and free-market competition. The laws of political economy were 'natural' – that ambiguous catchword of the Enlightenment – hence inexorable and prior to morality. The Physiocrats' theory told them that agriculture alone could yield a net product (a disposable surplus over the necessary costs of production). Manufactures and commerce were 'sterile' as they put it, because their activity was dependent on the supply of raw materials from agriculture and thus produced no net product. Physiocrats saw the monarchy as the main actor in increasing the net product. They advocated the establishment of a 'legal despotism', monarchial rule without the intervention of intermediary bodies such as the *Parlements*, as the guarantor of a strong force to hold the ring between different economic interests. They also advocated replacing the complex and unequal tax system of *ancien régime* France by a single tax on land, to fall equally on all, which they considered would raise royal revenues. In relation to the all-important topic of agricultural production, their aim was to replace inefficient agriculture of small peasant farms and share-cropping (a system whereby the peasant farmer paid as rent a fixed proportion of their produce), with what can only be called agricultural capitalism: large, heavily capitalised farms using day-labour and the latest farming techniques. Most importantly, they urged not only that the monarchy remove controls on trade in general, but especially that in grain, as the best means of raising the net product. By 1763, the royal court, with the vital backing of Mme de Pompadour, the king's mistress, had decided to support this idea.

The grain trade was of particular importance because the price of bread determined not only the amount of surplus available for taxation, but was also a major factor in public order issues. When in 1774–5 the *Guerre des Farines* (flour war) erupted, it was as a peasant insurgency against the rising price of bread. Bread riots were common in town and country alike if the price of a loaf rose too high. Above all, public order in Paris could be threatened if the price of grain in its agricultural hinterland made the cost of a loaf unsustainable for the working man. Physiocrats believed that bringing the grain trade out of strict controls and into competition on the open market would raise the price of corn, raise profits, and thus encourage agricultural investment, and the substitution of large-scale farming using modern methods for small farms using inefficient traditional methods. The Physiocrats seem to have regarded the impact of rising grain prices on the ordinary worker as secondary. In the long run, they argued, rising grain prices and thus agricultural profits would create new jobs, new wealth would circulate, and the revenue of the government would increase. An expansion of the agricultural market would – on the long term – make dearth less likely and a revitalised commerce would distribute grain more evenly, equalising prices and softening their oscillations. The problem was that for the poor and the working man, the price of bread was not a long-term economic goal, but a short-term necessity. Physiocracy provided no theory about how to tide the economy over the painful period of transition.[3]

Thus, when the Royal Declaration of 25 May 1763 and the edict of July 1764 authorised the free transport of grain from one province to another within the kingdom, it opened a Pandora's box of consequences. It demonstrated how the monarchy, hoping for higher revenues, had

[3] Steven L. Kaplan, *Bread, Politics and Political Economy in the Reign of Louis XV* (2 vols, The Hague, 1976), II, 677–82. The classic study of Physiocracy remains Georges Weulersse, *La physiocratie à l'aube de la Révolution, 1781–1792* (Paris, 1985), and Weulersse, *La physiocratie sous les ministères de Turgot et de Necker, 1774–1781* (Paris, 1950).

adopted not only the crucial Physiocrat demand for the liberalisation of the grain trade, but was also prepared to act as the 'legal despotism' which their theory had demanded. The increase and persistence of subsistence crises after liberalisation, however, led to the growth of an anti-physiocrat movement partly within and partly outside existing opposition movement from the *Parlements*. Nor were these dearths unique to France. Regions like Tuscany which had also implemented Physiocrat ideas found themselves faced with popular uprisings in the 1770s for that very reason.[4] Above all, the liberalisation of the grain trade broke the implicit compact between king and people that the royal government would control the grain trade in such a way as to alleviate dearth and famine.

Much of this opposition was given voice in the work of the Italian *philosophe* the Abbé Ferdinando Galiani, in his *Dialogues sur le commerce des bleds* (*Dialogues on the Grain Trade*), which was partly prepared for publication by Diderot. It became a bestseller. Its thesis was bold. The repudiation of controls on the grain trade was 'the most violent and dangerous shock that one can give to the state'. As Stephen Kaplan has noted, Galiani spoke in revolt against 'this spirit of enthusiasm and system which spoils everything', and argued that general rules could not be established for a question as complex as that of the grain trade.[5] In other words, the elaborate and pioneering macro-economic modeling of Quesnay's 1758 *Tableau économique* had mistaken the question. The grain trade was an object of the royal administration, not subject to the ordinary laws of political economy, and definitely not to *laissez-faire* commerce. Galiani argued that the grain trade had to be an 'object of administration' because grain was different from all other commodities. Crucial to prices and agricultural profits it might be: but it was also a matter of life and death. Demand for it was thus inelastic and always urgent. The monarchy through the police should intervene in the price of grain to prevent dearth. The rising cost of grain and hence of bread after liberalisation, argued Galiani, harmed industry by reducing purchasing power in the economy, which he, unlike the Physiocrats, saw as the real source of national wealth.[6]

The *philosophe* Abbé Morellet, commissioned by the monarchy to refute Galiani, denied that the monarchy had any duty to assure

[4] Wahnbaeck, *Luxury and Public Happiness*, 98–184; Mario Mirri, *La lotta politica in Toscana intorno alle 'riforme annonarie': 1764–1775* (Pisa, 1972).

[5] Kaplan, *Bread, Politics and Political Economy*, II, 594–5.

[6] Kaplan, *Bread, Politics and Political Economy*, II, 598.

subsistence and also denied the direct relationship between the political and social structure and the administration of the grain trade. The Controller of the Finances, Anne-Marie-Robert Turgot, sent hundreds of copies of Morellet's work into the provinces for distribution, and saw Morellet's work as a justification for the version of Physiocracy which he tried to implement in the 1770s, only to be met by the *Guerre des Farines*. The decree of December 1770, and the years between 1770 and 1771 saw the repudiation by the monarchy of the liberalisation of the grain trade in particular and physiocracy in general. It returned to conflict with the tax-ratifying *Parlements* as a means of working for modernisation and an increase in revenue.

Physiocracy was highly important in the evolution of political economy. It was the first attempt to model the concerns of an agricultural system at the macro level. Yet it was probably doomed to failure. The state remained obsessed with the relationship between subsistence crises and public order. The belief that grain distribution in times of dearth could not safely be left to market forces remained overwhelmingly strong and was seemingly justified by events. Even in times of good harvests, few believed with Turgot that grain prices would stabilise between the different regions of France. Few believed that there was no conflict of interest between producers and consumers of grain, or between agricultural capitalists and sharecroppers and day-labourers, or between the country and the town. Few believed with Turgot and the Physiocrats that there was an absolute property-right in grain for merchants and farmers.[7] Yet, as Kaplan notes, 'The peculiar merit of grain liberalization was that it proclaimed that the road to modernization passed through economic expansion, and that this was the only way to remove the social and economic blockage of the Ancien Régime.' This was undeniably correct.[8] The problem faced by Physiocracy was the management of the transition from regulation to *laissez-faire* without causing dearth or disorder.

Physiocracy also faced off against other and older ideologies of political economy. Foremost among these was Cameralism, the dominant version of political economy in the German states, Scandinavia, Austria and Russia. Cameralism, an ideology overwhelmingly held in parts of Europe without colonial empires, emphasised the drawing together of the state as an administrative unit and the regulation of the state's material relations with other polities through tariff barriers, export bans, especially on gold and specie, and state monopoly manufactures. There was also often an

[7] Kaplan, *Bread, Politics and Political Economy*, II, 596–7.
[8] Kaplan, *Bread, Politics and Political Economy*, II, 688.

emphasis on science to help with these projects.[9] In the Cameralist world, countries succeed if they have a positive balance of trade with other countries. Disagreeing with the idea that voluntary trade benefits all parties concerned, Cameralists saw the economy as a zero-sum game. Profits by one side lead to losses by another.

It was the Atlantic colonial empires, such as that of Britain, which used the ideology and practice of mercantilism. Producer monopolies were introduced such that the goods peculiar to the colony, be they spices, textiles, tea, coffee, sugar or naval supplies, had to be traded exclusively with the mother country. As captive markets, colonies were supposed to consume the products that the colonial state manufactured. In the case of Britain, just as in the case of the other Atlantic empires, Navigation Acts required trade between the colonies and the mother country to be carried only in British ships. British merchants could thus buy these commodities more cheaply, and resell them in other countries at a profit. Advanced manufactures such as that of woollen goods, were discouraged in the American colonies. There were advantages. The system gave the colonies a guaranteed market, and had the effect of encouraging agriculture. Thinkers like the Scots economist Adam Smith, friend and contemporary of Hume, argued that the mercantile system had encouraged high rates of growth in both Britain and the colonies, although he also believed that the rate of growth for Britain was less than it would have been without the Navigation Acts, which tended to divert British trade from European markets and made Britain dependent on the American market. Under this system, Britain could actually be endangered by the possession of a colonial empire. Smith also argued, in his work *The Nature and Causes of the Wealth of Nations* which was published as the same year as the American revolt, that in the long run the restrictions on American trade and manufactures would have become a crucial issue between Britain and the American colonies.[10]

But Smith's thinking of course extended far beyond the problems of mercantilism. It was just as much formed by the early stages of British industrialisation.[11] Probably the premier economic thinker of the Enlightenment, Smith's *The Nature and Causes of the Wealth of Nations*, had its genesis in Smith's visit to Paris in 1766, at the height of Physiocrat

[9] For an account of the Swedish naturalist Karl Linnaeus in a Cameralist context, see Lisbet Koerner, *Linnaeus: Nature and Nation* (Cambridge, MA, 1999).

[10] Adam Smith, *An Enquiry into the Nature and Causes of the Wealth of Nations*, Books IV–V, ed. Andrew Skinner (London, 1999), xxxix.

[11] Joel Mokyr, *The Enlightened Economy: An Economic History of Britain, 1700–1850* (New Haven, CT, 2009), well discusses the patchy nature of the early stages of industrialization.

influence. Smith met Diderot, Quesnay, Mirabeau and Dupont de Nemours, and it is to Quesnay that he dedicates Book I of the *Wealth of Nations*. For all that, Book IV reveals significant disagreements with the Physiocrats over their advocacy of a single tax, and over the idea of the economic 'sterility' of merchants and manufacturers. Yet their major idea, that of the virtues of *laissez-faire*, was very much Smith's, in spite of his argument in Book V that education should be state-funded. The mercantilist relationship between Britain and the American colonies, he argued, offended against the principle of *laissez-faire*. He also objected to the monopoly control of labour implied in the apprenticeship laws, seeing labour as 'the most sacred property' of every individual.[12] Indeed for Smith labour was the basis of the economy; as he says in the Introduction to the *Wealth of Nations*:

> The annual labour of every nation is the fund which originally supplies it with all the necessaries and conveniences of life which it annually consumes and which consist always, either in the immediate produce of that labour or in what is purchased with produce from other nations.

Smith has almost always been seen as the theorist of an expanding industrial economy. The division of labour (the breakdown of the production process of a given commodity into the smallest possible unit of time and movement) is one of the ideas most closely tied to Smith's name, though it is not original to him. Others such as the seventeenth-century political economist William Petty, Bernard Mandeville in his 1714 *Fable of the Bees*, and Diderot in the articles on industry in the *Encyclopédie*, had also previously seen it as necessary for economic growth.[13] In Book I of the *Wealth of Nations*, Smith sees the division of labour as key, though he is less happy with it in Book V, where he sees it as dulling the faculties of the worker and leading to the loss of martial spirit. The division of labour was crucial, as Smith wrote, to the great 'multiplication of the productions of all the different arts . . . which occasion that universal opulence which extends itself to the lowest ranks of the people.'[14] The division of labour even extended to the process of reasoning itself:

[12] Labour is the 'most sacred property' of every individual. Smith, *Wealth of Nations*, ed. Skinner, xli.

[13] Mandeville's work (1714) went into numerous editions and attracted considerable controversy. It discusses the paradox that private vices can benefit the economy as a whole. Women in particular cause the disjunction between consumerism and virtue: 'The variety of work that is performed and the number of hands employed to gratify the fickleness and luxury of women is prodigious' (Mandeville, 1723 edition, 236–8).

[14] Quoted in Kathryn Sutherland, 'The New Economics of the Enlightenment', in *The Enlightenment World*, ed. Martin Fitzpatrick, Peter Jones, Christa Knellwolf and Iain McCalman (London, 2004), 473–85; 478.

Like every other employment . . . it is subdivided into a great number of different branches, each of which affords occupation to a particular tribe or class of philosophers; and the subdivision of employment in philosophy, as well as in every other business, improves dexterity and saves time. Each individual becomes more expert in his own peculiar branch, more work is done upon the whole, and the quantity of science is considerably increased by it. (*Wealth of Nations* I, chapter 1, 9)

The division of labour, he noted, is limited by the extent of the market (*Wealth of Nations* I, chapter 3, 1–2). The increasing use of the division of labour is thus a sign of economic growth.

Like Hume, Smith saw economic activity as rooted in the deep impulses of human nature, in 'that principle in the mind which prompts to truck, barter and exchange one thing for another'. Smith continues with the less sanguine idea that economic activity, 'though it is the great foundation of arts, commerce and the division of labour, yet it is not marked with anything aimiable'.[15] Unlike Hume, he saw economic activity as accompanied by no corresponding moral advance. As he wrote:

man has almost constant occasion for the help of his brethren, and it is in vain for him to expect it from their benevolence only. He will be more likely to prevail if he can interest their self-love in his favour, and show them that it is for their own advantage to do for him what he requires of them . . . it is by . . . barter and by purchase that we obtain from one another the greater part of those mutual good offices which we stand in need of. (*Wealth of Nations* I, chapter 2, 1–5)

Because of this, Smith wrote,

Commerce and manufactures gradually introduce order and good government, and with them, the liberty and security of individuals . . . This, though it has been the least observed, is by far the most important of all their effects. Mr Hume is the only writer who, so far as I know has taken notice of it.[16] (*Wealth of Nations* I, 412)

Smith's ideas were not without their critics. His fellow Scot, Adam Ferguson, in his 1767 *Essay on the History of Civil Society*, points out that a commercial society does not necessarily generate freedom. For Ferguson, commerce can also give rise to an overwhelming desire for tranquillity, predictability and efficiency, and this may play into the rise of despotism. The Physiocrats had after all called for a 'legal despotism'. Commercial society can also generate a demand for luxury. Governments such

[15] *Lectures on Jurisprudence* (1766), 527.

[16] Adam Smith, *An Enquiry into the Nature and Causes of the Wealth of Nations*, ed. R. H. Campbell, A. S. Skinner and W. B. Todd (Oxford, 1976), I, 412.

as the Roman Republic have been corrupted through the 'luxury' that Hume and others such as Mandeville had seen as the motor of the economy, or the 'opulence' mentioned by Smith. As Hume however wrote, 'luxury nourishes commerce and industry'.[17] Here he was taking on the older Christian critique of luxury as mere gratification of the senses, as well as more recent opinions that Britain was being ruined by corrupt politicians whose avarice was encouraged by the pursuit of luxury. Public spirit and the love of liberty, the argument ran, would deteriorate in this chase after luxury.[18] Mercantilists also argued that luxury led to a general increase in wages, which resulted in an increase in the costs of production, and thus reduced the country's competitiveness in international trade.

Ferguson's comments also point to the importance of the study of human nature in the understanding of political economy. This topic, as Emma Rothschild and Albert O. Hirschman[19] have shown, was one of the great themes in the Enlightenment. Hume, though far from being the only writer on the subject as Smith had asserted, was certainly one of the most important. He wrote 'all the sciences have a relation, greater or less, to human nature . . . Even mathematics, natural philosophy and natural religion are in some measure dependent on the science of man'.[20] Hume's theory of the passions operated strongly on his thinking, fundamentally more optimistic than Smith's, about economics: 'Avarice, or the desire of gain, is a universal passion which operates at all times, in all places and upon all persons.' Hirschman has noted how in this period avarice began to be seen less as one among the seven deadly sins, and more as that passion which made fundamentally positive economic activity possible, and held all the others in check.[21] Later, Hume noted that, 'Everything in the world is purchased by labour and our passions are the only cause of labour.'[22] Yet if commercial society encouraged the desire for gain, it also encouraged sociability and learning:

[17] David Hume, 'Of Refinement in the Arts' (1772). Hume's *Essays Moral and Political* was printed in multiple editions from 1741. All quotations are taken from the edition of 1772, the last one to be published in Hume's lifetime.

[18] See also Wahnbaeck, *Luxury and Public Happiness*, *passim*.

[19] Emma Rothschild, *Economic Sentiments: Adam Smith, Condorcet and the Enlightenment* (Cambridge, MA, 2001); Albert O. Hirschman, *The Passions and the Interests: Political Arguments for Capitalism before Its Triumph* (Princeton, NJ, 1977).

[20] David Hume, *Treatise of Human Nature* (1739), 'Introduction'.

[21] Hume, 'Of the Rise and Progress of the Arts and Sciences', in *Essays* (1772 edn); Hirschman, *The Passions and the Interests*, *passim*.

[22] Hume, 'Of Commerce', in *Essays*.

> The minds of men, being once raised from their lethargy, and put into a fermentation . . . (by economic activity) turn themselves on all sides, and carry improvements into every art and science . . . they flock into cities, love to receive and communicate knowledge.[23]

Hume as an economist is not to be compared to Adam Smith or the Physiocrats. But he did make significant contributions to the study of money, especially by developing a quantity theory of money and of the flow of specie. He also contributed to the theory of international trade – so important for cameralism and mercantilism – between economies with different characteristics and different rates of growth. For him, unlike the Cameralists, international trade was not a zero-sum game, but brought mutual benefits.

Hume's opinion shows how contemporaries believed that the progress of the Enlightenment was linked to economic factors. It now remains to consider the reciprocal effects of the Enlightenment and political economy. We should also ask, as does Joel Mokyr in a recent book, what influence the Enlightenment had on the Industrial Revolution.[24] He points out that the exchange of ideas and techniques is easier in a relatively tolerant society like Britain, and that Britain had already rid itself of many features of the French monarchy such as internal tariffs and an unequal regime of taxation, which impeded economic growth. In Britain, this allowed the growth of an ideology of material improvement backed by a deep concern with Baconian programmes which emphasised utility as the objective of thought. A dense network of coffee-houses, newspapers and lending libraries carried new ideas and inventions, as did private meeting groups such as the Lunar Society in Birmingham, or the Glasgow Political Economy Club or the Society of Arts (1754) in London. Technology and science became an important part of the public realm and of the commercialisation of leisure, as people flocked to buy and read popular science books or to pay for and attend demonstrations in electricity or chemistry or natural history. Intellectual property laws had begun to protect inventors through the patent system. Gentlemen and inventors could come closer together, and new knowledge was created through such synergies.

As Mokyr says, Britain became the first country dedicated to ever-expanding consumption, and to that 'luxury' that Adam Ferguson, and Rousseau in his *First Discourse* decried, and Hume and Mandeville

23 Hume, 'Of the Balance of Trade', in *Essays*; Rothschild, 'The Atlantic Worlds of David Hume', in *Soundings in Atlantic History: Latent Structures and Intellectual Currents, 1500–1830*, ed. Bernard Bailyn and Patricia L. Denault (Cambridge, MA, 2009), 405–48.

24 See note 11.

admired. Mandeville tied the expansion of the economy to the desire of women for luxury goods.[25] Hume wrote in his essay, *Of Refinement* (1752): 'luxury nourishes commerce and industry . . . how inconsistent then is it to blame so violently a refinement in the arts, and to present it as the bane of liberty and public spirit'. This is why Mokyr can argue that the Enlightenment in England was 'the beginning of modern economic growth'.[26] It was certainly one of the major driving forces behind the formulation of political economy.

[25] Wahnbaeck, *Luxury and Public Happiness*; John E. Crowley, *The Invention of Comfort: Sensibilities and Design in Early Modern Britain and Early America* (Baltimore, MD, 2001).

[26] Mokyr, *The Enlightened Economy*, 62.

5 Exploration, cross-cultural contact, and the ambivalence of the Enlightenment

The eighteenth century was one of extraordinary geographical discovery. This is another way of saying that it was also an age of ever-increasing contacts between very different cultures. How those contacts took place, how they were received in Europe, and what debates they fostered, are the subjects of this chapter.

Exploration in order to gain new knowledge was a characteristic of the Enlightenment. Previous centuries had regarded new geographical knowledge as merely a by-product from voyages primarily aimed at loot and booty. At most, expedition leaders went to little-known territories as a way of interesting investors in parcels of land. The eighteenth century, however, began to regard exploration as a primary source of knowledge. Exploration in the Enlightenment was the first to be centrally concerned with the gathering of information about man and the natural world. Although geopolitical incentives, including taking possession of unknown lands, still motivated much travelling to unknown regions of the world, international cooperation between national scientific institutions to solve geophysical problems came very much more to the fore. In 1768, for example, observers were sent out from Lapland to Tahiti in order to observe the rare event of the passage of the planet Venus between the earth and the sun.

Such international effort in turn relied upon the progress of exploration. To send men, ships and scientific instruments to Tahiti, a small island in the Pacific, was nonsense unless that ocean was already sufficiently known. In spite of important land exploration in Siberia, in the frontier regions of the American colonies and in Lapland, the maritime exploration of the Pacific had far and away the largest impact on the popular imagination in Europe, the future history of their indigenous peoples, and debates about the nature of man. The Pacific Ocean was the Enlightenment's 'New World', as one historian has called it. Through the explorations of James Cook (1728–79), Louis-Anne de Bougainville (1729–1811) and others, Europeans were for the first time to gain an accurate knowledge of the Pacific, which contains over twenty-five thousand islands, and covers one-third of the earth's surface. Between 1769 and 1771, James Cook, sent into the Pacific in order to observe the transit of Venus from Tahiti, also discovered the east coast of Australia, and the two islands of New Zealand. On subsequent voyages, he was to discover Hawaii, and to prove the existence of Antarctica. He also filled in much of the North Pacific coastline, and sailed through the Bering Strait on the quest for the North-West Passage (a sea route from the Atlantic to the Pacific). In 1791, Vancouver, building on Cook's work of mapping and his contacts with indigenous peoples, extended the survey of the north Pacific coast of North America.

All this had the effect of drawing the Pacific for the first time into the developing system of global trade. The Pacific, which had scarcely seen three or four European ships a year until the 1790s, by the end of the century saw flotillas of American and European ships trading in an integrated system between the Pacific, and London or Salem, in Chinese teas, whale oil, sea-otter furs at Nootka Sound and tropical wood in the Marquesas islands many hundreds of miles away. None of this could have taken place without repeated contact between European explorers and indigenous peoples. The dependence of both land and maritime explorers on indigenous peoples for access to fresh food and water, and to their geographical knowledge, in any case forced contact. But encounters were more than that. Europeans were trying to gain precious commodities. They were also trying to gain knowledge of their unknown hosts.

Cook's companion on his second voyage, Johann Forster, wrote a famous essay called 'Cook the Discoverer'. Forster saw Cook as just as much an observer of peoples as a superb navigator:

> Let us look, however, at the most important object of our researches, at our own species; at just how many races, with whose very name we were formerly unacquainted, have been described down to their smallest characteristics, through the memorable efforts of this great man! Their physical diversity, their temperament, their customs, their modes of life and dress, their form of government, their religion, their ideas of science and works of art, in short everything was collected by Cook for his contemporaries and for posterity with fidelity and with tireless diligence.[1]

Forster's account shows that explorers like Cook were not coming empty-handed to their encounters with indigenous peoples. They had agendas of the information that they wanted, agendas which Forster clearly lists here. The encounters with indigenous peoples, however, were not so easily producers of knowledge. Problems of language were acute. From

[1] Cited in Alan Frost, 'The Pacific Ocean: The Eighteenth Century's New World', *Studies in Voltaire and the Eighteenth Century*, 1976 (15): 797–826.

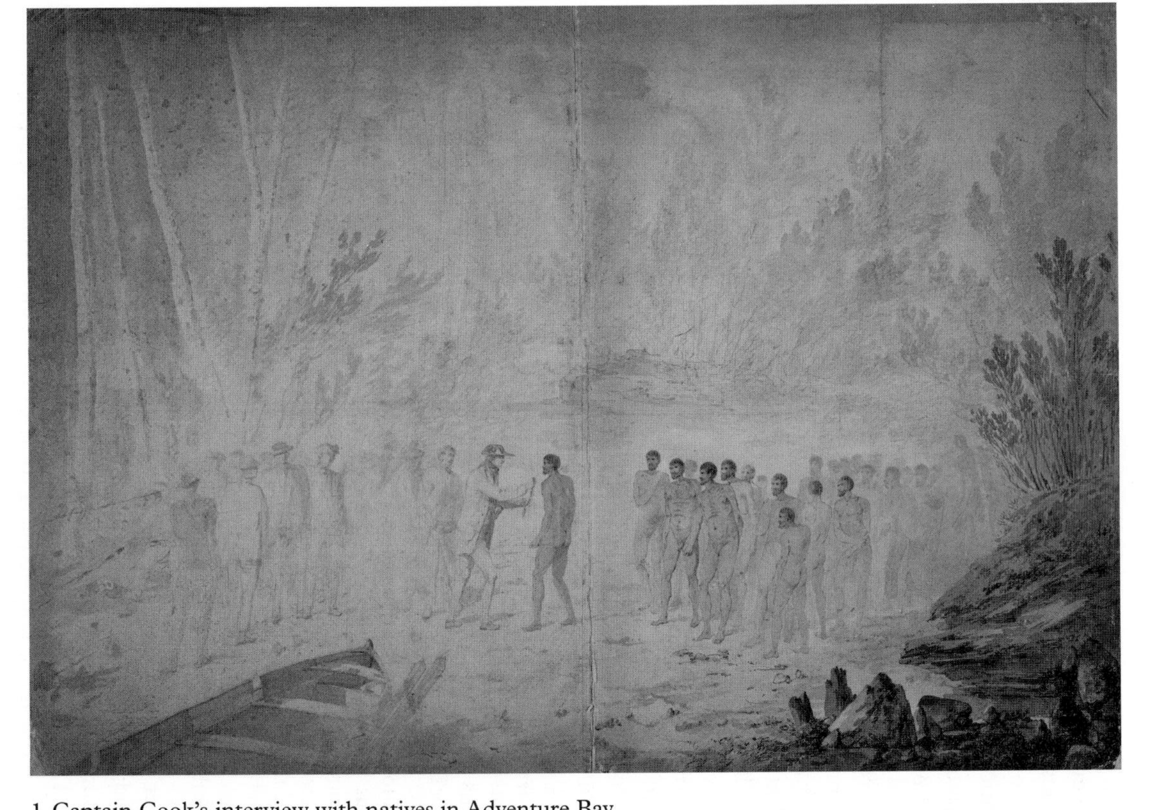

1 Captain Cook's interview with natives in Adventure Bay.
Cook is seen here at the moment of making contact with islanders on the beach at Adventure Bay, Van Diemen's Land (Tasmania) on 29 January 1777. The row-boat in which he arrived can be seen at the bottom left. The sketch well illustrates the formal nature of the encounter.

the Aleutians to Tahiti, no indigenous language resembled any spoken in Europe. Explorers often had only fleeting relations with the peoples they encountered. Cook's six-week stay on Tahiti was exceptional. It did result in the beginning of genuine language learning on both sides, and the beginning of relationships between islanders and the ship's crew. But even here, Cook confessed to James Boswell that

> he and his companions who visited the South Sea islands could not be certain of any information they got, or supposed they got, except as to objects falling under the observation of the senses, and anything which they learned about religion, government, or traditions might be quite erroneous.[2]

This episode shows Cook wrestling with the truth-value of the knowledge he had brought back, in much the same way that natural scientists, as we will see in Chapter 8, also were preoccupied with the possibility of obtaining truth from nature.

In these situations of uncertainty, gestures and objects carried the burden of meaning which words could not. Many encounters roughly follow the patterns of an attempt by James Cook to make contact with New Zealand Maoris who had never before seen a European. Cook knew how to make contact without words. Here is Forster's account of Cook making contact with a Maori in Dusky Bay.

> Captain Cook went to the head of the boat, called to him in a friendly manner, and threw him his own and some other handkerchiefs, which he would not pick up. The Captain, then taking some sheets of white paper in his hands, landed on the rock unarmed, and held the paper out to the native. The man now trembled very visibly, and having exhibited strong marks of fear in his countenance, took the paper; upon which Captain Cook coming up to him, took hold of his hand, and embraced him, touching the man's nose with his own, which is their mode of salutation. His apprehension was by this dissipated, and he called . . . to two women, who came and joined him, while several of us landed to keep the Captain company. A short conversation ensued, of which little was understood on both sides, for want of a complete knowledge of their language. (Forster, 1777: I, 137–8)[3]

In the absence of a common language, Cook uses small objects to make bridges between himself and the Maori. Objects were very important in these contact situations. Once objects have been exchanged, then physical contact can follow. Cook crosses the boundary between his own culture and that of the Maoris by adopting their greeting convention of rubbing noses. At the same time he makes the physical transition between the boat and the beach. In this island world of the Pacific, the place of

2 Frost, 'The Pacific Ocean', 798.

3 J. R. Forster, *Observations Made during a Voyage around the World*, ed. Nicholas Thomas Michael Dettelbach and Harriet Guest (Honolulu, 1996), 137–8.

contact is the beach, and the beach is also therefore the place of potential violence. Cook himself was to be killed on Kealakekua beach on Hawaii in February 1779. The absence of a common language also means that the potential for violence is always present in encounter situations. There are no words to explain intentions, and the meaning of the body-language and gestures of each culture is unclear to the other. Even a peaceful encounter, like this one between James Cook and the Maoris, could easily turn to violence. This is why members of his crew are there 'keeping him company'. On the other side, it was also clearly a situation of extreme fear and uncertainty. In this situation it is not surprising that so many contacts ended in violence from one side or another. The wonder is that any at all proceeded without it.

Exploration, and especially exploration in the Pacific, had a huge impact on public opinion in Europe. But the relation between the actual world of the Pacific and the images of it which so fascinated Enlightenment thinkers was often tenuous. Explorers themselves contributed to the problem of conveying any sort of real facts about Pacific island life. When Bougainville reached Tahiti he saw the island as the Homeric island of Cythera, the goddess of love. Native women were compared to Venus, and native men given names from classical mythology such as Ajax, Achilles or, for old men, Nestor. Many explorers saw the Pacific and its peoples through the lens of Greek and Roman epic. This was very much so in Bougainville's account, the *Voyage autour du Monde* (*Voyage around the World*) of 1771. In particular, the Homeric Odyssey seemed peculiarly appropriate as a source of understanding of the islands, since its hero Odysseus also wandered between unknown islands, this time in the Aegean Sea, in each of which a different adventure awaited him.

Cook was well aware of these problems. Returning from his first voyage, distrusting his own literary skills, he gave his notes to John Hawkesworth, a well-known populariser and ghost-writer, to be turned into a narrative of the voyage. On the publication of the text, Cook became furious, for Hawkesworth had inserted episodes which were not in Cook's text, had put in long and conventional reflections on Tahitian simplicity and virtue and, which angered Cook most of all, had introduced titillating sexual scenes which had no basis in reality.

In spite of Cook's disavowal, the book became an overnight bestseller, and was translated into several European languages. It became a bestseller because it gave its readers an image of the Pacific not as it was, but as they badly needed it to be. They needed to be able to believe in the existence of a utopian world whose inhabitants were peaceful, natural and pure, lived without intrusive government, and which contained only simple societies with no great distinctions of wealth or social status. At a time when governments were becoming more intrusive (see Chapter 3), it was therapeutic to think of a world where property owning and economic competition were absent or rare, and where above all life was free of the sexual controls which were so heavy in Europe. The beauty of the Pacific islands was also much appreciated at a time when, around the 1770s, many European societies began to see for the first time an aesthetic and moral value in landscape.

In fact, the islands functioned as a projection space for European hopes, frustrations and desires. They had the additional advantage of being real and current. The islands seemed to show that Utopia, instead of being a dream, actually existed. This certainty was increased by the fact that both Cook and Bougainville brought home real Tahitians (Omai with Cook, and Atouru with Bougainville). In the end, Europeans were less concerned with the 'getting it right', which had mattered so much to Cook, than with imaginatively constructing, on the basis of the travel accounts, a world they needed to believe was there.

Here we encounter an apparent paradox: the Utopian desires projected onto the islands were themselves the centre of a commercial industry in the eighteenth century. As mentioned before, Cook's and Bougainville's accounts were bestsellers. Travel literature was read more than any other genre, except that of novels. Stage plays with 'Tahitian' settings played to packed theatres in London. More images of the Pacific than ever before were available. Ships going into the Pacific for the first time carried professional artists, whose images of hitherto unknown peoples, plants and places could be cheaply reproduced as engravings. As Bernard Smith has demonstrated, these images gave a new and highly charged aesthetic dimension to exploration and to encounters with new peoples.[4] As well as pictures, artefacts were also brought back from the Pacific, often by sailors who looked to supplement their meagre pay by selling fish-hooks and feather cloaks, weapons of war or woven mats from the Pacific islands. These objects created the first markets in indigenous artefacts. They rapidly also entered publicly owned museums. Without them it is impossible to understand the impact of cross-cultural encounters on Enlightenment Europe.

The printed narratives, representations of distant parts of the world and artefacts shaped an important part of the European repertoire of ideas, images, hopes and feelings. All this flow of information and image was eagerly taken up by a reading public looking for living utopias. It was also a public which, as we have already seen in Chapter 2, defined itself as

[4] Bernard Smith, *European Vision and the South Pacific* (New Haven, CT, and London, 1988).

enlightened precisely in virtue of its encounter with the printed word, the theatrical performance and the representations given wide currency by engraving. It was this explosion of commercially produced images that allowed cross-cultural encounters on the edges of the known world to become the imaginative property of ordinary Europeans who thought of themselves as enlightened yet never ventured far from home.

These then were the equivocal bases on which Europeans acquired knowledge of newly discovered parts of the world, knowledge which they used as empirical examples in discussions, and as the bases of theories. Rousseau, for example began the discussion of the worth of 'civilisation' in his 1750 *Discours sur les sciences et les arts*, and his 1755 *Discours sur l'origine de l'inégalité parmi les hommes*. He sought to answer his questions about the worth of 'civilisation' by contrasting it with a portrayal of life in primitive societies. What would the life of man without the mixed benefits of western civilisation actually look like? Could existing exotic peoples, living outside the complex urbanised civilisations of China or India, be taken as representing what a natural man would be like? Would such a person be a 'noble savage', or would his life be as 'nasty, brutish and short' as many, such as the famous political theorist Thomas Hobbes (1588–1679), alleged that of the American Indians to be? If man is 'better' outside civilisation, as Rousseau thought, then how is he to exercise his 'natural' capacities such as reason and invention, without inevitably recreating the very civilisation from which he fled?

Many of these debates on the worth of civilisation were highlighted by the Pacific discoveries of the 1770s. Much discussion about the effects of the contact between two incompatible 'civilisations', the European and the Pacific islander, led increasingly to doubts and ambiguous feelings. Cook summed up much contemporary feeling when he wrote:

> What is still more to our shame as civilised Christians, we debauch their morals already too prone to vice, and we introduce among them wants and perhaps disease which they never before knew, and which serve only to disturb that happy tranquillity which they and their forefathers enjoyed. If anyone denies the truth of this assertion, let him tell me what the natives of the whole extent of America have gained by the commerce they have had with Europeans.[5]

Cook, hardly a philosopher or social theorist, nonetheless quite accurately reflects ambiguities about culture (it is ours and makes us civilised and Christian: yet it somehow harms others who come into contact with it). He reflects the almost universal belief that indigenous societies are corrupted out of a state of innocence into wants which they had never

[5] Cited in Frost, 'The Pacific Ocean'.

previously had. Here Cook echoes Rousseau's argument that civilisation inevitably corrupts because it fills us with inauthentic desires (which are also what propel the economies of the corrupt societies). These inauthentic desires are what cause the wish for luxury.

James Cook's ideas were convergent with those of a major figure of the Enlightenment, Denis Diderot, whose *Supplément au voyage de Bougainville* (*Supplement to the Voyage of Bougainville*) was written in 1772 (but only published in 1796) in response to Bougainville's account of his circumnavigation. Diderot moves the debate on the 'noble savage' and on 'civilisation' away from its previous focus on the 'savages' of the New World, onto the very different descriptions of the Pacific islanders. Diderot too saw Tahiti as an earthly Paradise, or a Utopia, where the islanders were better and happier, because more natural than the Europeans who had discovered them.

> The life of savages is so simple, and our societies are such complicated machines! The Tahitian is close to the origin of the world, while the European is closer to its old age . . . They understand nothing about our manners or our laws, and they are bound to see in them nothing but shackles disguised in a hundred different ways. Those shackles could only provoke the indignation and scorn of creatures in whom the most profound feeling is a love of liberty.[6]

It is no accident that the 1770s were in France a time of political conflict between the royal government and the privileged law courts, widely interpreted as a struggle between royal despotism and personal liberties. Talk about idealised Tahitians could be turned to serve the purposes of any European internal political conflict. Diderot also saw the Tahitians as the inhabitants of a time capsule, living 'closer to the origin of the world'. Like many Enlightenment writers, Diderot saw the 'noble savages' as spyglasses into the distant heroic phases of Europe's own history. Their simple, natural culture replicated those of Greece and Republican Rome. In the same way, the historian Jean Lafitau had argued in his 1727 *Moeurs des sauvages américains comparées aux moeurs des premiers temps* (*Customs of American savages compared to the customs of the earliest times*) that American Indian society could be seen as a living model of those of the classical world.

Such identification between the Pacific islanders or American Indians and the heroic age of the classical world could only come about because the Enlightenment viewed society and history as morality. Classical civilisation was seen by most educated people as exemplifying a particular

[6] In *Political Writings*, ed. John Hope Mason and Robert Wokler (Cambridge, 1992). See also *Le Neveu de Rameau* (1762), ed. J. Barzun and R. H. Bowen (New York, 1956), 194, 233–4.

range of virtues, such as civic spirit, self-control, self-sacrifice and stoicism in the face of pain and danger. If even some of these characteristics could be identified by Europeans in the exotic peoples they encountered, it was very easy to conflate their distance in space from Europe with their distance in time from the classical world. This view was especially important for those who, like Rousseau, were most strongly convinced of the imperfections of European society, and could not accept the view held by thinkers like Condorcet that history could be understood as the story of the progressive advancement of humanity.

All this meant that exotic societies were often viewed by Europeans as both the ultimate opposite or other to themselves, and also a replication of Europe's own origins. Little effort was made to see these societies on their own terms. This reminds us of the way in which audiences flocked to see theatrical performances, or bought engravings with allegedly Tahitian themes, not because they wanted to find out about authentic Tahiti, but because they needed Tahiti as a projection space for their own concerns.

Another question raised by the European encounter with the new world of the Pacific was the nature of humanity itself. On the one hand, it was perfectly clear that the Pacific islanders or the American Indians were men. But in that case, why was it that they were so different in history and culture, and even looked so different? Here we see why many Enlightenment debates on race begin to come to the fore, and why they become more active than before. Previously, exotic peoples had been classified in terms of their customs or religious beliefs. The Enlightenment relied to a greater extent on physical characteristics as a way of defining the boundaries of the human species, though without approaching Victorian levels of classification of human beings by appearance and anatomy alone. As usual, there was no consensus in the Enlightenment on the definition of the races of man. Some, such as the French naturalist Georges-Louis Buffon (1707–88), argued that the human race was a unity. If some humans looked different from others, they did so only because of contingent factors such as exposure to particular climates. Anyone who lived in a fierce tropical climate was bound to respond to the action of the sun, and to have a dark skin. If Europeans did the same, they too would develop a dark skin. But there was nothing which made some men inherently black, and some inherently white. Environment and climate were the determining factors, not some inborn characteristic of man. Buffon's work offered no support to anyone who wished to argue that black Africans or American Indians or Pacific Islanders were in some fundamental way inferior or different.

Buffon's contemporary, the Swedish naturalist Carl Linnaeus (1707–78), however, argued differently in his 1740 *Systema Naturae* (*System of*

Nature), that far from having a basic unity, man could be divided into four different classificatory groups: white Europeans, red American Indians, black Africans and brown Asians. But in his 1758 edition of the same work, he introduced new groups into the classifications which he used to subdivide the human race. These groups were wild men, pygmies and giants. Such categories were none of them the same kind of classification as the others, and it was difficult to explain their relation to the colour classifications introduced in early editions of the *Systema*. Such examples show the tentative and unstable character of Enlightenment attempts to classify the members of the human race. They also show how difficult it was to find out where the boundaries of humanity were. The Scots jurist Lord Monboddo, for example, argued that orang-outangs were really men, because they used tools and seemed to have language. Linnaeus, on the other hand was unsure whether pygmies qualified for membership of the human race.

Thinking on race in the Enlightenment also raised theological issues. Buffon's arguments for the unity of mankind would have been acceptable to those who believed that all men were ultimately descended from the original human couple, Adam and Eve. The Bible account also explained the different skin colour of black Africans by seeing it as the punishment meted out to the descendants of Ham, the banished son of Noah. Unfortunately, these monogenists were opposed by those who rejected the authority of the Biblical account, and argued that the races of man were fundamentally different from each other, and had sprung up independently at different times and places, some perhaps even before the creation of Adam himself. There was also a historical aspect to racial thinking in the Enlightenment. Scottish thinkers such as Adam Ferguson, in his 1766 *Essay on the History of Civil Society*, linked differences in race with the idea that human societies all progressed through four major stages (hunting, pastoralism, agriculture and commerce), and each stage was characteristic of a particular race.

Enlightenment attempts to classify the varieties of mankind were ultimately inconclusive. Though there was intense interest in the debates on race in the Enlightenment, paradoxically the debates were of little applicability to the practical problems of the Enlightenment. They were not conclusive enough either to oppose or to justify slavery. The idea of a universal human subject at the heart of the science of man could not be reconciled with seeing blacks as inferior, and enslaving them in large numbers.

The same ambiguities were present in the Enlightenment discussion of colonialism. James Cook clearly saw that indigenous peoples had made only questionable gains as a result of being discovered and colonised.

On the other side, many accepted that it was the duty of man to exploit the earth's resources (if necessary by forced labour), or viewed commerce itself, including the growing colonial trade, as a positive ethical value. Unanswerable problems abounded. What would be the cost of ending slavery? what would be the cost of ending colonialism? Others, like Rousseau, insisted on the way in which slavery, and the colonial regimes which rested on it, were an affront to central Enlightenment ideas. The existence of slavery contradicted the increasingly important idea that human beings had universal rights in virtue of their common humanity. Rousseau in his *Discourse on Inequality* pointed out that colonialism simply became a mechanism for the perpetuation of inequality, and thus constituted a barrier to the realisation of Enlightenment.

In 1770, the Abbé Guillaume Thomas Raynal (1713–96), assisted by Diderot, published his massive *Histoire philosophique et politique des établissements et du commerce des européens dans les deux Indes* (*Philosophical and Political History of European Institutions and Commerce in the East and West Indies*). The book enjoyed instant success, and was read far down the social scale. For us today it is valuable not only as a compendium of Enlightenment knowledge on colonial geography and economics, but also as a compendium of the ambivalent attitudes which underpinned its economic relationships with large areas of the non-European world. As he wrote:

> There has never been any event which has had more impact on the human race in general and for Europeans in particular as that of the discovery of the new world, and the passage to the Indies around the Cape of Good Hope. It was then that a commercial revolution began, a revolution in the balance of power, and in the customs, the industries and the government of every nation. It was through this event that men in the most distant lands were linked by new relationships and new needs. The produce of equatorial regions was consumed in polar climes . . . everywhere men mutually exchanged their opinions, their laws, their customs, their illnesses and their medicines, their virtues and their vices. Everything changed and will go on changing. But will the changes of the past and those that are to come, be useful to humanity? Will his condition be better, or will it be simply one of constant change?[7]

Raynal admits that in principle reason and equity do not provide any justification for colonisation. Yet he then argues that in practice it can be justified in the previously uninhabited areas of the globe, or to spread 'civilisation', or permit the better exploitation of natural resources. Yet

[7] Cited in Gabriel Esquer (ed.), *L'anti-colonialisme au XVIIIe siècle: Histoire philosophique et politique des établissements et du commerce des européennes dans les deux Indes, par l'Abbé Reynal* (Paris, 1951), 43 (opening paragraphs of the work).

Raynal still admitted that little good had come from the contact between European and native peoples. Confusedly, he saw most native peoples as closer to nature, happier, more innocent, in fact morally superior to Europeans. Yet this very closeness to nature also justified European colonisation as a way of spreading 'civilisation'. As we see in Chapter 6, reactions to slavery show similar ambivalences. Raynal acknowledges that slavery is unjustifiable. Nonetheless, he fell short of demanding its immediate abolition: slaves would not know what to do with their freedom, and the collapse of the plantation economies would unleash disorder and violence. By the end of the century, pressure groups, like the elite French Society for the Friends of Black People, founded in 1788, or the British Society for the Abolition of the Slave Trade, which organised mass petitions of Parliament against slavery, had begun to overcome these ambivalences in at least trying to bring about the end of slavery as an institution. Yet it was clear that these abolitionists worked from the same strongly primitivist idea as their opponents. Abolitionism had no necessary links with seeing Africans as they really were.

Utopian ideas of other exotic peoples began to change by the end of the eighteenth century. By the time of the French Revolution unresolved political and economic problems could no longer be hidden behind the utopia of the South Seas, or exported into the metaphor of the 'exotic'. By the 1790s, the image of the islands had in any case been tarnished by the murder of James Cook on Hawaii in 1779. Ideas that primitive and natural peoples were somehow happy, natural and models for Europeans had been superceded by one of islands corrupted, whose societies faced extinction as a result of the importation of European diseases.

The German thinker Johann Gottfried Herder (1774–1803) began to explore European impact on exotic societies as a way of beginning a critique of the Enlightenment as a whole. Herder challenged the optimistic view of human history as a progression towards perfection. It was thought by Condorcet and Turgot, for example, that human beings, by virtue of their common humanity, would all possess reason, and would gradually discard irrational superstitions, and bring human affairs into harmony with the universal natural order. The progress of history would therefore result in increasing harmonisation of world culture, so that mankind, instead of being divided between many different cultural groups, maybe differing as widely as did Tahitians and British, would become a truly cosmopolitan whole. These considerations are essential for a theory of globalisation.

Herder also rejected the idea that there existed a human nature somehow unchanged by history, geography and climate:

> The general philosophical, philanthropic tone of our century which wishes to extend our own ideal of virtue and happiness to each distant nation, to even the remotest age of history . . . It has taken words for works, Enlightenment for happiness, greater sophistication for virtues, and in this way invented the fiction of the general amelioration of the world.

Herder believed that in this way the high-minded men of the Enlightenment had justified the dominance of European culture over others:

> The ferment of generalities which characterise our philosophy, can conceal oppressions and infringements of the freedom of men and countries, of citizens and peoples.[8]

Herder was exposing the contradiction which lay at the heart of Enlightenment thinking about newly discovered non-European peoples. Europeans regarded them simultaneously as exotic and familiar, exemplary and exploitable. Nor were these mere quirks of Enlightenment thinking. They could result in the devastation of the non-European world. Raynal's equivocations made it easier to tolerate slavery. The idea of a single grand movement of progress lying behind human history obscured the possibility of there being many cultures, each driven by its own dynamic, and made it easier to tolerate the attack on different cultures, and their homogenisation into the European world. While Herder accepted the idea of a common human nature, his major concern was the extent of its variability. Unlike Condorcet, who saw human beings as basically of one kind, Herder saw them as having a basic unity, but also as deeply altered by geography and climate, until they became separate peoples, speaking different languages, looking physically different, telling different folk stories, reciting different poetry, making different laws.

Enlightenment reactions to exotic worlds and peoples were thus extraordinarily contradictory. Huron Indians and Pacific islanders were called to do work in solving European political problems. Many descriptions of a common humanity did nothing to end the slave trade. The list could be multiplied. One important overall point remains: that the contradictions and equivocations of European attitudes were also the pattern for the process of globalisation in the Enlightenment.[9]

[8] Cited in F. Barnard (ed.), *Herder on Social and Political Culture* (Cambridge, 1969), 187, 320.

[9] See Christian Joppke and Steven Lukes (eds.), *Multicultural Questions* (Oxford, 1999).

6 When people are property: the problem of slavery in the Enlightenment

Slavery has existed as the most extreme form of unfree labour in most human societies. It has assumed a myriad of legal, economic and social forms, and still exists today in many countries. Slavery has not only existed in almost all human societies, but has historically also done so without arousing outrage or abhorrence, or undergoing any radical challenge to its existence. Even the Greek philosopher Aristotle had argued that for some men, slavery was natural to their being.[1]

In the centuries between Aristotle and the Enlightenment no one argued that the slave's lot was enviable, and many had pleaded for the humane treatment of slaves. But it was not until the eighteenth century that there were more than isolated attacks on the institution of slavery itself. The complex history of the growth of radical opposition to slavery as an institution from around the time of the French thinker Montesquieu's attacks in his 1748 *De l'esprit des lois*, will be one of the main themes of this chapter. Even so, it was only from the 1770s onwards that compassion for the lot of the slave began to coalesce into organised pressure groups such as the *Société des Amis des Noirs* (Society of the Friends of Black People), which attacked the institution of slavery itself. In the young United States of America, this growing feeling was

1 On slavery in the ancient world, see Moses Finley, *Ancient Slavery and Modern Ideology* (London, 1980). This chapter will not cover the slave trade or its impact on African society, or slave life in the Americas, in any depth. On these topics there exists already a substantial literature. See Orlando Patterson, *Slavery and Social Death: A Comparative Study* (Cambridge, MA, 1982); Herbert S. Klein, *The Atlantic Slave Trade* (Cambridge, 1999); Joseph E. Inikori and Stanley L. Engerman (eds.), *The Atlantic Slave Trade: Effects on Economies, Societies and Peoples in Africa, the Americas and Europe* (Durham, NC, 1982); Eugene D. Genovese, *Roll, Jordan, Roll: The World the Slaves Made* (New York, 1974); Robert William Fogel and Stanley L. Engerman, *Time on the Cross: the Economics of American Negro Slavery* (Boston, MA, 1974). Comparatively little work exists on Ottoman and North African slavery, which continued in full force also in this period. It is very difficult to reconstruct the experience of the slaves themselves. Slave autobiographies exist, but most were written under guidance of literate whites. An account generally accepted as authentic is *The Interesting Narrative of the Life of Olaudah Equiano, Written by Himself* [1789], ed. Robert J. Allison (Boston, MA, 1995).

sometimes put into practice. Quakers in Pennsylvania and Massachusetts refused to hold slaves. In Pennsylvania gradual emancipation began in 1780, and in Rhode Island and Connecticut in 1784. There were bans on participation in the slave trade in Connecticut, Massachusetts, New York and Pennsylvania in 1788, and in Delaware in 1789.

However, the only actual large-scale liberation of slaves during the French Revolution began in the same year of 1789. On the French Caribbean colony of St Domingue came a violent, sustained resistance by the slaves themselves, which in the end for a short time procured their freedom. Slaves on the other French Caribbean possession of Guadeloupe were freed for about eight years during the Revolution.[2] Though slavery was ended legally during the French Revolution, in 1794, that piece of legislation was soon revoked by a French government torn between the demands of white planters, free persons of colour and the fear of slave revolt as violent as had happened in Guadeloupe and St Domingue. Equally, the mass abolitionist movement in England failed in 1792 to carry a parliamentary Bill which would have banned the slave trade, and had to wait until 1807 before the trade was legally banned. It was not until 1834 that slavery itself was banned in British possessions in the Caribbean. Slave-holding did not become illegal in the United States until the adoption of the thirteenth amendment to the Constitution in 1865. It did not end in Brazil, which employed a far larger number of slaves, until 1888. The reasons for the failure of the Enlightenment to procure the end of slavery, in spite of its significant changes in attitudes towards it, will be another major theme of this chapter.

At first sight, the continuing presence of slavery in the Enlightenment seems to present us with a paradox. This was an age in which many thinkers, such as Jean Jacques Rousseau in his *Discourse on the Origins of Inequality* (1754), centrally concerned themselves with equality, freedom, and with controls on arbitrary power. Yet at the same time a system of labour in which human beings were legally treated as chattels of their owners was tolerated, and recognised as a necessity for the plantation economies of the Caribbean. The continuing and expanding use of African slaves in some European colonies was obvious to contemporaries. By treating people as commodities, slavery raised more sharply than before such questions as the definition of a person, and the importance, both economic and political, of property. As debates over the justifications of slavery heightened, they called into question the

[2] C. L. R. James, *The Black Jacobins: Toussaint L'Ouverture and the San Domingo Revolution* (New York, 1963 and 1989); Eugene Genovese, *From Rebellion to Revolution: Afro-American Slave Revolts in the Making of the Modern World* (Baton Rouge, LA, 1979).

	£
Boston Distiller & Driver	100
Prince a Boiler	150
Gilbert	25
Jacob Ruptured	25
Money	20
Ned	65
Jupiter Superannuated	6
Billy Boiler	80
Toby Carter & field Worker	130
Sam Ditto	115
Andrew Ditto	125
Robin	90
Stephen	130
Abraham	90
Cuffy	90
Will	110
Jemmy	100
Stepney	85
Casar	95
Pimbah	6
Phillis & 1 child India	90
Nancy Daughter of Phillis	85
Penny Ditto	85
Molly	75
Violet	60
Cherry	90
Daphne	90
Peggy	90
Grace Peggy's Daughter	70
Venus ditto	40
Jenny a Girl Peggy's children	40
Daniel a Boy	20
Joe a child of Hagers	12
Peter a child of Peggy's	10
Seppy	75
Amber	65
Elsey a Girl	50
Cudjoe a Boy	75
Cuffy ditto	65
Isaac	20
[illegible]	100

	£
Joe	85
Hager & female child	90
Nelly	75
Total £	3590.2

56 Negroes in 1782

2 A Valuation of Estate Slaves, Antigua, 1782.
This financial document well illustrates the extent to which slaves were regarded as marketable property. Most slaves are referred to by Christian name only, making it hard to reconstruct slave genealogies.

status of very different authorities, ranging from the Bible to natural and positive law, which were used by different interest groups either to contest or to justify the institution of slavery. As missionary activity on the plantations increased, more slaves were baptised and became Christians. The problem thus further arose of combining spiritual equality and legal servitude. This was a problem that concerned the justification of the subjection not only of slaves but also of European women, whose membership of Christian churches and the equality of whose souls equally counted for little against their legal subordination. Debates on slavery became deeply bound up with, or even stood in for, debates about the boundaries of the civil community, about who was really inside and who, like slaves, was outside any given group.

The problems posed by the relationship between slavery and the Enlightenment are in any case hard to resolve. There were not only intractable paradoxes in the relationship between the existence of slavery and the Enlightenment. It is also impossible to say whether it was the diffusion of Enlightenment ideas or the growth of slavery itself that forced these paradoxes into the open. As so often it may be that each worked on the other. Objective changes in the organisation and economic importance of African slavery in European colonies in this period did not make any easier the path to their resolution or to the abolition of slavery.

Slavery in the eighteenth century was far from being a failing institution in economic terms, and yet it increasingly came to be an obnoxious one in moral terms. As Herbert Klein has shown, importation of slaves from West African ports to the Caribbean, the vast Portuguese colony of Brazil, and the English colonies in North America, reached its numerical peak in this period. The Caribbean islands, such as the English possessions of Jamaica and Barbados, the French possessions of Guadeloupe, Martinique, St Domingue (present-day Haiti) and French Guiana, and the Danish establishments in the Virgin Islands, were devoted to exceptionally profitable plantation agriculture. They specialised in the cultivation of crops such as sugar, tobacco, coffee and the dye-stuff indigo. These were products which demanded labour-intensive agriculture, and for which the demand in Europe appeared to be insatiable. This high and continuous demand meant that something different happened than the usual economic pattern of over-supplied markets reaching saturation point, demand beginning to drop and prices to fall. Quite differently, in the case of these tropical commodities profits for plantation owners could rise apparently forever.

Not only was demand insatiable. The plantations were supplied by a labour force composed of slave workers who lacked any ties to the surrounding society and were thus completely disposable at their owners' wish. Slaves gave their owners a supply of labour whose purchase price, food, clothing and lodging still put the cost of their labour at well below the market rate. The apparently inexhaustible supply of slaves liberated the planters from the labour shortage endemic in the Americas. Slave labour was thus an integral part of the rising profits of colonial plantation agriculture.

That colonial economies and profits depended on the existence of slavery meant that segments of metropolitan economies did as well. The British port cities of Liverpool and Bristol, or French port cities such as Nantes and Bordeaux, had economies that were influenced by the slave trade. Merchants and financiers lived by investing in the trade, as did the shipbuilders who constructed the specially designed slaving vessels, the carpenters, metalworkers and rope-makers, sail-makers and labourers who built them. In turn their wages helped to keep the local economy buoyant.

The slave trade also encouraged the growth of sophisticated financial systems. Voyages to the coast of West Africa to buy slaves for the Caribbean market might well last more than a year. Long-term credit arrangements from bankers and financiers to the captains of slaving ships made such voyages possible, and at the same time integrated the slave trade with the expansion of credit mechanisms which took place more broadly at this time. A loan made in Nantes or Bristol triggered events in distant continents. The certainty of payment made it worth the while of Arab and African slavers to bring slaves, often captured as prisoners of war deep in the African interior, to be sold to white traders on the coast of West Africa. From there, the slaves were shipped across the Atlantic in specially built ships, and set to work in the Caribbean or Brazil to produce colonial products for London, Paris, Milan and Boston.[3] The slave trade had global consequences made possible by its financial structures.

Slavery and the slave trade, and especially the version of it that reached its peak in the Caribbean and Brazil, were essential to the increasingly

[3] It is worth remembering that the traditional slave markets of North Africa and the Ottoman Empire were also still in full operation, and provided alternate pathways by which African slaves could reach Europe. See, for one such case, Wilhelm A. Bauer, *Angelo Soliman, der hochfürstliche Mohr: Ein exotisches Kapitel Alt-Wien* (Berlin, 1993). Historians of slavery have tended to concentrate on Caribbean and US slavery, because it was there that slavery was at its harshest and most inflexible. This contrasts with the very variable conditions of slavery in Ottoman lands, which did not exclude slaves rising to high civil and military office. It was also in the Americas that most dramatic changes in slavery occurred. But the persistence and flourishing of slavery outside the Americas shows how mono-focal the late eighteenth-century movements for the abolition of slavery actually were. For a more wide-ranging comparative approach with extensive citations from original documents, see Stanley L. Engerman, Seymour Drescher and Robert Paquette (eds.), *Slavery* (Oxford, 2001).

integrated world economy of the Enlightenment. They were embedded in powerful, highly organised, economic structures. Slave labour returned high profits to those in the slave trade, and also to those involved in colonial plantation production. While these profits might not have been the key to the industrial revolution, they certainly primed the economic pump, and provided higher tax revenues to the ever-expanding governments discussed in Chapter 3. To begin to question the existence of slavery itself, rather than deploring the situation of individual slaves, was thus in Enlightenment terms to have to think thoughts which were not only difficult but which also logically involved the dismantling of a profitable, successful, and globally organised economic structure. It is not difficult to see why anti-slavery mobilisation took so long to come together.

The Enlightenment not only saw the economic integration of the world; it opened up enormous moral and intellectual problems that did not become easier to solve once they were projected onto a world stage. Economic integration often, as in this case, works against the moral integration of the globe. Nowhere was this more clearly demonstrated than in relation to slavery. There were strong economic interests pushing for the continuing existence of slavery. The moral ground for abolition could seem ambiguous. Reactions to slavery acted almost as a discloser fluid for the contradictions and paradoxes of Enlightenment thought. Even those opposed to slavery could, like Thomas Jefferson, often sound very like their opponents. The increase of anti-slavery sentiment in the eighteenth century was in fact a long, and often confused, process. Mass petitioning against slavery began in Britain in the 1770s. Elite anti-slavery societies emerged in France, such as the *Société des Amis des Noirs*, founded in 1787. Yet the arguments of both pro- and anti-slavery thinkers in fact were and remained ambiguous throughout this period. The path to abolition in both Europe and North America by the mid nineteenth century was very long.[4]

Mass opposition to slavery was a novel phenomenon even in late eighteenth-century Britain, and never occurred in France. Radical protests against slavery (rather than against individual instances of inhumanity to slaves) can be traced as far back as 1688, in the Moravian

[4] Seymour Drescher, *Capitalism and Anti-Slavery: British Mobilisation in Comparative Perspective* (New York, 1987); *The Mighty Experiment: Free Labour and Slavery in British Emancipation* (Oxford, 2002); *From Slavery to Freedom: Abolition of Slavery and the Aftermath of Emancipation in Brazil* (Madison, WI, 1999); Sue Peabody, *"There are No Slaves in France": The Political Culture of Race and Slavery in the Ancien Régime* (New York, 1996); Gert Ostindie (ed.), *Fifty Years Later: Capitalism, Modernity and Anti-Slavery in the Dutch Orbit* (Leiden, 1995).

colony of Germantown, then outside Philadelphia. This might seem like a promising beginning, but in fact even such communities often backslid into slave ownership.[5] Neither did this happen simply for economic reasons. While the non-conformist churches were often the first to make radical anti-slavery protests, they faced several problems in finding legitimation for doing so. Churches such as the Moravians were tied to Biblical authority, yet there was no Biblical support for abolition. Numerous Old Testament passages showed the patriarchs holding slaves. There was no divine pronouncement against it. In the New Testament, there is no explicit discussion of the issue, and anti-slavery opinion had to fall back for legitimation on allegorical interpretations of the 'freedom' which comes to us from Christ. The Bible, authoritative though it still was, could thus be a slippery text for those who looked there for decisive pronouncements against slavery. As late as 1785, for example, 266 slave-owners petitioned the Virginia General Assembly against a measure facilitating the manumission of slaves. They based their case squarely on the Bible. Abraham, after all, had kept slaves, and 'Christ while on earth and giving instructions for things necessary for salvation, did not forbid it, but instead left behind injunctions to regulate masters and servants'. The Virginia petitioners also remark that they are trying to meet their opponents on their own ground 'who make bold to petition your August Assembly for a general emancipation of them [slaves] in pretending to be moved by religious principles and taking for their motive universal charity'. These comments were made in direct response to Methodist resolutions of 1784, excluding slave-owners from their congregations.[6] The Virginia case is interesting because it well exemplifies the slipperiness of religious arguments as bases of both pro- and anti-slavery positions. It also shows that so strong were the Biblical arguments for slavery, that for these pro-slavery Virginians there was no felt need to bring up arguments based on race for additional support of their position. This indicates also the difficult position in the Enlightenment of the Bible as a source of authority. Was it possible to use the Bible to intervene in the making of positive law in Virginia in the 1780s, as both Methodists and slaveholders seemed to assume? And how much authority had the new Enlightenment ideals of 'benevolence' or 'universal charity' against the Bible text? Pro- and anti-slavery groups did not necessarily dispose of sharply differentiated argumentation or use different evidence to legitimate their cause.

5 Jon F. Sensbach, *A Separate Canaan: The Making of an Afro-Moravian World in North Carolina, 1763–1840* (Chapel Hill, NC, 1998).

6 Fredrika Teute Schmidt and Barbara Ripel Wilhelm, 'Early Pro-slavery Petitions in Virginia', *William and Mary Quarterly*, 30 (1973), 143–4.

Religious groups also faced other problems in making a convincing case for abolition. The 'Afro-Moravians' described by Jon Sensbach, the converted and baptised slaves held by Moravian small farmers in Virginia, are an example.[7] Far from the plantations of the Caribbean, these slaves worked beside their masters on the small farms of the Virginia hinterland. Baptised, they worshipped together in the same buildings, sitting on the same benches for the communal meals, and eventually being buried in the same graveyard. This situation posed in acute form the contradiction between the spiritual equality with their masters of the baptised slaves. The daily interweaving of their lives in church and work, on the one hand, and on the other, the slaves' legal situation of total submission to their white masters, were difficult to reconcile. Spiritual equality and legal inequality to the highest degree were supposed to co-exist in one person. It should come as no surprise that early feminists such as Mary Wollstonecraft should point out the similarities between the position of European women and of slaves, as we shall see in Chapter 7. European women were baptised too; but spiritual equality gave them no legal equality with men. 'Equality' was as slippery a word as 'freedom'. Neither did different forms of freedom or of equality line up neatly with each other.

This is no less true in relation to the way in which arguments about race intervened in arguments about slavery. By the end of the century, assertions that black Africans formed a 'race' whose characteristics uniquely fitted them for slavery and justified its imposition as 'natural', had become a common – though as the Virginia petition example shows, not a necessary – part of pro-slavery positions. To understand why this happened, we need to go back to the way racial thinking was structured in the Enlightenment, which we began to discuss in Chapter 5.

It became easier for Europeans to link race and slavery, first of all, because, from the end of the seventeenth century, those slaves reaching the Caribbean, North America and Brazil were almost all black Africans (just as were the slaves seen by Europeans in Arab North Africa). Indentured labour, most of it European, began to be less common and then almost completely disappeared as a system of unfree labour in the Americas by the late eighteenth century. This allowed debates on slavery, in the absence of other forms of unfree labour usually confined to white people, to become connected with debates about the racial characteristics of sub-Saharan Africans. Early on, Montesquieu in his *De l'esprit des lois* of 1748, satirised those who believed that the physical characteristics

[7] Sensbach, *A Separate Canaan*.

of Africans justified their enslavement. He remarked ironically that had he to defend slavery, he would argue that:

> Those concerned are black from head to toe, and they have such flat noses that it is almost impossible to feel sorry for them. One cannot get into one's mind that God, who is a very wise being, should have put a soul, above all a good soul, in a body that was entirely black. It is impossible for us to assume that these people are men because if we assumed they were men one would begin to believe that we ourselves were not Christians.

Race and slavery became linked because of two further developments: the decreasing reliance in the Enlightenment on the possession of a soul as a definition of a human being; and the rise in interest in all things involving the classification of natural objects in the eighteenth century. What Michel Foucault once called the 'taxonomic impulse', the impulse to classify natural objects, led natural philosophers to ask where the line between men and primates should be drawn, and whether man himself could be divided into different species, and if so on the bases of what criteria. This is the time at which man himself became 'an object of natural history' as Jefferson was later to express it in his 1781–2 *Notes on the State of Virginia*.

It was not easy to find a way to systematically analyse the different varieties of man. Even the most famous taxonomist of the age, Linnaeus, sometimes classified orang-outangs as men (because of their upright posture, use of tools and, some contended, speech) and sometimes did not; and sometimes included and sometimes excluded 'giants', 'hairy men' and so on as separate categories of man. Debate raged as to where to put the boundary between the primates and man. Should it be on the basis of skeleton, external appearance or social behaviour? The question 'What is a man?' became increasingly difficult to answer in the Enlightenment. It became difficult to answer exactly as the century increasingly made the human being the locus of the possession of the very rights and legal identity denied to slaves.[8]

Thinking about the obvious apparent physical differences between humans from different parts of the world was very different in the eighteenth century than it had been previously. Older 'pre-formationist' ideas received since Descartes, that human beings were pre-formed from all eternity by God, that in other words the dark skin of the African or the straight dark hair of the Japanese was set from all time for each individual, no longer seemed so convincing. Both Montesquieu and Buffon

[8] Christopher Fox, Roy Porter and Robert Wokler (eds.), *Inventing Human Science: Eighteenth-Century Domains* (Berkeley and London, 1995), 112–51.

argued that appearance, disposition and temperament were shaped by climate and geography. Believing, too, that man had a single origin in the descendants of Adam, Montesquieu, like Buffon, thought that skin colour could only be an acquired characteristic shaped by climate. Both believed that the human race 'must' originally have been white (a belief of course without any biblical basis), and that dark-skinned peoples were so because of their exposure to hot climates, not because they really differed from the original archetype of humanity. Such ideas carried the implication that if racial characteristics were so shaped by climate and environment, they had not been fixed by God from all time, but could be changed if a race altered what we would now call its habitat.

But by the end of the century, ideas were changing once again. Anatomists like Petrus Camper and Johann Friedrich Blumenbach now concentrated not on external characteristics like skin colour and hair conformation, but on the internal structures of the body, especially the skeleton and cranium. These works gave legitimacy to a notion of a natural hierarchy of the races on the strength of the scrutiny of anatomical form, cranial angles and skin pigmentation. This was a very new way of thinking about race. Camper and Blumenbach argued that differences between the races in skeletal structure seemed to go well beyond what might plausibly be argued to be effects of climate and environment. After such studies, the differences between races seemed less flexible than they had earlier in the century. Racial difference began to seem far more inevitable and ineluctable. It was also at this time that increased scientific attention began to be paid to the anatomical conformation of women, especially skeleton and cranial size and shape. Skeletal evidence was used to 'prove' that women had smaller cranial cavities and were thus 'naturally' intellectually inferior to men. It is no accident that slaves and women were argued to be inferior on the basis of 'scientific' evidence. They were the two groups who most dangerously embodied the two extremes of legal inequality and spiritual equality.

As we will see in Chapter 8, the natural was also emerging as a moral category of great force in the Enlightenment. What was natural was also (usually) what was good; it was also what was ineluctable. In spite of Hume's protests, therefore, it was difficult for eighteenth-century people not to leap from the *is* to the *ought*, from what was natural to what was socially defined, in the case of thinking about women as much as in the case of thinking about slaves. In effect, the 'natural' became a new way of designating classes of humans as outsiders, at points where taxonomy alone failed to achieve this objective. While anatomists were not in the pay of Caribbean slave-holders, the theories of human difference which they sponsored certainly did not weaken the pro-slavery cause. They functioned to revamp Aristotelian arguments about the way in which some men, 'Barbarians', were in fact 'natural slaves' and thus, if enslaved, would be living in accord with their own true nature. Slavery could thus, from these arguments, be seen as maintaining the order of nature. Such arguments had been widely used in the Spanish colonies in the Americas from their foundation. The arguments of the late eighteenth-century anatomists were a way of saying the same thing.[9]

What was new, however, was the way in which the new anatomy turned all those whom it anatomised into the 'objects' of science, that is as having an existence only in so far as they were seen and anatomised by the scientist. This made it possible to treat inhumanly humans who became 'objects' of science, and thus enforce their position as outsiders. An important source here is Thomas Jefferson's 1781–2 *Notes on the State of Virginia*. This text is important not only because its author was the third President of the young United States, but also because it shows how hard it was to think clearly about slavery, especially for those who, like Jefferson, lived in the middle of flourishing slave societies. He had originally inserted clauses outlawing slavery and the slave trade into the Declaration of Independence that he drafted in 1776. The resistance of delegations from Georgia and South Carolina had caused these clauses to be removed.

Yet in the *Notes on the State of Virginia* he remarked, 'To our reproach it must be said that though for a century and a half we have had under our eyes the races of black and of red men, they have never yet been viewed by us as objects of natural history.' This text, which was not originally intended for a Virginia audience, expatiates on the moral horror of slavery, and describes its corrupting effect on the whole of white slave-owning society (though Jefferson devoted little attention to its bad effects on the slaves themselves). But Jefferson apparently sees no incongruence in pointing out the importance of scientific studies of racial difference. Due to inadequate scientific study Jefferson feels able

> to advance it therefore as a suspicion only, that the blacks, whether originally a distinct race, or made distinct by time and circumstances, are inferior to the whites in the endowments both of body and mind. It is not against experience to suppose that different species of the same genus, or variations of the same species, may possess different qualifications . . . This unfortunate difference of colour and perhaps of faculty, is a powerful obstacle to the emancipation of these people.

[9] Anthony Pagden, *The Fall of Natural Man: The American Indian and the Origins of Comparative Ethnology* (Cambridge, 1982).

This passage is interesting because it shows that opposition to slavery and the slave trade did not necessarily involve a belief in equality between black and white people.

The appeal to 'scientific evidence' shows very clearly the increasing authority of science by the late century as a force that could legitimate arguments. But like arguments from biblical authority, science was likely to give inconclusive directions. The work of the anatomists and those working on the science of man gave no clear basis for either pro- or anti-slavery arguments. Blumenbach, for example, produced an anatomy which allowed ideas of race as ineluctable to emerge. But his work begins with the idea that human beings have universal characteristics, like the possession of mind. Jefferson is another example. He uses the language of natural history and taxonomy (the science of classification) to argue that emancipation must be immediately followed by the deportation of all former slaves. He exclaims:

> Will not a lover of natural history then, one who views the gradations in all the races of animals with the eye of philosophy, excuse an effort to keep those in the department of man as distinct as Nature has formed them? . . . Among the Romans, emancipation required but one effort. The slave, when made free, might mix with, without staining, the blood of his master. But with us a second is necessary, unknown to history. When freed, he is to be removed beyond the reach of mixing.

The emancipated slave is to be immediately deported, before any sexual relation with white people can occur. Jefferson here both acknowledges and denies that Africans were of the same race as whites. Species were not defined alone by their physical resemblance, but on their ability to interbreed. Jefferson wants to believe that African slaves are humans, because they look enough like white humans; but he does not want them to interbreed with whites, and thus is ambiguous about whether they are the same species as whites.

Jefferson wanted the abolition of slavery, as far as it could be achieved without the 'irritation' of social and economic turmoil – which is to say, never. He thought slaves were human, but did not want to face the consequences of seeing them as so human that they could form sexual relationships with whites. Jefferson's thinking on slavery was fragile and conflicted. In that he was hardly unique. Like many others who detested slavery, he went on holding slaves, and like many others who detested racial mixture, continued a long relationship with a slave woman. But the contradictions could have consequences that went well beyond the personal level. As one of the architects of the American Revolution, as mainly responsible for the drafting of the Declaration of Independence, and as third President of the new United States, he helped bring into being a new state undermined by contradiction from the start by the issue of slavery. In a letter to a French friend, Jean Nicholas Meunier, of June 1786, he bemoaned Virginia's failure to legislate for slave emancipation, thus inflicting on slaves 'bondage more dreadful than that which they had risen against from England'.[10] The new state, whose founders claimed liberty for themselves as an inalienable right, but simultaneously denied it to their slaves, was left with a serious problem not to be resolved except by the Civil War more than seventy years later.

Neither scientific arguments, nor arguments from biblical authority provided a firm basis for the views of pro- or anti-slavery groups. Neither, as we will see, did political ideologies of property and liberty or even legal decisions. The very fact that so many attempts were made, from so many different quarters, to legitimate both anti-slavery and slavery, shows, firstly, the extent to which slavery articulated vital Enlightenment issues; secondly, it shows how unclear the authority of such legitimations was. The debate on slavery is an exemplification of an even wider crisis of authority in the Enlightenment. Yet the very contradictions evident in thinking about slavery in the Enlightenment may also have had more benign long-term consequences as well. For slavery to be maintained, it is helpful if those enslaved can be seen as totally 'enslavable outsiders'. But slaves were increasingly often baptised members of the same churches as their masters, albeit their equality of soul did not lead to civil freedom. There were many who, like Jefferson, acknowledged the humanity of slaves, albeit taking no direct action to end slavery. And legal decisions at the end of the century left it less than clear that slaves were property rather than persons. So in some respects, and in spite of the work of contemporary anatomists, the 'outsiders' were becoming less wholly so in the Enlightenment, and this also must have contributed to weakening slavery as a legitimate institution, at least in Europe and North America.

When we look at how the Enlightenment integrated slaves and slavery into its thinking about property, the situation is no less complex. Slaves were property. They were bought and sold in a clearly defined market, in just the same way that cattle or books might be. Property holding and liberty were closely connected in the Enlightenment. In the 'classical republican' tradition of political ideology, the right to hold property, and actual property holding, particularly tenure of freehold land unencumbered by rent or lease, protected subjects against the whims of overbearing monarchs. It gave men a 'stake in the country', stabilised society and politics alike, preventing the collapse of order which would leave no one with liberty – an important point for those living in the century after the

[10] Thomas Jefferson, *Writings* (New York, 1900).

English civil war and the Frondes of France. This was not simply an elite political ideology. It was a belief held at most levels of society, particularly in England and its North American colonies.

In France, similarly, few endorsed the teachings of Rousseau who in his 1754 *Discours sur l'origine et les fondements de l'inégalité parmi les hommes* saw property as the cause of a harmful inequality amongst men who were created naturally equal. In the *Encyclopédie* article 'Inégalité naturelle', for example, the Chevalier de Jaucourt affirmed the right to hold property, as one that was natural and absolute, and the foundation of all society. But any scheme of slave emancipation, let alone any attack on the slave trade itself, would undermine property rights, and increase the powers of government – since only government could order and organise slave emancipation – and thus endanger the very foundations of liberty. These were sensitive issues when all across Europe, as we have seen in Chapter 3, governments trying to stay afloat in the international competition of the period attempted increasingly to expand their powers, and extract more of surplus property, in the shape of taxes, than they had ever done before. The rights and liberties of subjects were widely perceived as being under threat in all of the major monarchical states. It is thus one of the numerous paradoxes surrounding this subject that it was exactly at this time that an organised anti-slavery movement began to mobilise in England.

Anti-slavery sentiment also succeeded in creating legal cases whose judgments reveal all the problems and ambiguities we have so far discussed. Undoubtedly the most famous case concerned James Somerset, a slave held by a planter, Charles Stuart. Stuart brought Somerset with him to England in 1769. When in October 1771 their return to Virginia drew near, Somerset deserted his master. Stuart had him recaptured, and forcibly imprisoned on a ship waiting at anchor in the Port of London and bound for Jamaica, where Somerset was to be sold. In doing so Stuart was asserting his rights as a property-owner to dispose absolutely of his slave. Anti-slavery activists such as Granville Sharpe organised lawyers to act on Somerset's behalf, and the case opened before Lord Justice Mansfield in 1772. Somerset's lawyers argued that by condemning the return, 'the revival of domestic slavery will be rendered as impracticable by introduction from our colonies and from other countries as it is by commencement here'. Mansfield ruled, with reluctance, that Somerset could not be forced to return to Virginia against his will.

> The state of slavery is of such a nature that it is incapable of being introduced on any reasons, moral or political; but only by positive law, which preserves its force long after the reason, occasion and time itself from whence it was created, is erased from memory: it's so odious that nothing can be suffered to support it, but positive law . . . therefore, the black must be discharged.

Somerset was discharged partly as a solution of the conflict of laws between England, which had no provision for slavery, and those of Virginia, which did. Mansfield's reasoning also contained the argument that slavery was so odious that it could only be upheld by a positive legal system, and received no support from natural law. However reluctant Mansfield's judgment, Somerset was no longer to be treated like a piece of inanimate property, as his master argued the status of slave implied, but as a person. Anti-slavery activists hailed the Somerset case as a great victory. But it should be noted that the case did not make statute law. It only resolved the particular issue between Somerset and his master. Nor did the case abolish either slavery or the slave trade, nor did it make illegal the holding of slaves either in England or in its colonies. But Somerset's case was a publicity success for the anti-slavery side. It contributed thus to the mass-mobilisation against slavery that was unique to Britain at this time. It also captured the attention of the Methodist leader John Wesley, and led to the Methodist movement's 'awakening' against slavery and slave owning.[11]

By now, we have assembled a large number of issues around the problem of slavery: the normative power of racial difference; the relation between property and liberty; the degree of authority to be given to biblical teaching on slavery, and hence the degree of authority to be given to the Bible itself; the limits of spiritual equality; the grounding of social and legal inferiority in physical difference. These are all problems at the heart of Enlightenment thinking, which is centrally concerned with the meaning and manipulation of difference. They also illustrate the ways in which Enlightenment thought, which often dealt in powerful abstractions, also often failed to offer a clear basis for action. The Enlightenment was trying to create a 'universal' human subject, one possessed of rationality, a free actor economically, who could be used as the basis of the 'science of man'. Slavery showed how far such an ideal was from being achieved. And yet slavery changed from being a practice acceptable to most people at the beginning of the Enlightenment to being progressively less acceptable and more problematic by the end. By mid-century it was increasingly being seen, even by ordinary people, not only as cruel and wrong, but also as somehow unalterable. By the end of the century, the Somerset case and its consequences, such as the 'awakening' of Methodism against slavery, and increased mass petitioning against it in England,

[11] This account draws on David Brion Davis, *The Problem of Slavery in the Age of Revolution* (Ithaca, NY, and London, 1975), 470–86, and Ruth Paley, 'After Somerset: Mansfield, Slavery and the Law in England, 1772–1830', in Norma Landau (ed.), *Law, Crime and English Society, 1660–1830* (Cambridge, 2002).

were showing how the tide of opinion was beginning to turn against slavery as an institution even at the height of its economic importance in the Caribbean.

The Methodist turn against slavery was part of a general mobilisation of opinion in Britain and, to a limited extent, in its North American colonies. The origins of this change are still obscure. Religious motivations were undoubtedly important, but the most powerful condemnations of slavery came not from the majority churches, but precisely from those denominations with fewest members. Even so, probably more people were influenced directly or indirectly by Methodism or Quakerism, than could claim a close knowledge of Voltaire's or Montesquieu's arguments on slavery. Yet in asking what caused the dramatic shifts in attitudes towards slavery, it is in fact difficult to ascribe this to religious factors. It is true that the Protestant 'witnessing' churches such as Moravianism and Quakerism, at angular relationships with the established churches, took an early lead in challenging slavery. But in the established churches themselves, there is no evidence of a religious divide. The Calvinist Dutch had little sympathy for abolition, neither did the Catholic French, and nor did the Protestant South of the American Republic.

More important for the majority of people than religious or economic motives, or scientific discussion of racial characteristics, may have been the growing diffusion of Enlightenment ideologies which valorised sentiment, humanity and benevolence. Others argued that slavery was a danger to the preservation of the liberty of non-slave societies. All these points of view paid due service to the sufferings of the slaves. But the basis of their opinions had in the end more to do with securing the self-esteem of liberal whites, or the security of white societies that felt 'liberties' under threat.

The mobilisation against slavery at the end of the century seems to have had some real effects. The chronology of legal abolition looks impressive. In England, the slave trade, though not slave holding, was declared illegal in 1807, and slavery was illegal in the British Caribbean islands from 1833. Several states in the new American Republic, such as New York State in 1799, also adopted graduated emancipation laws. But in reality, the record of abolition was patchy. The only part of the Caribbean which achieved the outright liberation of slaves was the French possession of St Domingue, where liberation was achieved by the slaves themselves in a series of violent conflicts lasting from 1792 to 1804. In 1802, the French restored slavery in Guadeloupe, and to all French colonies in 1803, having previously outlawed slavery in their colonies in 1794. In the new United States of America, those states which 'abolished' slavery had in any case previously very low ratios of slaves to whites in comparison to the plantation islands of the Caribbean. Even such states always liberated slaves gradually over periods of up to twenty-five years rather than fully and outright. In the largest slave society of all, Brazil, outright emancipation did not occur until 1888, and in the United States not until the Civil War and the thirteenth Amendment to the Constitution in 1865. Historians have also argued that the use of slavery may in fact have actually expanded in places like Louisiana, other southern states of the United States, the Guianas and Trinidad in the period between the French Revolution and the American Civil War.[12]

It must also be remembered that emancipation and abolitionism do not necessarily go together. Virginia planters, whose slave population was self-reproducing, not only had no need for the existence of the slave trade, but campaigned against it, seeing slave-traders as a commercial class who aimed to create indebtedness. The Virginia example shows that it was well possible to campaign against the trade, and still with conviction possess slaves. Even mass support for abolition in England might have been connected more with a concern for the maintenance of liberty at home. It did not necessarily imply a wish to see former slaves living in England, or a great sympathy for the plight of slaves elsewhere. Finally, mass abolitionism was confined to England. Pressure groups in France like the *Société des Amis des Noirs* were founded later, just before the Revolution, and remained elite organisations. Abolitionism was not a popular cause in the general population of France.

Anti-slavery appeared very late in the day as 'issue politics' in the Enlightenment, far later than campaigns in press and public opinion against, for example, judicial torture, tax inequality, or civil rights for Protestants in Catholic countries, the end of villeinage, and the reduction of the economic and cultural power of the Catholic Church. Even after the opening of the French Revolution, the new ideology of equal rights did not bring immediate or permanent or effective emancipation. Other excluded groups, such as women, also had to wait to be ascribed rights, often achieved them briefly, and were then deprived of them again. The problem posed to reformers was how to give equal and universal rights, in the face of economic and political forces, such as slavery, with vested interests in maintaining difference; and in the face of the 'facts' of human biological difference. This is a problem that is still with us.

[12] David Barry Gaspar and David Patrick Geggus (eds.), *A Turbulent Time: The French Revolution and the Greater Caribbean* (Bloomington, IN, and Indianapolis, 1997).

7 Enlightenment thinking about gender

> Who made man the exclusive judge, if woman partake with him of the gift of reason?
>
> For man and woman, truth, if I understand the meaning of the word, must be the same; yet for the fanciful female character, so prettily drawn by poets and novelists, demanding the sacrifice of truth and sincerity, virtue becomes a relative idea, having no other foundation but utility, and of that utility, men pretend arbitrarily to judge, shaping it to their own convenience.
>
> The male is male only at certain moments. The female is female her whole life . . . everything constantly recalls her sex to her . . . a perfect woman and a perfect man ought not to resemble each other in mind any more than in looks.[1]

The Enlightenment devoted great energies to the definition of gender, so great in fact that some historians have seen this period as a watershed in European culture's attempts to define difference between the sexes.[2] Gender, like the exotic, was an area of difference. It therefore challenged some very strong strands in Enlightenment thought, the strands that emphasised the idea of a universal human nature, and a universal human history, both validated by the possession of a single universal human form of rationality. It was no accident that by the end of the eighteenth century many thinkers such as Mary Wollstonecraft were to equate the denial of rights to slaves and the denial of rights to women. Each destabilised crucial Enlightenment assumptions. Yet in practice as well as in much

[1] Mary Wollstonecraft, *Vindication of the Rights of Women* [1792], ed. M. B. Kramnick (London, 1982), 87, 139; Jean Jacques Rousseau, *Emile, ou de l'éducation* [1762] (Paris, 1964), book V, 446, 450.

[2] Rita Goldberg, *Sex and Enlightenment: Women in Richardson and Diderot* (Cambridge, 1984); Thomas Laqueur, *Making Sex: Body and Gender from the Greeks to Freud* (Cambridge, MA, 1990), 5. 'By around 1800, writers of all sorts were determined to base what they insisted were fundamental differences between the male and female sexes, and thus between man and woman, on discoverable biological distinctions, and to express these in a radically different rhetoric.'

Enlightenment writing, each was insisted upon. This chapter attempts to understand this contradiction.

A great deal of effort in the Enlightenment focussed on the definition of femininity. Images powerful in former times of women as shrews, harlots or Amazons retreated, and were replaced by numerous medical and scientific attempts to define social and cultural differences between men and women as 'natural' and therefore right and inevitable. Much debate focussed on the physical constitution of the female sex and on the importance of women's role as mothers.[3] In these debates science and medicine contributed an increasingly important voice.

Increasingly, medical writings seemed to imply that women were virtually a separate species within the human race, characterised by their reproductive functions, and by a sexuality which was often denied or repressed. Paradoxically, however, women were often ascribed the role of custodians of morality and religion within the domestic setting. This was a view of women which obviously contains many inconsistent elements. It was one which also denied women full status as individuals, at precisely the time that men were increasingly defining themselves as autonomous individual actors in the legal and economic spheres, even in those countries, such as France, whose political structures were overwhelmingly based on corporate, not individual identities.[4] Enlightenment thinking about gender thus confronted many internal inconsistencies. It set up a wide gap between the rights and autonomy increasingly demanded by men and the dependence still demanded from women. It was discrepancies such as these which were to shape the arguments which were to be put forward at the end of the century by such writers as Mary Wollstonecraft, Theodor von Hippel or the Marquis de Condorcet.[5]

Wollstonecraft's book was important, not only because of the classic status it has acquired in contemporary feminist thought, but also because it was one of the first books squarely to confront the contradictions implicit in Enlightenment ideas of gender, and point out their problems for the structure of Enlightenment thought. Wollstonecraft pointed out that ideas of femininity supported by writers such as Rousseau, which designated women as inferior to and different from men, did nothing

[3] Pierre Fauchéry, *La destinée féminine dans le roman européen du dix-huitième siècle, 1713–1807: Essai de gynécomythie romanesque* (Paris, 1972); Nancy K. Miller, *The Heroine's Text: Readings in the French and English Novel 1722–1782* (New York, 1980).

[4] Elizabeth Fox-Genovese and Eugene D. Genovese, *Fruits of Merchant Capital* (Oxford, 1983), especially chapter II, 'The Ideological Bases of Domestic Economy'.

[5] Wollstonecraft, *Vindication*; Theodor von Hippel, *Über die Bürgerliche Verbesserung der Weiber* (Berlin, 1792), reprinted Vaduz, Switzerland, 1981; Nicolas Caritat, Marquis de Condorcet, 'Lettres d'un bourgeois de New Haven', in *Oeuvres complètes de Condorcet* (Paris, 1804), XII, 19–20; 'Déclaration des Droits: Egalité', in *Oeuvres complètes*, 286–8.

more, as Voltaire had previously noted, than replicate in domestic life the political system based on privilege and arbitrary power, enjoyed by monarchs and aristocrats over their subjects, or slave owners over their slaves, which those same thinkers were so ready to criticise in other contexts.[6] Wollstonecraft also identified yet more serious contradictions in Enlightenment thought as it clustered around gender. She pointed out that Enlightenment was based on ideals such as 'reason' and 'virtue' which were alleged to be innate in, or attainable by, all human beings. But rationality was precisely what was denied to women by writers such as Rousseau, and by the medical writers, while 'virtue' was defined for women in an exclusively sexual sense. As Wollstonecraft points out, however, such manoeuvres can only lead to a dangerous moral relativism which will also impede the progress of Enlightenment, by 'giving a sex to morals'.[7] By defining 'virtue' as one thing for men and another for women, any attempt to link Enlightenment and religion could also be undermined. As she says:

> If women are by nature inferior to men, their virtues must be the same in quality, if not in degree, or virtue is a relative idea . . . virtue has only one eternal standard.[8]
>
> It is a farce to call any being virtuous whose virtues do not result from the exercise of its own reason.[9]

To say that virtue for some human beings (women) is not founded on rationality and is differently defined from that practised by other human beings (men) is to give it characteristics which mean it cannot grow from God, since he is one, eternal and rational.

If women were in fact not rational, Wollstonecraft argued, it would be far preferable to abandon pretence, and exclude them altogether from social life, in the same way that animals are. If they *are* rational, then they should take part in the same moral and intellectual life that men do:

> Contending for the rights of woman, my main argument is but on this simple principle, that if she be not prepared by education to become the companion of man, she will stop the progress of knowledge and virtue: for truth must be common to all, or it will be inefficacious with respect to its influence on general practice.[10]

Without a universal, non-gendered standard of morals and rationality, it would not be possible to sustain the Enlightenment project of emancipation through universal value systems based on reason and virtue, if one half of the human race were held to lack a capacity for either quality. In other words, the way the Enlightenment thought about gender

[6] Wollstonecraft, *Vindication*, 121–2. [7] *Ibid.*, 121.
[8] *Ibid.*, 108; see also 109, 139. [9] *Ibid.*, 103. [10] *Ibid.*, 86.

contradicted, undermined, and challenged its claims to legitimacy as a universally applicable project.

It has often been pointed out that many of these contradictions arose from the way in which the Enlightenment connected discussion of gender with the ambiguous concept of nature. The concern of Rousseau and others like him was to define femininity as 'natural' and hence as both 'right' and ineluctable. In doing so, they were attaching the debate on femininity to one of the central concerns of the Enlightenment. 'Natural' could mean many different things: it could mean 'not socially defined'; not 'artificial'; 'based on the external physical world'. Overwhelmingly, 'natural' was used, often in a mixture of all these meanings, to legitimate and control arrangements which we in the twenty-first century would see as socially created, and hence subject to change and criticism.[11] 'Naturalness' was also often used to legitimate arguments aimed to bring into being a state of affairs which did not yet fully exist. 'Natural' in other words was a very good way to argue for points of view that were in fact often novel and always highly prescriptive. Social arrangements could be given additional validation by being presented as 'natural'. Arguments for the 'naturalness' of feminine roles could thus, because of the ambiguity of the term, gain force from biological arguments about created 'nature' and, at the same time, from repeated Enlightenment polemics against 'artificiality' in society, by which was meant social practices which were held to be at odds with the 'real' or true structures of 'human nature'.[12]

The extreme ambiguity of the term 'nature' could be thus used in multiple ways to define femininity in this period. Women were increasingly defined as closer to 'nature' than were men, as well as being more determined by 'nature', meaning anatomy and physiology. Women were especially affected by a definition of 'nature' as meaning the external, created world, as that realm upon which mankind acts, partly to manipulate, partly to render intelligible. 'Nature' could be taken to be that part of the world, which human beings have understood, mastered and made their own.[13] Equally the notion that women are closer to nature than men included *both* the claim that because of their physical 'nature' they were emotional, credulous, and incapable of objective reasoning; and at the same time that they were the carriers, within the family, of a new morality through which the *un*-naturalness of civilisation, its artificiality, could be transcended and a society created which was natural, polite and

[11] L. J. Jordanova, *Sexual Visions: Images of Gender in Science and Medicine between the Eighteenth and Twentieth Centuries* (London and New York, 1989), 19–42, esp. 41.

[12] The most celebrated controversy of the Enlightenment on this issue was that caused by Rousseau's own 1750 *Discours sur les sciences et les arts*.

[13] Jordanova, *Sexual Visions*, 41.

modern.[14] Cultural images of this complex relation between femininity and the natural could range from the ultimate subjection of superstition by reason, and women by men in Mozart's opera *The Magic Flute* (1791), or in the promises of regeneration *through* women expressed in Bernadin de St-Pierre's 1788 bestseller *Paul et Virginie*:

> Women lay down the first foundations of natural laws. The first founder of a human society was a mother of a family. They are scattered among men to remind them that above all they are men, and to uphold, despite political laws, the fundamental law of nature . . . Not only do women bind men together by the bonds of nature, but also by those of society.[15]

However, in spite of all these ambiguities, one point clearly stands out. In spite of the Enlightenment tendency to define 'the natural' as 'the good', women's equation with 'nature' did not operate in such a way as to give her equality with or superiority over men: rather, paradoxically, it operated to place women at one remove from men, to define them as 'the other': as that which has to be defined, rather than that whose nature is obvious and right. It is also important that once the definitions of 'femininity' and of 'nature' are brought together, each becomes problematic. Why should women be more 'natural' than men? Especially at a time when, in other contexts, humanity as a whole was often urged in the Enlightenment to abjure artificiality and convention, and become more 'natural'. The important point here is that the project of defining femininity perturbs and renders problematic very many key Enlightenment concepts, like 'nature'.

Perhaps it was an attempt to tie down 'nature' that led to such interest in the Enlightenment in scientific and medical definitions of gender. Recently, historians such as Thomas Laqueur have argued that from the seventeenth to the eighteenth century, the definition of male and female began to undergo a redefinition much influenced by medical definitions of the gendered body. A rising cultural status for science and medicine allowed the 'truths of biology' to replace 'divinely ordained hierarchies or immemorial custom as the basis for the creation or distribution of power in relations between men and women.'[16] Put briefly, older ideas that the female body was essentially another version of that of the male, with the female organs of reproduction being seen as inversions or homologies of

14 Sylvana Tomaselli, 'The Enlightenment Debate on Women', *History Workshop Journal*, 20 (1985), 101–24. Women's role in creating a new and decent society was especially emphasised in the context of the American Revolution: Jan Lewis, 'The Republican Wife: Virtue and Seduction in the Early Republic', *William & Mary Quarterly*, 44 (1987), 689–721.

15 J. H. Bernadin de St-Pierre, *Paul et Virginie* (Paris, 1788); preface to 1806 edition.

16 Laqueur, *Making Sex*, 193.

male equivalents, was replaced, Laqueur argues, by the idea that male or female bodies were absolutely different.[17] In anatomy, structures that had been thought common to men and women, like the skeleton and the nervous system, were now differentiated. Organs such as ovaries and testes, which had previously shared a name, were now separately labelled.[18] Anatomical studies on women's brains argued that they were of smaller size, and thus conclusively demonstrated women's unfitness for intellectual pursuits.[19] Many women themselves seem to have accepted these ideas. For example, in direct response to Wollstonecraft's *Vindication*, Laetitia Hawkins stated in her 1792 *Letters on the Female Mind*:

> It cannot, I think, be truly asserted, that the intellectual powers know no difference of sex. Nature certainly intended a distinction . . . In general, and almost universally, the feminine intellect has less strength and more acuteness. Consequently in our exercise of it, we show less perseverance and more vivacity.[20]

Writers like Hawkins were by the 1790s only echoing very similar ideas used by influential writers like Jean Jacques Rousseau earlier in the century. Describing Sophie as the 'ideal woman' he created in his educational tract *Emile* (1762), Rousseau talks of the way in which Sophie's physical make-up both sharply distinguishes her from Emile, her intended mate, and operates to ensure firstly her subjection to him, and secondly her definition as maternal and domestic:

> The male is male only at certain moments; the female is female her whole life . . . everything constantly recalls her sex to her, and to fulfill its functions, an appropriate physical constitution is necessary to her . . . she needs a soft sedentary life to suckle her babies. How much care and tenderness does she need to hold her family together! . . . The rigid strictness of the duties owed by the sexes is not and cannot be the same.[21]

For writers like Rousseau, basing themselves on the implications of contemporary medical texts, women's occupations 'were taken to be rooted in, restricted to, and a necessary consequence of their

[17] Laqueur, *Making Sex*, 149–50.

[18] Londa Schiebinger, 'Skeletons in the Closet: The First Illustrations of the Female Skeleton in Eighteenth-Century Anatomy', *Representations* 14 (1986), 42–82; *The Mind Has No Sex? Women in the Origins of Modern Science* (Cambridge, MA, 1989), 191–200; Laqueur, *Making Sex*, 152. The second half of the article 'Squelette' in Diderot's *Encyclopédie* is entirely devoted to the female skeleton.

[19] Elizabeth Fee, 'Nineteenth-Century Craniology: The Study of the Female Skull', *Bulletin of the History of Medicine*, 53 (1979), 415–33; Schiebinger, 'Skeletons', 206–7.

[20] Laetitia Hawkins, *Letters on the Female Mind* (London, 1792).

[21] Rousseau, *Emile*, 450.

reproductive functions'.[22] The fact that ideas of gender *could* be discussed in this way is also an important pointer to the way in which thinking about gender in the twenty-first century differs from that of the eighteenth. In our own day, most people have come to believe that differences between the genders are due as much, if not more, to differences in training, education and social expectations than they are rooted in the different biology of men and women. For the Enlightenment, on the other hand, biological difference and culturally induced sex roles were seen as one and the same thing. For most eighteenth-century thinkers, biological difference *directly* generated the social roles assigned to each sex, such as the increasing stress on women's unique fitness for the role of wife and mother. Another crucial difference with our own way of thinking is the explicit generalisation of gender roles, whereas today it is often stated that each individual is unique in his or her mixture of 'masculine' or 'feminine' attributes.

Laqueur's arguments, and those of the historians who follow his lead, about the increasing tendency to define gender as absolute difference through biological and medical 'evidence' sound convincing. But do they cover the entire problem of changes in thinking about gender in this period? We may point out, first of all, that Laqueur admits quite freely that we shall probably never know how many people actually believed the scientific and medical theories put forward to redefine femininity.[23] He himself points out that many older beliefs about gender seem to have co-existed with the Enlightenment redefinitions.[24] The increasing differentiation between physiological models of male and female produced by medical and scientific literature co-existed, for most people outside the elites addressed by medical arguments, with much older ideas of masculinity and femininity. As Laqueur also admits, the new, medically driven ideas of sexual difference also did not derive from a scientific consensus based on overwhelming evidence. No single account of sexual difference triumphed and new knowledge about human anatomy and physiology did not support the claims about gender difference which were made.[25] It is not logically possible to move from the 'Is' of scientific fact to the 'Ought' of gender roles in society: or put in another way, from the descriptive to the prescriptive. Laqueur does not really tackle

[22] L. Jordanova, *Sexual Visions: Images of Gender in Science and Medicine between the Eighteenth and Twentieth Centuries* (London and New York, 1989), 29: 'Women's capacity to bear and suckle children was taken to define their physical, psychological and social lives'. See also Yvonne Knibichler, 'Les médecins et la "nature féminine" au temps du Code Civil', *Annales*, ESC, 31(1976), 824–45.

[23] Laqueur, *Making Sex*, 152. [24] Laqueur, *Making Sex*, 153–4.

[25] Laqueur, *Making Sex*, 152.

the question of why it was, in that case, that eighteenth-century writers expended so much energy in making precisely this connection between the different biological nature of women and their social roles.

Many historians have pointed to large-scale industrial change and development as the motor for changes in women's social roles. They argue that industrialisation and the construction of global markets necessitated the construction of a 'sexual division of labour' which assigned to women, especially middle-class women, the task of consuming the increased array of goods made available by industrialisation.[26] This 'division of labour', they argue, led inexorably to the construction of a 'domestic sphere' which was to be the main place of consumption, and peculiarly the domain of women. Such historians also point out, as Laqueur does not, that much Enlightenment thinking about women's biological nature was inherently class based; that what was being described in the medical accounts of the female body was not the body of *all* women, and certainly not the bodies of hardworking farm women or urban artisans, but much more the frail and soft bodies which could with more plausibility be ascribed to middle-class women. Some historians like Nancy Armstrong have carried this argument so far as to assert that the new economic role assigned to domestic, middle-class women meant that the first truly modern economic person was a female, because the female role was the first to be described as an economic function.[27]

However, the idea that women's sphere was the domestic world was hardly new in the eighteenth century, and had frequently been stated in historical eras which long antedated either industrialisation or the biological redefinition of femininity.[28] What had changed in the Enlightenment was the increasing reliance on medical 'evidence' to back up this idea. It must always be noted that such medical justifications also co-existed with much older justifications for women's role as defined by their family responsibilities, through the means of scriptural injunctions, and traditional precedent. Historians who thus emphasise the Enlightenment attitude to gender as unique or new, thus often encounter real problems in justifying their views in the light of specific historical contexts in the eighteenth century. It is also far from clear that the majority of women

26 E.g., Fox-Genovese and Fox-Genovese, *Fruits*; V. Jones, *Women in the Eighteenth Century: Constructions of Femininity* (London, 1990); J. B. Elshtain, *Public Man, Private Woman* (Oxford, 1981).

27 N. Armstrong, *Desire and Domestic Fiction: A Political History of the Novel* (Oxford, 1987).

28 Steven Ozment, *When Fathers Ruled: Family Life in Reformation Europe* (Cambridge, MA, 1983); B. Niestroj, 'Modern Individuality and the Social Isolation of Mother and Child', *Comparative Civilisations' Review*, 16 (1987), 23–40 points out the medieval and early Renaissance roots of much that has been taken to be specific to Enlightenment ideologies of gender, and materialism.

even in the middle and upper classes which were most exposed to such debates on 'women's role' in society, and on the definition of femininity, really accepted such teachings and allowed them to influence their lives. Great controversy surrounded even the 'new' social role for women as wife and mother which many historians have seen as central to the redefinition of femininity in this period.[29]

Women's economic role was increasingly replaced by an emotional one, and the image of woman 'naturally' fitted for domestic duties, particularly of providing warm maternal care to her children and loving companionship for her spouse, was increasingly argued for by eighteenth-century writers, and depicted by artists.[30] Such theorists of the family paid particular attention to the practice of wet-nursing or sending infants, often to distant villages, to be suckled and cared for by paid foster-mothers. This practice was current in continental Europe, and involved all social classes except the very poorest. Historically already well established by the Enlightenment, it was to survive as a socially acceptable practice in France, at least, right up to 1914.[31] In the 1760s, however, writers such as Rousseau increasingly argued against it. In his *Emile*, Rousseau echoed many contemporaries when he argued that mothers who sent their children away to be nursed were 'unnatural', rejecting the duties of maternity which her physiological construction indicated to her: 'The sweet mothers who give themselves over to the gay pleasures of the town, do they pause to think what treatment their children are receiving in their swaddling bands out in the villages?'[32] Yet this was an ideology, which those women who absorbed these diatribes in favour of maternal breastfeeding obeyed at some cost. As Rousseau made clear, the price of a clear maternal conscience on the matter of breastfeeding and intimate maternal relationships with infants and small children was increased confinement within the family circle, in exchange for freedom to taste the attractions of the city or the world outside the family.

Rousseau's arguments, and the arguments of the many writers whom he echoed, are also interesting in another way. The versions of femininity

[29] D. G. Charlton, 'The New Eve', in *New Images of the Natural in France: A Study in European Cultural History 1750–1800* (Cambridge, 1984); Mary Sherriff, 'Fragonard's Erotic Mothers and the Politics of Reproduction', in L. Hunt (ed.), *Eroticism and the Body Politic* (Baltimore, MD, and London, 1991), 14–40; Carole Duncan, 'Happy Mothers and Other New Ideas in French Art', *Art Bulletin*, 55 (1973), 570–83.

[30] Sherriff, 'Fragonard's Erotic Mothers'; Duncan, 'Happy Mothers'.

[31] Mary Lindeman, 'Love for Hire: The Regulation of the Wet-Nursing Business in Eighteenth-Century Hamburg', *Journal of Family History*, 6 (1981), 379–95; G. Sussman, *Selling Mother's Milk: The Wet-Nursing Business in France, 1715–1914* (Urbana, IL, 1982).

[32] Rousseau, *Emile*, 45.

they argue for can often be shown to have far older roots. But it is certainly also the case that arguments about gender do intersect with other concerns in Enlightenment thinking in ways which *are* specific to that period. This is an important point to make, because it allows us to pinpoint better ways of saying that the Enlightenment *did* bring something new to debates on gender, and secondly to say why it was that such debates were of consequence in the overall pattern of Enlightenment thinking.

It was not simply that the problem of gender disturbed some of the deep structures of Enlightenment thought. That was also true of the way in which any group conceived of as 'different', such as slaves or the poor, could also only be received with difficulty into Enlightenment universalism. It was also the case with women, however, that it was far less easy to exclude the problem of gender because women themselves persisted in participating in the formation of Enlightenment culture. The eighteenth century saw the emergence, for the first time, of a sizeable body of women earning an independent living by various forms of cultural production, whether as members of 'Grub Street', as free intellectuals such as Mary Wollstonecraft herself, or as painters such as Angelica Kauffmann or Elisabeth Vigée-Lebrun. Such independent women, as was remarked in Chapter 2, posed a major problem for the emerging independent male intellectual class. As women, they were defined as intellectually inferior and intrinsically lacking in the social and political authority which they implicitly laid claim to by the very act of writing. The numerous aggressive attacks on women's intellectual capacities, and specifically on women's writing, produced by male intellectuals, show their worry that women's admission to the ranks of independent intellectuals might tar their male colleagues with the stigma of dependency and irrationalism which was so commonly alleged to be an intrinsic part of the female character by writers such as Rousseau. So 'gender' was not simply a difficult topic for reflection by the Enlightenment, it was also a theme which affected who and what the Enlightenment thought it was. Was it genuinely a movement of autonomous, rational, objective, hence legitimate, and hence also male thinkers, whose right to criticise the order of society lay in the very characteristics which also defined their male gender; or did it also include women, the reverse of the masculine? For the thinkers of the Enlightenment, the question raised by Mary Wollstonecraft of whether rationality was a universal human characteristic or was confined only to men, was a profoundly political as well as a philosophical one: because in the answer to that question lay the entire right of the *philosophes* to carry out the business of critique with legitimacy.

Women in the Enlightenment did, however, carry out more traditional roles which connected them both to the production of 'opinion' and 'knowledge', as well as to the 'public realm' theorised by Habermas (Chapter 1). Women were crucial to the organisation of one of the most characteristic intellectual institutions of the Enlightenment in continental Europe: the *salon*. Our analysis so far of the economic structures and the sociability crucial to the making and diffusion of Enlightenment ideas has emphasised so far public, commercial, and predominantly male-controlled markets for ideas, and diffusion networks. The *salons* were quite other. The *salon* as a social form concerned with ideas had its roots in the seventeenth century, and in court society, particularly in France. Aristocratic ladies had begun to gather around themselves groups of both women and men, often of a somewhat lower status than themselves, and to encourage the production within and by those groups of an elaborate, literary, common culture. Members of the groups met to discuss topics often designated in advance by the *salon* hostess. Plays, poems and prose works were produced, read aloud in the groups, and often substantially altered in response to criticism by other *salon* members before being presented to a wider public. For some, *salon* presentation was seen not merely as an essential part of the creative process, but as an acceptable equivalent to publication in print. *Salons* in the seventeenth century were thus crucial because they set intellectual agendas, and provided a social forum for what often amounted to group literary and intellectual production, amongst the social elite. In all this, women were crucial. Each *salon* was a distinctive creation of the hostess, with its own character and programme, and group culture. It was the hostess who provided the meeting place for the group, usually in the family residence. It was she (or indirectly her husband) who met the costs of entertainment. It was she who chose the members of the *salon*, and oversaw the relationships they formed; it was she who largely controlled thereby the intellectual agendas of the group. The social status of the *salon* hostess, in other words, as well as her financial capital, legitimated the intellectual production of the *salon* members, who tended to be of a lower social class. The *salons* also thereby legitimated the intellectual style, and agendas of their women members. In the seventeenth century, such female *salon* hostesses and female members were often described as *précieuses*, women whose particular, distinctive, highly mannered and controlled way of speaking and writing, whose predilection for verbal games, was the high point of development of the distinctive literary culture of the *salon*.

By the eighteenth century, therefore, the *salon* already had a long history, and a history which enshrined women as shapers of elite culture. The *salon* by this point had also begun to create a common verbal, literary, allusive culture which helped to eliminate the gulf between the sexes caused by their very different educations and social roles. But the eighteenth century saw also significant changes for the *salons*. They began to move out of court society. The aristocratic hostess began to be replaced by women like Mme du Deffand, wife of a successful financier, or Mme du Tencin, d'Alembert's mother, whose reputation as a novelist was only exceeded by the scandal which surrounded her, and effectively excluded her from the court; or Julie de Lespinasse, the beloved of d'Alembert, and poor relation and protégée of Mme du Deffand. Many of the functions of the hostess in recruiting and organising the *salons*, setting their agendas, and managing the personal relationships of their members, remained the same. But their wider social basis during the Enlightenment manifested how, very gradually, control of intellectual agendas was passing from the court to a far wider social and intellectual elite. It also meant that the *salons* were able to bring into their membership many who like Diderot began life outside the aristocratic, legal, or administrative elites. By *salon* membership such non-elite members not only gained audience for, and contribution to, their own work, but also access to a social capital of relationships which could allow them ascension into the elite itself through the operation of patronage. It was also the case that the increasing numbers of non-aristocratic *salons* widened the intellectual agenda from the culture of the *précieuses*, to a wider focus on critical writing in history, economics and politics, from the word game to the message itself. In this way, the changing focus of the *salon* mirrored the changing orientation of cultural creation as a whole, whose project was decreasingly aimed at the capture of the apex of the social and political pyramid and increasingly at the more and more heterogeneous elites who shaped public opinion outside the reach of the court. The court had ceased to be the single most significant arbiter of and actor in the public realm. This erosion of the intellectual dominance of the court happened at the same time as the erosion of its political control. This was no coincidence.

But what was the importance of gender in the *salons*? Why did they remain a powerful force at a time when so much else in the way that culture was transmitted and created seemed to be defined in such a different way, and defined in ways which undermined women's cultural and intellectual roles? Partly, the *salons* remained as a viable social and intellectual form because of the very expansion of the surrounding public realm. Increasing numbers of career intellectuals born well outside the old court aristocracy needed a mechanism for the social ascension which would allow them to transform their gifts into visible social and political recognition. Nor was the 'collective' creation characteristic of salon culture incompatible with eventual publication for a broad market; it could even be seen as a safe way of advance testing audience reaction.

But why do women, and not men, emerge as the *salon* organisers? A large part of the answer to this should refer back to the discussion of gender earlier in the chapter. This was partly because of the way women's roles had been defined in the eighteenth century in ways which in fact were far wider than their reproductive roles: as being the agents and bearers of the civilised state, whether through their role as actual mothers or as intellectual mothers transmitting cultural values to the next generation. This role as the organiser, facilitator, and if necessary inspirer of male knowledge production is of course as old as that of the nine muses. But it was also a role which women, whose intellectual independence was challenged in other ways, as we have already seen, could turn into one which put them into close contact with other intellectual figures, contact necessary for the enhancement of their own public careers, and yet leave them in control of the (predominantly male) members of the *salon*. The increasing numbers of women who, as the seventeenth-century hostesses had in the main not been, were literary producers as well, shows that women were realising the flexibility of the role of the *salonnière* to place a purchase on the intellectual community which might well otherwise have been denied them on grounds of their sex.

It may be because of the nature and antecedents of the *salon*, with its legacy of feminine dominance and of the *précieuses*' interest in elaborate, artificial, language, that the *salons* also attracted the wrath of political writers such as Rousseau. Rousseau inveighed against the *salons* because these very factors, their feminine dominance, and historical links with a decaying and highly artificial court culture, were enough to attract his anger. For him, their artificiality was an open affront to the transparency and 'naturalness' which ought to govern human relations as well as define the human polity. For the same reasons, Rousseau also inveighed against the public theatre. For those who like Rousseau believed that women were dominated by their sexual and reproductive roles, women controlling any social institution was equivalent to it being riddled with sexual corruption. His attacks on the *salons* thus also fed into the increasing propensity to define the monarchy itself as corrupt because of the alleged dominance of its policy by women's sexual bargaining. The polemic over women's intellectual role and capacities in the Enlightenment was therefore intimately linked with attempts to reshape the very culture and power relationships of government itself, which as we have seen was a strong concern in the Enlightenment.

Recent historical scholarship, while usefully highlighting the importance of biological definitions of female 'nature' as well as indicating new, if controversial, ways in which economic change may have contributed to the Enlightenment redefinition of gender, has also perhaps neglected the complexity of the Enlightenment response to this issue. The stress which the gender debate placed on key concepts such as 'nature' was mirrored by intense discussion on femininity which was neither so concerned with biology or economics, nor so avowedly restrictive as current emphases on Rousseau's teachings in *Emile* would have us believe. We should not forget, after all, that *Emile* was condemned upon publication by the Paris Parliament, and publicly burnt (although not because of its view on gender), and remained controversial ever after. In fact, the views of other *philosophes* on women were very different.[33] Voltaire, Montesquieu and Diderot all noted the discrepancy between the legal codes which excluded women from any position in public life, and the actual extent of the power women were capable of wielding.[34] Diderot, unlike the doctors and natural scientists, argued that men and women were not very different, though certain characteristics were more often found in one sex than the other.[35] In the realm of intellect, Voltaire maintained, unlike Rousseau, that 'women are capable of all that men are'. Such views did not stop such men of letters justifying a double standard of sexual morality, justified by women's special role in the family, but they did show a most un-Rousseau-like concern with moving towards an affirmation of the common humanity of men and women, which should override the reproductive roles so stressed by Rousseau and the medical definitions of femininity. Voltaire objected to the idea of the husband as sole master in the home; he, Diderot and Montesquieu pictured maternity not as a woman's whole character but as a single and temporary aspect of life.[36] Recognition of such thinking can act as a valuable corrective to concerns now current in historical and literary scholarship relating to gender in the Enlightenment.

Conclusion

The Enlightenment debate on gender was conducted with such energy because of the contradictions and challenges it imported into the heart of Enlightenment thinking. Examination of the debates around gender shows us that Enlightenment, for all its universalist claims, had much difficulty in finding a place for social groups – not just women, but also lower social classes, and other races – which previous historical periods

33 Paul Hoffman, *La Femme dans la pensée des Lumières* (Paris, 1977); M. Hunt, Margaret Jacob, Phyllis Mack and Ruth Perry (eds.), *Women and the Enlightenment* (New York, 1984), survey the often contradictory attitudes of the Enlightenment towards women.

34 F. M. A. de Voltaire, 'Femmes, soyez soumises à vos maris', *Dialogues et anecdotes philosophiques*, ed. Raymond Nares (Paris, 1955), 216; Denis Diderot, 'Sur les Femmes', *Oeuvres*, ed. André Billy (Paris, 1951), 985.

35 Diderot, 'Sur les femmes'.

36 Diderot, 'Sur les femmes'; Voltaire, 'Femmes, soyez soumises'; Montesquieu, *Spirit of the Laws*, Book XXIII, I (Paris, 1748).

had equally defined as outside the central human community. In the case of women, the problem of the definition of gender cut across such key Enlightenment terms as 'nature', 'reason' and 'virtue'. With particular insistence new attempts were made to present social differences between the genders as based on 'natural', physiological and medical 'facts'. This showed a new tendency for social debates to be legitimated by science in a way which was to become commonplace in the following century. By problematising women's intellectual capacities, Enlightenment debates also introduced fractures into the 'republic of letters' or 'public opinion'. All these fractures, as Wollstonecraft noted, made it difficult to sustain Enlightenment claims to be the 'party of humanity', sustained by the universal project of reason and virtue.

Furthermore, such claims also rendered the place of women in public life highly problematic. Enlightenment thinkers seemed to assert, on the one hand, that women, as human beings, could have rights; but also, on the other, that because of their alleged irrationality and lack of autonomy, they should not be allowed to take part in politics.[37] Writers such as Rousseau went further, and argued that women's participation in politics was actively harmful. Such assertions fed into a rising tide of hostility especially in France, directed at the real if informal power enjoyed by women royal favourites, and towards queens such as Marie Antoinette.[38]

As a resource for the future, the Enlightenment showed similar ambiguities. The practice of the Enlightenment set the stage for the creation of an entirely masculine political culture during the French Revolution; but its theory of universalism also gave ammunition to those who were to struggle to free women from restrictive definitions of gender.[39] The debate over women thus contributed to the reshaping of power in the Enlightenment which is the subject of Chapter 3.

[37] This argument is developed in Joan Landes, *Women and the Public Sphere in the Age of the French Revolution* (Ithaca, NY, and London, 1988). Writers like Diderot who commended the work of exceptional female rulers such as Catherine the Great of Russia still argued that wives should be subject to husbands.

[38] Sara Maza, 'The Diamond Necklace Affair Revisited (1785–86): The Case of the Missing Queen', in L. Hunt (ed.), *Eroticism and the Body Politic* (Baltimore, MD, 1991), 63–89; Sara Maza, 'Le tribunal de la nation', *Annales* ESC, 42 (1987), 73–90.

[39] D. Outram, *The Body and the French Revolution: Sex, Class and Political Culture* (New Haven, CT, and London, 1989).

8 Science and the Enlightenment: God's order and man's understanding

> The Creator doubtless did not bestow so much curiosity and exquisite workmanship and skill upon his creatures, to be looked upon with a careless or incurious eye, especially to have them slighted or condemned; but to be admired by the rational part of the world, to magnify his own power, wisdom and goodness throughout all the world, and the ages thereof... my text commends God's works, not only for being great, but also approves of those curious and ingenious enquirers, that seek them out, or pry into them. And the more we pry into and discover of them, the greater and more glorious we find them to be, the more worthy of, and the more expressly to proclaim their great Creator.

> The first man I saw was of a meagre aspect, with sooty hands and face, his hair and beard long, ragged and singed in several places. His clothes, shirt, and skin were all of the same colour. He had been eight years upon a project for extracting sunbeams out of cucumbers, which were to be put into vials hermetically sealed, and let out to warm the air in raw inclement summers. He told me, he did not doubt in eight years more, that he should be able to supply the Governor's gardens with sunshine at a reasonable rate; but he complained that his stock was low, and entreated me to give him something as an encouragement to ingenuity, especially since this had been a very dear season for cucumbers. I made him a small present, for my Lord had furnished me with money on purpose, because he knew their practice of begging from all who go to see them.[1]

Science is today probably the most powerful force in twenty-first-century culture. It determines our potential for technological control of the environment, many of our cultural and intellectual assumptions, and our economic, technological and agricultural base. In the twentieth century almost all science receives some form of public funding, and scientific practices and assumptions have also heavily influenced much current

[1] William Derham, *Physico-Theology: or, a Demonstration of the Being and Attributes of God, from His Works of Creation* (2 vols., London 1798) II, 394, first published, 1713; Jonathan Swift, *Gulliver's Travels* (1726) (London, 1967), 223–4 ('A Voyage to Laputa', part III, section 5).

thinking about the way governments should be run. None of this was the case in the eighteenth century. The intellectual status of science was contested, its institutional organisations often weak, and certainly thin on the ground, and the nature of its relations with the economy and with government often tenuous. No institution of science was a major employer of labour, and educational structures in most countries paid little attention to disseminating scientific knowledge. Only a few men could support themselves by full-time work in science.

Nonetheless, science in this period is still an important topic, and not only because of its forerunner status to the expansion of science in subsequent centuries. Precisely because science *was* an insecure form of knowledge in the eighteenth century, it had to confront many crucial questions in the way that the established science of today, which can concentrate on problem solving within a clearly delineated intellectual area, often does not. Eighteenth-century science had to grapple with such larger issues as the relationship of man to nature, the very possibility of knowledge of the external world, and of the best way to organise such knowledge. Science also acted as the link between many apparently diverse areas of Enlightenment thought. As we will see, it was also deeply implicated in contemporary religious development (Chapter 9). 'Nature', the very subject matter of science, has also been described by many as an 'ethical norm' in the Enlightenment. What was 'natural' must be 'good'. Others have argued that science embodied the central Enlightenment value of 'reason' or 'rationality'. By 'rationality' was usually meant objective thinking, without passion, prejudice or superstition, and without reference to non-verifiable statements such as those of religious revelation. More recently, the French philosopher Michel Foucault put forward the controversial but influential view that the development of Enlightenment science was paradigmatic of deep changes in the structures of *all* knowledge in this period.[2] Thus, for some historians science is the cultural category of the Enlightenment, rather than that of religion which seemed so central to Hegel.

There thus seems to be ample reason to devote attention to science in the Enlightenment. But a word of warning is necessary. In using this word 'science' at all, we are in fact committing the sin of anachronism. The words 'science' and 'scientist' were not invented until the 1830s in England. Before that 'natural philosophy' was probably the term most

[2] A. O. Lovejoy, 'Nature as an Aesthetic Norm', in *Essays in the History of Ideas* (New York, 1960), 69–77; Michel Foucault, *The Order of Things: An Archaeology of the Human Sciences* (New York, 1973). According to Foucault, taxonomy served during this period not only as the dominant impulse for the pursuit of natural history, but as the organising principle for *all* intellectual activity.

in use. In French *science*, like the German *Wissenschaft*, meant 'knowledge' or 'knowing', and was not necessarily connected with knowledge of nature. The term *scientifique* to label specifically those involved in such investigation was a coinage of the late nineteenth century.[3] Thus, in two major languages there was no word specifically to describe enquiry into nature, or its practitioners. This should alert us to the extent to which 'science' was not yet separated out from other intellectual areas, nor were its practitioners readily distinguished from practitioners of other forms of intellectual enquiry. Enlightenment normality was typified by Voltaire, who worked on a popularisation of Newtonian mathematical physics, while also producing plays, poems, short stories, and political criticism; or by Diderot, whose speculations on the organisation of nature and the nature of human perception occurred in the midst of other enquiries and discussions, such as those contained in *Rameau's Nephew* or on colonialism in his *Supplément au Voyage de Bougainville*.

The linguistic point also reveals the extent to which 'science' was not yet a defined body of knowledge, not yet a 'discipline', a body of knowledge separate from other bodies of knowledge, with its own subject matter, let alone divided into sub-disciplines such as 'physiology' or 'geology'. The study of what we now call 'science' still took place in the eighteenth century within other disciplines, linked together under the heading of 'natural philosophy'. In turn, as a recent historian has noted 'the whole point of "natural philosophy" was to look at nature and the world as created by God, and thus as capable of being understood as embodying God's powers and purposes'.[4]

This statement is particularly true for the 'natural philosophy' practised in the English-speaking Enlightenment, but it was also a strong factor in much of the natural philosophy undertaken in continental Europe. In an age much concerned with the construction of a 'reasonable Christianity' (Chapter 9) which could offer information about God and his purposes independent of 'irrational' sources such as faith and revelation, science, with its appeal to the evidence of the senses, was an essential reference in theological debate. For example, the title of John Ray's 1692 *The Wisdom of God Manifested in the Works of the Creation* could stand for many others of the time. The natural order was also implicated in the arguments of those Deists who thought of God as little more than the original force

[3] Sydney Ross,'"Scientist": The Story of a Word', *Annals of Science*, 18 (1962), 65–86; Raymond Williams, *Keywords: A Vocabulary of Culture and Society* (London, 1976), s.v. 'science'.

[4] A. Cunningham and P. Williams, 'De-centring the Big Picture', *British Journal for the History of Science*, 26 (1993), 407–32.

behind the laws of nature, to the extent that the Deity and the laws of nature often seemed little more than synonyms.

'Natural philosophy' thus functioned within this wider framework to a greater or lesser extent, in most European states. This often made it nearly impossible to establish where 'natural philosophy' ended, and where theology, 'the Queen of the sciences', began. It was not easy for the study of nature to become a separate intellectual discipline, with a separate body of practitioners. The link between natural philosophy and theology was tightened by the fact that much natural philosophy, particularly in Protestant states, was done by members of the clergy. Leisure, education and a rural vicarage were the sources of much observational science.

The quest for a 'reasonable Christianity' thus did throw natural philosophy into a place of increasing importance in the Enlightenment. But, 'Nature' also started to assume importance in a rather different sense. For 'natural philosophy', 'nature' was seen as an expression of God's ordering hand and was, therefore, largely represented, despite considerable evidence to the contrary, as ordered, as obeying 'laws' and as providing a benevolent habitat for man, who was thus enabled by God to carry out His purposes. 'Nature', however, also had other important meanings in the Enlightenment, many of which were extensions and secularisations of the ideas behind 'natural philosophy'. The 'natural' was seen as the 'good', meaning original, authentic, simple, uncorrupted, and, by extension, in the works of Rousseau and others, as a state opposed to 'civilisation' with all its artificiality and corruption (Chapter 5). Thus 'nature' became a description of a moral ideal as well as of a scientifically discernible order, and was seen as something which could reside in the hearts of men, as much as being an external order visible and tangible and measurable to natural philosophers. The meaning of 'nature' was thus notoriously imprecise. It and the search for 'reasonable Christianity' together heightened the importance of enquiry into 'nature' in Enlightenment thinking. They certainly did not provide a secure methodology for the actual conduct of science.

But if 'nature' was to function either as an ethical norm or as a Christian image, natural philosophy had to be underpinned by ideas about how it was possible to know 'nature' at all. Older intellectual traditions which denigrated knowledge of the external world still had considerable force in this period, traditions which greatly pre-dated the popular Enlightenment idea that it was not only possible but proper to deduce the existence and nature of the creator from that of his creation. Among ordinary people, science was often seen as ridiculous or even useless. In 1740, for example, the Swedish naturalist Carl Linnaeus, whose nomenclature systems still survive in botany, felt impelled to answer critics who questioned the very purpose of science. He wrote:

> one question is always asked, one objection always made to those who are curious about nature, when ill-educated people (*le vulgaire*) see natural philosophers examining the products of nature. They ask, often with mocking laughter, 'What's the use of it' . . . Such people think that natural philosophy is only about the gratification of curiosity, only an amusement to pass the time for lazy and thoughtless people.[5]

Linnaeus, like Swift's depiction of Laputa, gives a picture of the serious natural philosopher as besieged not only by the ridicule and incomprehension of the uneducated, but also by a strong prejudice *against* the gratification of intellectual curiosity. In the middle ages and the Renaissance, curiosity had a bad name, both as a form of lust and as the impulse which had resulted in the expulsion of Adam and Eve from Paradise. This was a point of view which the continuous publication of earlier theological writings kept firmly alive. Even by 1762, Rousseau was still having to argue in his influential educational text, *Emile*, that curiosity was a virtue which could bring benefits by enhancing knowledge.[6]

Even sections of society which had jettisoned moral qualms over curiosity about the created world faced other problems concerning the status of scientific knowledge. How, philosophers asked, could men ever know the external world of nature, or, knowing it, how could they be certain that their knowledge *was* accurate? How was it possible to reduce the dazzling succession of events and entities in nature to general laws which might be predictive? Many argued, as did the Neopolitan historian Giambattista Vico (1688–1744) in his aptly named *Scienza Nuova* (1725), that 'natural philosophy' could never really be a secure form of knowledge. Vico argued that if one is seeking universal and eternal principles in a field of knowledge, principles that make it proper to call it a 'science', one must look to things of *human* creation, such as human history and human institutions. Physical 'science', for example, deals with entities, of which we can never have direct experience, and which are thus completely foreign to us. We can only make up theories which are more or less *probable* about physical objects. But we can have an intuitive *certainty* in our understanding of the needs and desires that unite the human

[5] B. Jasmin and Camille Limoges (eds.), C. Linné, 'A Quoi Sert-il?' in *L'Equilibre de la nature* (Paris, 1972), 145–6.

[6] J. Céard (ed.), *La curiosité à la Renaissance* (Paris, 1986); [M. Landois], 'Curieux'; [Chevalier de Jaucourt], 'Curiosité', in d'Alembert and Diderot (eds.), *Encyclopédie* (Paris, 1754), 577–8; Jacques-Bénigne Bossuet, *Traîté de la concupiscence* (1731) eds. C. Urbain and E. Lenesque (Paris, 1930), esp. chapter 8. Jean Jacques Rousseau, *Emile ou de l'éducation* (1762), ed. F. and P. Richard (Paris, 1964), 185, 271.

race across the ages, and which can be checked against common human experience. Vico's arguments were to be echoed by many others down the century, and it remained a commonplace that historical and literary judgements, for Vico's reasons, were far more stable than knowledge of nature, and thus represented a superior kind of intellectual outcome.

Those Enlightenment thinkers who did try to find a basis for knowledge of the external world, such as John Locke or Etienne Condillac (1715–80), broke away from previous thinking and emphasised the role of sense impressions of the external world in the formation of abstract concepts. A consequence of this belief was that man could know only appearances, not the real essences of external things:

> Ideas in no way allow us to know beings as they actually are; they merely depict them in terms of their relationship with us, and this alone is enough to prove the vanity of the efforts of those philosophers who pretend to penetrate into the nature of things.[7]

Because of the way in which our ideas of the external world were formed, natural philosophy, in other words, could never explain 'first principles', the causes of causes. And so, while many continued to accept that natural philosophy and theology should operate cooperatively, philosophy in practice laid more emphasis on the constraints on the possibility of human beings gaining any deep knowledge of the natural order. Paradoxically, this was to be a first step along the road to science becoming an entirely distinct form of intellectual endeavour, of its gradual separation from the 'first order' questions dominant in theology, the 'Queen of Sciences'.

But if science could not peer into the heart of things, could it at least construct a picture of the external world which would be coherent and orderly and law governed – a picture which might not be deeply 'true', but could at least be self-consistent? Here too, however, the philosophers did not make things easy for those interested in the natural world. Statements that one thing causes another are clearly highly important in 'natural philosophy'. Chemists, for example, like to be able to say that the presence of certain chemicals causes a certain reaction. But even the validity of such causal statements was challenged. The Scots philosopher David Hume contested the belief held by Descartes – and, for different reasons, by later thinkers such as Locke and Condillac – that there was an easy way of guaranteeing the validity of any transition from the fragmentary and transient world our sense impressions reveal to us to the orderly and 'lawful' world described especially in the physical sciences. Hume

[7] Etienne Bonnot de Condillac, *Traîté des sensations* (Paris, 1754).

explains the fact that human beings do seem routinely able to make this transition, by reference to what he calls 'custom', socially agreed ways which act as facilitators for humans to make the leap from the world of sense impressions to the ordered depiction of the natural world which they portray as the 'natural order'.

Because of this the causal claims so central to some branches of natural philosophy, particularly in the cosmological and physical sciences, could not be given absolute legitimation, once science shifted from *describing* a divinely instituted natural order, to enquiring into its causal relations. While scientific accounts of causal relationships could claim to be more or less self-consistent, their truth-value had to remain debatable. Hume argued that the only thing which impels us to connect events in terms of causation is previous experiences of similar sequences. Our *habit* is to reason causally; but nothing guarantees that causal reasoning produces truth, rather than consistency with appearances; and nothing guarantees that these appearances will always appear in the same sequence. That the sun has risen for millions of days before today does not guarantee that the sun will rise tomorrow.

It is difficult to reconcile these ideas, which had a great impact on European philosophers such as Immanuel Kant, with the presupposition central to theology, that nature as God's creation really could be said to be actually existing 'out there', reflecting the order, contrivance and plenitude of the Divine mind itself, and that that natural order would gradually become more and more accessible to human beings. In Hume's account, there was no obstacle to this actually being the case; but it also seemed that a huge number of obstacles inherent in man's own perceptions had been created to men ever being able to perceive the natural order in a way they could guarantee was 'true' rather than 'probable'. Thus, it seemed unlikely that knowledge of God, or 'reasonable Christianity', could be supported by the findings of 'natural philosophy'. Because of this, Hume also argued that it was impossible to reason from the character of the natural order, as constructed by human natural philosophers, to the character of the Deity. The creator could not be presumed from His creation.

Thus, 'natural philosophy' operated in an increasingly strained relationship with philosophical enquiry which undercut its capacity to carry out the objectives of theology. This did not prevent natural philosophy, with all its theological presuppositions, from being enthusiastically endorsed in actual practice, particularly in English-speaking and Protestant countries. But it does mean that we cannot say that the Enlightenment unanimously endorsed scientific enquiry as the best or most 'rational' form of knowledge. There were severe and persistent doubts about its standing and 'truth value', as well as its utility and stability in comparison to the historical and literary, let alone theological 'sciences'.

Yet, enquiry into nature did develop in this period, and did end the century with a higher status than at the beginning, though never approaching the dominant place in culture which it has assumed in our own times. Partly, this was because the doubts expressed by even well-known writers like Hume, who was better known in his own day as an historian, seem to have had little impact on the actual practice of science, or on the cultural importance of natural theology in English-speaking countries. The reason for this might be that philosophers almost always began their questioning of science not from the actual practice or utility of science, but from the predicament of an individual 'observer' facing 'nature'. Men like Hume and Kant, in spite of the importance of their legacy, did not address the questions of how and why science *can* operate as an activity pursued in common by human beings in a social setting. In this they reflected the comparative social and institutional weaknesses of science in the world around them, as well as reflecting the common emphasis placed by Enlightenment philosophy on an ideal, solitary, representative individual as encapsulating truth.

It is now time to look at what 'science' was actually doing in the Enlightenment.[8] At many points, we can see that natural philosophy was gradually separating itself from theological ends. This is one interpretation of the work of the century's most famous scientific figure, Isaac Newton (1643–1727). It is certainly possible to argue that the Enlightenment opens not only with John Locke's attempts to understand the human mind and human society, but also with Newton's attempts in his 1687 *Mathematical Principles of Natural Philosophy* (*Philosophiae Naturalis Principia Mathematica*) to produce mathematical descriptions of the cosmic order, the motions of planets, the famous law of universal gravitation, and the idea of planetary space as infinite. Newton's achievements were transmitted down the century by a host of popularisers in most European countries, which, as we have seen, even included Voltaire,

[8] It is impossible in a single chapter to present the entire range of scientific activity in the Enlightenment and this chapter concentrates on two areas: Newtonian cosmology and natural history. Information on other important fields of science can be found in, e.g., G. S. Rousseau and R. S. Porter (eds.), *The Ferment of Knowledge: Studies in the Historiography of Eighteenth-Century Science* (Cambridge, 1980); R. Porter, *The Making of Geology: Earth Science in Britain, 1660–1815* (Cambridge, 1979); L. J. Jordanova and R. Porter (eds.), *Images of the Earth: Essays in the History of the Environmental Sciences* (Chalfont St Giles, 1978); J. Roger, *Les sciences de la vie dans la penseé française au dix-huitième siècle* (Paris, 1963); J. Heilbron, *Electricity in the Seventeenth and Eighteenth Centuries: A Study of Early Modern Physics* (Berkeley, 1979); F. L. Holmes, *Lavoisier and the Chemistry of Life: An Exploration of Scientific Creativity* (Madison, WI, 1985).

and which played into a growing market for popular science. Each populariser introduced his own distortions as they produced verbal equivalents to what were complex and demanding mathematical expressions.[9] Most contrived to produce an idea that Newton had described the whole of the created universe and had described that order as a self-regulating balanced system of lawful movement. In many of these popular accounts, it might appear that whatever the theoretical objections to the possibility of our knowledge of the external world might be, at least physical laws of motion could be completely described by self-consistent mathematical systems.

Newton's views were in fact much more complex. He stated that while it was possible to describe the cosmos mathematically, it was not possible to use mathematics to answer 'first-order' questions as to how the cosmos was kept in being and in motion. Newton himself also denied that his laws did describe a self-generating, self-regulating universe. As he said, motion 'is much more apt to be lost than got, it is always upon the decay'. Energy, he thought, could only be restored to the cosmic system by the direct, periodic intervention of its creator. Newton's ideas seemed to have shown the necessity of some First Cause to keep the cosmos functioning; but in spite of the statements of some of the popularisers, it provided no guarantee that that First Cause in any way resembled the God of the Old or New Testaments, or that there was any scientific grounding for the tenets of Christianity.[10]

Newton's impact was mixed. In the 1690s, the theologian Richard Bentley preached sermons which enlisted Newton in defence of religion. By 1734, the divine and philosopher George Berkeley (1685–1753) saw Newtonianism as conducive to heresy and atheism. There was even disagreement as to how Newton had actually achieved his results. D'Alembert, in his 1751 Introduction to the *Encyclopédie*, invoked Newton to show the supremacy of mathematical analysis in science, while others saw Newton's work as a triumph of pure observation. Others hoped that Newton's prestige could legitimate a 'science of man' that would be as lawful as his natural philosophy. Even as late as 1802, the French Utopian thinker Claude-Henri St-Simon (1760–1825), whom many have seen as one of the grandfathers of Socialism, proposed a social system based on 'Newtonian' principles of reason, order and universal law.

[9] Popularisations include such European bestsellers as Francesco Algarotti, *Il newtonismo per le Dame* (1737), and for children, John Newberry, *Tom Telescope's Philosophy of Tops and Balls* (London, 1761).

[10] The literature on Newton is vast. I. B. Cohen, *The Newtonian Revolution* (Cambridge, 1980) is probably the most accessible and comprehensive account.

22 MATHEMATICAL PRINCIPLES

A X I O M S,

O R,

L A W S O F M O T I O N *(o)*.

L A W I.

Axioms, or

That every body perſeveres in its ſtate of reſting, or of moving uniformly in a right line, as far as it is not compelled to change that ſtate by external forces impreſſed upon it.

PROJECTILES perſevere in their motions ſo far as they are not retarded by the reſiſtance of the air, and impelled downwards by the force of gravity. A top, whoſe parts by their cohesion are perpetually drawn aſide from rectilinear motions, does

COMMENTARY.

(o) 14. The end and deſign of Sir *Iſaac Newton*'s philoſophy is, to inveſtigate the laws obſerved in the production of natural effects, to diſcover their conformity and agreement, and to deduce the various phenomena of nature from the moſt ſimple and general principles, into which theſe laws can be reſolved. Theſe general principles are diſcovered only by experiments upon ſuch bodies, as are within our reach; and by reaſonings, from obſervation and analogy, to thoſe that are at a diſtance.

That there is a certain invariable order in which every appearance of nature is preſented to our view, is evident to the moſt common obſerver: while the philoſopher, in tracing them to the original principles from which they flow, diſcovers a regular ſeries and train of events, preceding, in an eſtabliſhed order, the

3 Axioms, or Laws of Motion, 1777.
This page from a later translation of the *Principia mathematica* (1687) shows the first of Newton's laws of motion. It is interesting to compare this form of the law with the modern forms of it which are slimmed down and more mathematical.

Newton's achievement, great though it was, also had little to say about the nature of living beings on earth itself. This was the second area towards which Enlightenment science directed much effort. How was man to understand the order of nature? Was there such an order? Were there relationships between different living beings, and, if so, of what kind? Could nature simply be understood as a two-dimensional 'Great Chain of Being', stretching down from God and his angels, through to man and, in a descending order of complexity, ending in worms and stones?[11] Or were the relationships between living beings more complex?

Enlightenment natural philosophers tended increasingly to ignore those parts of the Great Chain above man, and to visualise nature, rather, as being headed by man, usually represented as outside and above the natural order. Enquirers such as Linnaeus also started to distinguish sharply between living and non-living beings, a distinction which was to make it possible for the 'earth-sciences' such as geology and mineralogy, on the one hand, to distinguish themselves from 'life-sciences' like botany and zoology, on the other. Linnaeus and his pupils produced a new binomial classification for living beings based on their reproductive characteristics. While extremely successful in the case of plants, Linnaeus' classifications were less so in relation to other living beings. Linnaeus' approach to nature was also very largely *a*-historical, although by 1744 he was ready to speculate in his *Oratio de telluris habilitabilis incremento* (Lecture on the increase of the habitable earth) that new groups of plants and animals might have developed over time by hybridisation. But Linnaeus in the end still saw nature as a whole, as a harmonious and balanced system created by God, in much the same way that Newton's popularisers represented his view of the cosmos itself.

Linnaeus' views were challenged by the equally well-known and influential naturalist Georges-Louis Leclerc, Comte de Buffon (1708–88). In his *Histoire Naturelle*, which began publication in 1749 and rapidly became a popular publishing success, Buffon challenged the very possibility of classifying living beings in such a way as to reveal thereby the 'real' structure of nature. Whereas Linnaeus believed that species could reveal *truths* about nature, Buffon remained convinced that individuals in nature could not be classified in ways which revealed such 'truths', and that classifications were merely heuristic devices.[12]

Buffon was also much more interested than Linnaeus in the idea that nature had a history, that its present state was not the state in which God

[11] The 'Great Chain' is described in A. O. Lovejoy, *The Great Chain of Being* (New York, 1936).

[12] Jacques Roger, *Buffon: un philosophe au Jardin du Roi* (Paris, 1989).

had created it. Buffon used fossil evidence, and physical experimentation, to argue that the world and life itself were far older than was indicated by strict adherence to the chronology indicated by the account of the creation in the Book of Genesis. This importation of historical thinking into natural history has been seen by Michel Foucault as one of the essential ways in which Enlightenment science started to differ in a quite basic way from that of preceding periods, which were much more concerned to place living beings in static taxonomic relationships with each other.[13] Foucault sees this idea that nature too had a history, that species did not emerge perfect and immutable from the Divine hand, but changed in response to other pressures, over far longer periods than were indicated by current understandings of Biblical chronology, as the essential precondition for the emergence of Darwinian theory in the next century and thus for the beginning of scientific modernity. More appositely for our purposes, the question of nature's history also shows divisions emerging between the objectives of theology and scientific enquiry. Buffon's work on the rates of the earth's cooling was condemned by the Paris theology faculty, the Sorbonne, because his results implied that the earth was far older than had previously been realised, but were still reprinted in his best-selling *Epoques de la Nature* (Eras of Nature).

Still other *philosophes*, such as Diderot, applied themselves to the nature of 'life' itself, and produced a picture of 'life' as the constitutive force of nature, an impulsion within living beings themselves to survive, to reproduce, and to obey the laws of their own existence. This picture of life as a dynamic force was emphasised by Diderot, among others, and the idea of living beings as having their own purposes, or teleology, was to be advanced by Kant. Neither did much to prop up an idea of nature as fixed, immutable, perfect, and energised from outside itself, by the will of its creator in the hierarchical order of the Great Chain of Being.

By the end of the century it had become impossible to sustain the calm and stable view of nature left by many theologians. Nature began to be seen as an economy of dynamic processes, changing over time. Far from being described by a 'Great Chain of Being', it became divided into discrete classification groups. Even man's own place in nature began to be questioned. Was man, God's highest creation, securely placed above a natural order, created for his exploitation and profit, or was he to be seen as an integral part of that order? In spite of his unique possession of a soul, after all, he also seemed startlingly similar in general conformation

[13] Foucault, *The Order of Things*. Werner's *Short Classification and Description of the Rocks* (Freiburg, 1787) suggested that geological strata followed a regular order of deposition which could be used as a guide to the history of different epochs in the history of life.

to the major apes. Was the earth itself still changing? If so, would it do so in a stable way? If God was benevolent and all knowing, why had so many species which he had created become extinct? The questions dragged on, with increasing resonance as the century progressed, and increasingly, especially in continental Europe, gulfs opened up between the objectives and assumptions of theology and those of 'natural philosophy'. In creating this gap, questions about the history of nature played a major role, and meant the mythical 'ordinary person's' view of nature was markedly different from what it would have been at the beginning of the century. Increasingly acceptable was the idea of nature having a history, and a long one at that, which might have seen change occurring as much by violent upheavals as by the slow accretion of the daily operations of nature. While the theological view of nature as reflecting the positive attributes of the Deity still seemed acceptable to many, especially in Great Britain, it seemed increasingly possible for men to hold simultaneously views of nature which were quite divorced from theological objectives; one where nature functioned as a secular sort of emotional therapy, and where knowledge of nature, in spite of the charges of the philosophers, had started to seem more valid and more important.

Social changes in science itself helped this process along. While it remained true well into the next century that few men could hope to make a career in full-time scientific work or even by teaching science, yet science did become much more visible and accessible. The booming publications market began to include many books of popular science, spearheaded by the popularisations of Newton discussed earlier. Popular science lectures became a regular part of urban life in Britain, the Netherlands, France and Italy.[14] In the German states, a wave of new universities founded from the 1740s onwards, like the University of Göttingen, trained future bureaucrats in forestry, agricultural science, engineering and mining, as well as in law and history. This was also the great age of the scientific society. Beginning in the 1660s, which saw the foundation of both the Royal Society of London, and the Paris *Académie des Sciences*, all over Europe, and especially in Germany and Italy, both private and publicly chartered learned societies and academies sheltered and encouraged the scientific research of enthusiastic amateurs, or even, in the Paris case, of the few full-time paid workers in science.[15]

[14] R. Porter, 'Science, Provincial Culture and Public Opinion in Enlightenment England', *British Journal of Eighteenth-Century Studies*, 3 (1980), 16–25. Best-selling popularisations of science included the Abbé Pluche, *Spectacle de la Nature* (1732–50).

[15] R. Hahn, *The Anatomy of a Scientific Institution: the Paris Academy of Sciences, 1666–1803* (Berkeley, CA, 1971); R. E. Schofield, *The Lunar Society of Birmingham* (Oxford, 1963);

Zoological gardens, and botanical gardens, such as the Jardin des Plantes in Paris directed by Buffon, allowed public access for the first time. New scientific journals were founded. Certain branches of science, particularly botany, began to be popular amongst women, who were often banned from the education in classical languages and history which was still standard for their brothers. The technological aspects of science such as forestry, mining, veterinary medicine, and agriculture began to appeal more to governments attempting to exert more control than ever over natural environments, and more than ever beset by problems in engineering, in agriculture, and in public health. By the end of the century, science had thus become implicated in the business of government itself, and especially new sciences like that of statistics and probability began to offer the possibility of controlling and predicting the need for social and natural resources on which governments depended (see Chapter 3).[16]

Paradoxically, the 'profile' of science was also raised because all this happened at a time when science was still not dominated by experimentalism. There was much rhetoric about the importance of direct observation of nature, and of careful public experimentation; but it was still perfectly possible to engage in speculative writings about Nature, such as those produced by Diderot, which were not based on an experimental approach. This was discursive science, written to be read by lay people, and diffused through the print media. The evidence of library catalogues shows that, at the beginning of the century, the most widely purchased books were theological; by the end of the century, they were fiction or popular science. Science-based crazes such as Mesmerism started to appear.[17] We may dispute Foucault's claim for the dominance of the 'taxonomic impulse' in European thought as a whole, and certainly in terms of the specific concerns of natural history. Where Foucault does appear to be on stronger ground, is with the contention that the Enlightenment earth and life sciences had a new, historical, component which was to drive a wedge between science and its former theological justifications. All this shows the extent to which science was slowly replacing religion as a dominant cultural 'plot', was inculcating as a cultural value the idea that knowledge was secular, concerned with the world as it is, and that

J. E. McClellan, *Science Reorganised: Scientific Societies in the Eighteenth Century* (New York, 1985).

16 L. Daston, *Classical Probability in the Enlightenment* (Princeton, NJ, 1988); G. Gigerenzer *et al.* (eds.), *The Empire of Chance: How Probability Changed Science and Everyday Life* (Cambridge, 1989); H. Mitchel, 'Rationality and Control in French Eighteenth Century Medical Views of the Peasantry', *Comparative Studies in Society and History*, 21 (1979), 81–112.

17 R. Darnton, *Mesmerism and the End of the Enlightenment in France* (Princeton, NJ, 1964).

it is to this world that men's curiosity might best be turned. Science was becoming acceptable as a form of knowledge worth pursuing in spite of both the jeers of the unlearned, and the *caveats* of the philosophers.

By the end of the century, idealisation of nature, particularly of plants and of wild mountain scenery, had come to provide a new, secular form of therapy, formerly provided by religious means for emotional disturbance. From a different direction, other forms of science – technology and statistics – began to seem increasingly important as means of control and exploitation available to governments. In spite of philosophical objections, and internal conflicts over methodology, such as the struggle between 'observation' and 'experimentation', science was increasingly successful, if not in putting forward claims to 'truth', or even consistently to objectivity, at least in putting forward claims to both consistency and practical utility.[18] It had begun to offer claims to control, exploit and predict nature and society, to provide secular knowledge, where man's knowledge of the universe could become independent from that of its creator. Science had come a long way from Laputa.

[18] L. Daston, 'Baconian Facts, Academic Civility, and the Pre-history of Objectivity', *Annals of Scholarship* (Spring, 1992).

9 The rise of modern paganism? Religion and the Enlightenment

> The greatest number still believe that the Enlightenment is concerned with almost nothing but religion.
>
> (Johann Pezzl)

> When all prejudice and superstition has been banished, the question arises: Now what? What is the truth which the Enlightenment has disseminated in place of these prejudices and superstitions?
>
> (Georg Wilhelm Friedrich Hegel)

> I knew a real theologian once . . . He knew the Brahmins, the Chaldeans . . . the Syrians, the Egyptians, as well as he knew the Jews; he was familiar with the various readings of the Bible . . . The more he grew truly learned, the more he distrusted everything he knew. As long as he lived, he was forebearing; and at his death, he confessed he had squandered his life uselessly.
>
> (Voltaire)[1]

As we have seen, 'Enlightenment' is a term which has been defined in many different ways both by contemporaries and by later historians. But nowhere is the divergence between contemporary and later definitions wider than in the area of religion. Until recently, few historians would have echoed Johann Pezzl's contemporary judgement on the centrality of religious issues to the Enlightenment. Indeed, in the nineteenth century, many conservative historians saw the Enlightenment as a time characterised by deliberate efforts to undermine religious belief and organisations. Some went so far as to link anti-religious attitudes fostered by the Enlightenment with the outbreak of the French Revolution itself in 1789 (see Chapter 10). This is a view taken also by many modern historians. It is Peter Gay who significantly subtitles one volume of his synthetic study of the Enlightenment as the 'rise of modern paganism'. Similarly, Keith

[1] Johann Pezzl, *Marokkanische Briefe* (Frankfurt and Leipzig, 1784), 174–5; G. W. F. Hegel, *Phänomenologie des Geistes*, ed. Johannes Hoffmeister (Hamburg, 1952), 397. English version, *The Phenomenology of Mind*, trans. J. B. Baillie (New York and Evanston, 1967), 576; Voltaire, *Philosophical Dictionary* (1764), article 'Theologian'.

Thomas has seen the eighteenth century as a time of 'disenchantment of the world', meaning the collapse of a way of seeing the world as full of magical or spiritual powers and forces organising a mysterious cosmos. Thomas argues that this change in religious values had very important consequences. From being seen as a power moving outside and beyond the created world, God, he argues, 'was confined to working through natural causes' and 'obeyed natural laws accessible to human study'.[2] While Thomas is certainly not arguing that the Enlightenment saw an end of religious belief, he is arguing for a radical shift in religious conceptions from the beginning of the eighteenth century. Nor is this perception of the Enlightenment as a time of the decline of supernatural, 'mysterious' religion confined to English-speaking historians. Michel Vovelle has also seen a slow decline in religious belief, which he somewhat dramatically describes as 'dechristianisation' in the south of France, which he finds evidenced by the declining use of religious phrases in wills, and declining numbers of bequests with religious objectives. In spite of the controversy his work has attracted, mainly due to his choice of sources, it has seemed nevertheless attractive to many because it seems to point to a connection between declining religious belief pre-1789, and the attempts made during the French Revolution both to stamp out Christian belief in France, and to produce new forms of 'rational' or 'natural' religion.[3]

Gay, Vovelle and Thomas have thus all produced work arguing that the Enlightenment saw either an absolute decline in religious belief, or a radical shift in its meaning and context. Nor is this a new view of the Enlightenment. Genealogy for this view is provided not merely by the conservative historians who considered the relationship between Enlightenment and Revolution in the previous century. It is also supported by the contemporary analysis of the impact of the Enlightenment on religion by the great German philosopher, G. W. F. Hegel (1770–1831), many of whose arguments on this point are also adopted by Horkheimer's and Adorno's *Dialectic of Enlightenment*.[4] Hegel's analysis pinpoints religious issues as indicative of fundamental shifts in Enlightenment thought. For Hegel, the Enlightenment, especially in France, was an inherently religious movement, where the *philosophes* 'carried out the Lutheran Reformation in a different form'. For him, both Reformation and Enlightenment were contributions to the same objective, that of human spiritual freedom: 'What Luther had initiated in the heart, was freedom of spirit.' Nonetheless,

[2] Keith Thomas, *Religion and the Decline of Magic: Studies in Popular Belief in Sixteenth and Seventeenth-Century England* (London, 1983), 640, 659.

[3] Michel Vovelle, *Piété baroque et déchristianisation en Provence au XVIII*[e] *siècle: Les attitudes devant la mort d'après les clauses des testaments* (Paris, 1973).

[4] Max Horkheimer and Theodor Adorno, *Dialectic of Enlightenment* (New York, 1972).

Hegel argued that the Enlightenment had mistaken its path, in arguing that faith should be assessed by rationality. Hegel is also concerned that attacks by *philosophes* on the reality of spiritual experience also rely on the view that all real ideas ultimately come only from sense experience. For Hegel this meant that the Enlightenment, instead of completing its historical mission to complete the Reformation, was in severe danger of destroying faith altogether. In doing so, it would, according to Hegel, be destroying a crucial aspect of man's self-knowledge, its relation to the absolute and the spiritual:

> Formerly, they had a heaven adorned with a vast wealth of thoughts and imagery. The meaning of all that is, hung on the thread of light by which it was linked to that of heaven. Instead of dwelling in this world, presence, men looked beyond it, following the thread to an other-worldly presence, so to speak. The eye of the spirit had to be forcibly turned and held fast to the things of this world; and it has taken a long time before the lucidity which only heavenly beings used to have could penetrate the dullness and confusion in which the sense of worldly things was enveloped, and so make attention to the here and now as such, attention to what has been called 'experience', an interesting and valid enterprise. Now, we seem to heed just the opposite: sense is so fast rooted in earthly things that it requires just as much force to raise it. The Spirit shows itself so impoverished that, like a wanderer in the desert craving for a mouthful of water, it seems to crave for its refreshment only the bare feelings of the divine in general.

Furthermore, Hegel alleged that the Enlightenment failed to produce any set of beliefs which could possibly replace religious faith. Enlightenment had in fact, he thought, changed the grounds of debate about religion away from questions of religious/theological *truth*, which obsessed the Reformation era of the sixteenth and seventeenth centuries, to become equally obsessed with the *utility* of religion, in the sense of providing social stability. Alternatively, according to Hegel, the Enlightenment simply saw religion as an outcrop of other phenomena such as the laws of nature, which were knowable by man. In any case, religion ceased to have an independent status as relating to a world of faith only partially knowable by man, and became totally assimilated to human needs and human understanding. Once man became an end in himself, as Hegel alleged he was in Enlightenment thought, once he lost religious aspiration, then he becomes trapped in his own solipsism, unable to judge himself aright, or to form non-utilitarian ties to other human beings. Thus, Hegel like Kant saw the Enlightenment as an uncompleted project for intellectual and spiritual freedom. But for Hegel, the Enlightenment had betrayed itself, left unfulfilled its religious mission, because of the nature of the image of man which it produced, which emphasised human autonomy and self-sufficiency.[5]

These are views of the relationship between Enlightenment and religion which have been enormously influential. Nor was Hegel's view of the religious thought of the Enlightenment without considerable substance, especially in the case of France. Religious movements such as Deism, especially strong in Britain and France, denied that man could gain any knowledge of the Creator apart from the mere fact of 'his' existence. Writers such as Voltaire alternately crusaded against all organised religion, or argued that religious observance was only to be tolerated because of its utility in producing social stability, not because its claims were actually true. Materialists such as Julien de la Mettrie (1709–51) argued in his *L'Homme Machine* of 1747 that there was no such thing as a soul, and that all knowledge came ultimately from sense impressions of the surrounding physical world.[6] Men, the Baron d'Holbach argued in another notorious materialist treatise, the *Système de la Nature* (1771), should abandon religion completely, to reconcile themselves with 'nature'.[7] And again, economic thought in the Enlightenment in the works of such men as Adam Smith did define individuals as autonomous seekers of self-interest rather than of salvation.

However, our picture of the Enlightenment as 'modern paganism' starts to become considerably more complex once we abandon this focus on the small group of determinedly anti-religious thinkers who are almost confined to the French Enlightenment. As we have already seen, thinkers of the stature of Hegel saw the Enlightenment as a movement which could not be understood except within religious categories, however one assesses his claim that the Enlightenment had betrayed man's religious nature. In fact the Enlightenment produced a wide variety of responses to organised religion, ranging all the way from violent Voltairean hostility to religion, through to attempts to bolster orthodox belief by demonstrating its rationality and accordance with natural law. The century can also be seen as one of great religious creativity, even creating the characteristic and new religious idea, that of toleration, which was possibly its most important legacy to succeeding centuries. The Enlightenment saw not

[5] This analysis is considerably indebted to Lewis Hinchman, *Hegel's Critique of the Enlightenment* (Gainesville, FL, 1984), chapter 5. See also H. R. Trevor-Roper, 'The Religious Origin of the Enlightenment', in his *Religion, Reformation and Social Change*, 3rd edn (London, 1984). Quotation from Hegel, *Phenomenology of Spirit*, translated A. V. Miller (Oxford, 1977), 5.

[6] Julien Offray de la Mettrie, *L'Homme Machine* (Paris, 1747), ed. Paul Laurent Assoun (Paris, 1981).

[7] Paul-Henri Thomas d'Holbach, *Système de la nature ou des lois du monde physique et du monde moral* (Paris, 1769).

only attempts to stabilise orthodox belief by demonstrating its acceptability to human reason, but also powerful religious movements, such as English Methodism, the 'Great Awakening' in the North American colonies, the rise of the mystical sect known as Hassidism within Polish Judaism, and the Pietist movement in the German states, which all emphasised a personal and emotional faith. Religious controversy within Christianity and Judaism also had a powerful reciprocal impact on the development of historical scholarship in this period, involving a complete reworking of thinking about the historical development of human society. At the same time, Deism, the belief that little or nothing could be known about the creator except the fact of his existence as a precondition for that of the workings of the natural laws governing the cosmos, posed in an acute form the relationship between science and religion. The century is one of powerful multivariant religious debate and innovation, which certainly cannot be encapsulated in Voltaire's famous battle-cry of *Ecrasez l'infâme*: wipe out the infamy of organised religion.

Let us turn first to that most characteristic Enlightenment idea: that of the importance of religious toleration. Though some voices had been raised, particularly in England and France, in the seventeenth century on the side of toleration, it was to be the eighteenth century which saw the determining debates and decisions on this issue. Indeed in terms of religion, the century of the Enlightenment can be seen as framed by two important measures for toleration: in 1689 the English Parliament passed the Toleration Act in Great Britain, which greatly decreased (without altogether removing) legal penalties against those who did not subscribe to the Church of England, especially Catholics and Dissenters. In 1787, the monarchy in France issued decrees allowing limited toleration and some lessening of civil disabilities to Protestants. In between these two decrees lay a long period of struggle and argument over the issue.

Why should the issue of religious toleration have aroused such strong passions, and such continuous debate in the Enlightenment? This happened to a large extent because the Enlightenment was also heir to the Reformation in a different sense to that understood by Hegel. It was the heir not only to its potential legacy of intellectual freedom, but also to the military and political conflicts, which had been aroused by Luther's attempts to reform the Catholic church in the sixteenth century. From the sixteenth century until the Peace of Westphalia in 1648, states whose rulers were of opposing religious convictions had fought each other, at least partly to impose their religious convictions on their opponents. At the same time, as conflict broke out between states, religious dissent proliferated within states. Catholic states, such as France, produced embattled Protestant minorities. Protestant states, such as England, persecuted Catholics, and faced a proliferation of mutually hostile Protestant sects within their own borders. Such internal religious conflict was fertile ground for foreign intervention. In both the Protestant and Catholic camps it was widely held that error had no rights, and that those who held religious views which differed from those of the reigning monarch were disloyal subjects whose very existence challenged the unity and stability of state and society. To a large extent, the Enlightenment's attempt to come to grips with the issue of toleration was also an attempt to confront its immediate past and to influence future outcomes. Enlightenment thinkers grappled with a past full of religious intolerance with the same urgency that the late twentieth century grappled with the issues raised by the Holocaust.

Some of this began to change when Westphalia brought to a close a prolonged period of warfare in Europe, known as the Thirty Years' War, some of whose most important causes were to be found in hostility between Catholic and Protestant states. The year 1648 saw the end of war between states with the objective of enforcing religious allegiances. Some rulers still were to attempt to impose religious uniformity within their own borders, for, of course, the prolonged religious conflict before 1648 had not produced religious homogeneity within *any* state. But the changed international situation meant that the confessions and the dynasties were no longer so embattled over the religious issue. In the eighteenth century, states were increasingly faced with real decisions as to whether to continue to strive for confessional uniformity within their own borders, or whether to tolerate religious diversity, and, if so, to what extent. At the same time, a rising tide of opinion looked back with revulsion at the devastation and chaos caused by religious conflict between and within states in the past. Was conflict and instability too high a price to pay for religious uniformity? Increasingly, it was also pointed out that religious belief could not in any case be compelled. Religious belief was increasingly seen as something that should not dominate man like a foreign power, but freely arise from interior forces such as conscience and reason. Thus attempts to impose uniformity by force were nonsensical.

Nonetheless, in spite of this rising tide of opinion in favour of religious toleration, manifested for example in Voltaire's 1763 *Traîté de la tolérance*, it was not easy for many rulers to take decisive steps towards legally implementing it. Religious toleration, which seems so obviously acceptable to us, in fact raised many issues about the nature of state and monarchy, which were not easy to resolve. The victory for religious toleration was thus not immediate or speedy, as the gap of a century between the Toleration Act in Britain and the Toleration Decrees in France should remind us.

For many, toleration posed as many problems as it answered. How could subjects of a faith different from that of the ruler or the established church be seen as truly loyal? How could they take binding oaths? How far would the extension of religious toleration change the nature of state and monarchy? This was a particularly important question at a time when the great majority of states were governed by monarchies whose legitimacy stemmed at least in part from their claims to allegiance to a particular church. To give only a few examples the French monarch, whose subjects included a sizeable number of Protestants, took a coronation oath to extirpate heresy. The English monarch was secular head of the Church of England. The King of Prussia was *summus episcopus* of the Lutheran church. Thus, at stake in the struggle for state-supported religious toleration was a transition from the idea of a monarchal state as necessarily involving also a uniform community of believers, to the idea of an impersonal state where religious loyalties could be separated from loyalty to the state itself: in other words, the transition from a distinctively *ancien régime* political order to one more typically modern. This was not a particularly attractive option, for example, for a ruler like Maria Theresa of Austria who saw her role as that of acting as a specifically Catholic monarch and was willing to deport many thousands of her Bohemian Protestant subjects in order to work still towards the creation of a uniformly Catholic state.

This was an issue about which there were thus great variations of viewpoint. Maria Theresa and her son and successor Joseph II, for example, held strongly opposing views on the issue of toleration, views which reflected different ideals about the nature of a modern polity, and thus of the role of the ruler. Joseph wanted to be able to define his subjects apart from their religious allegiance, Maria Theresa looked for a polity which still had something to do with the ideal of a unified Christendom which the Reformation had broken down. Opposing each other here were two different world views.[8] Each possessed valid arguments; neither of them was negligible.

Thinking about toleration thus did not have foregone conclusions. While Maria Theresa (1717–80) and Joseph II (1741–90) struggled over the issue, their contemporary Frederick II (1712–86) of Prussia, who

8 Joseph II wrote to Maria Theresa in June 1777, 'with freedom of religion, one religion will remain, that of guiding all citizens alike to the welfare of the state. Without this approach we shall not save any greater number of souls, and we shall lose a great many more useful and essential people.' A. von Arneth, *Maria Theresa und Joseph II: Ihr Correspondenz* (2 vols, Vienna, 1864), II, 141–2.

came to the throne in 1740, the same year as Maria Theresa, adopted a quite different line. In spite of the fact that Frederick was *summus episcopus* within the majority Lutheran church in Prussia, he established policies of wide religious toleration within his kingdom, immediately on his accession. Frederick defined his functions as holding the ring between the many different religious groups in Prussia, to the extent of even allotting state funds for the building of a new Catholic Cathedral in his capital city, Berlin, in 1747. Heresy enquiries, and public exposition of theological controversy were forbidden. In 1750, a revised General Privilege and Regulation for the Jews in Prussia increased Jewish rights, though not to the level of full toleration, though they were given the right to be tried by their own laws, and given the possession of their own schools, cemeteries and synagogues. Religious toleration was enforced in the Prussian army. As Frederick – who was personally an unbeliever – put it in a famous letter of June 1740: 'All must be tolerated . . . here everyone must be allowed to choose his own road to salvation.'[9]

Why was Frederick's reaction so different from that of Maria Theresa? Can we find the answer to this simply in the political context of his kingdom? His territories were certainly, from 1740 until at least the mid 1760s, being continually expanded, not only by warfare but also by a continuous process of exchange and negotiation aimed at bringing together widely scattered territories in as united a territorial bloc as possible. Frederick was also recruiting skilled labour from all over Europe to aid the economic and industrial development of Prussia. To enforce religious uniformity in all these circumstances would have been very difficult.

But arguments for toleration based on its economic utility or political convenience, strongly though they were made, are not enough to explain differences in attitudes between rulers on this issue. The argument for toleration on economic grounds seemed overwhelming to Joseph II, and was undoubtedly accepted by Frederick the Great; it did not impress Maria Theresa enough for her to cease large-scale state persecution of Protestants residing in Bohemia and in Hungary. Nor is it other than misleading to draw distinctions between Catholic and Protestant rulers on this issue. If Maria Theresa persecuted non-Catholics, non-Protestants certainly did not gain full equality of status and rights (though they were usually less dramatically mistreated), in any majority Protestant state, apart from the British North American colonies, which had no established state church, and possibly in the Netherlands. Everywhere, Jews laboured under more disadvantages than did their Christian neighbours of any denomination. In fact, Frederick's view in Prussia that all sects

[9] Quoted in H. W. Koch, *A History of Prussia* (London, 1978), 41.

would be tolerated, as long as they made no special claims, was highly unusual in the eighteenth century. It pointed the way in which Frederick's monarchy showed a more rapid evolution away from traditional models than any other, with the possible exception of the British. In religious terms, this meant that Frederick explored, perhaps more thoroughly than any other ruler, the freedoms conferred by the ending of interstate confessional warfare at the end of the seventeenth century.

The religious denominations themselves also had to explore this new situation. After 1648, it was not only international conflict over religion that began to die down; so did, though with some important exceptions, internecine conflict between the sects. Over a hundred years of conflict since Luther had demonstrated to many the impossibility of convincing others of religious truths by appeals either to the authority of the churches, or to revelation, supernatural knowledge of things spiritual which could only be told to men by God through specially chosen human channels such as the prophets. Many in all religious denominations became anxious to construct a version of their faith which could be apprehended by human *reason*, which would thus be accessible to all men alike, and should thus convince without the need to resort to force. It is no accident that in 1695, John Locke should publish a book entitled *The Reasonableness of Christianity*.

Behind the push to construct a 'reasonable' Christianity lay the hideous memory of sectarian strife, often accompanied by threat of social revolution, which had been so prevalent in the seventeenth century. It was also motivated by continuous, sporadic outbursts of religious hostilities within states, even in the eighteenth century itself. Protestants in Lithuania were persecuted by their Polish rulers in the 1720s. Protestants in Hungary and Bohemia were harried. There were renewed outbursts against Protestants in France from the 1740s at least until the famous Calas and Sirvin cases of the mid 1760s. The drive to construct a 'reasonable' version of Christianity was fuelled by those outbursts as much as by the memories of the preceding century.[10]

But 'reasonable Christianity' also brought along new problems of its own. If Christianity was to be recast in a form which any rational person could accept, what happened to the status of the Bible, so full of the irrational, and of the personal testimony of the prophets and apostles, who had certainly not received the revelation of 'a new heaven and a new earth' through rationality? What happened to apparently irrational occurrences, such as the miracles performed by Christ which overturned

[10] D. Bien, *The Calas Affair: Reason, Tolerance and Heresy in Eighteenth-Century Toulouse* (Princeton, NJ, 1960).

the laws of nature? Thus a questioning of the status and authority of the Bible was to be a major – if unintended – by-product of the attempt to establish 'reasonable' Christianity.

The attempt to downplay revelation in favour of reason also had other consequences. Revelation was, by definition, that which Christianity did not share with other faiths. As the century progressed, and knowledge of other religions grew, it was increasingly and unforgettably realised that much of what had been seen as specific to the Christian religion had in fact many analogues in other faiths. Legends of a great flood, for example, appeared in many oriental cultures without historical links to Judaism or Christianity.[11] Increasing interest in other religions was also to lead to the study of religion as a human creation, rather than a revelation by the Divine of itself. This new focus is revealed, for example, in David Hume's 1757 *Natural History of Religion*, and in the growing interest throughout the century in what we would now call the field of 'comparative religion'. Voltaire's theologian was not a unique figure in the Enlightenment; nor was his increasing uncertainty surrounding the status of Christian belief in relation to that of other religions.

If the new field of the study of comparative religion was unsettling, science itself sent ambiguous messages into the religious thinking of the Enlightenment. For centuries it had been customary to point to nature and to cosmology as evidence of God's power and benevolence. The earth had been created, it was argued, as a benevolently ordered habitat for man, who had the right to control and exploit other created beings in his own interest.[12] Astronomical work in the sixteenth century by Copernicus and Kepler, however, had demonstrated that far from being the stable centre of the cosmos, planet earth revolved around a sun and was itself only one of many planetary systems.

In 1687, Isaac Newton (1642–1727) published his *Mathematical Principles of Natural Philosophy*. In spite of its difficult mathematics, this work had tremendous impact throughout the Enlightenment, as it seemed to provide a basis for answering the question of what *sort* of interest God actually displayed in his creation. Did he intervene daily in the lives of his chosen, as the Old Testament seemed to imply? Or was his interest far more remote, or non-existent? Newton himself portrayed an ordered cosmos subject to mathematical laws, not only originally set in motion by its creator, but also requiring considerable intervention from him to

[11] Hans Frei, *The Eclipse of Biblical Narrative* (New Haven, CT, 1977); P. J. Marshall, *The British Discovery of Hinduism in the Eighteenth Century* (Cambridge, 1970); G. R. Cragg, *Reason and Authority in Eighteenth-Century England* (Cambridge, 1964).

[12] K. Thomas, *Man and the Natural World* (London, 1983).

correct irregularities and supply energy. The cosmos, as Newton originally envisaged it, could be seen as a vast proof both of God's existence, and of his continuing concern at least for his physical creation, if not in the day-to-day doings of men.

Many of Newton's popularisers, whose work reached an audience far larger than did Newton's original text, interpreted the *Mathematical Principles* as showing God's *distance* from his creation. Newton's work thus was used in ways far removed from his original intentions, to support those whom the century called Deists, who believed in God only as the creator of the universe, a Being thus virtually equivalent to the laws of nature itself. Such a God displayed no interest in the moral choices of men, but existed only as a First Cause.[13] Meanwhile, the Scots historian and philosopher David Hume pointed out that the existence of the order of nature, or of the laws of the cosmos did not necessarily betray anything about the nature of its creator, or indeed that there had been a creator at all. However, this eminently logical conclusion was read by relatively few people. While popularisations of Newton's work received a much larger audience throughout Europe and the Americas, and undoubtedly provided fruitful ammunition for doubters and Deists, most eighteenth-century people still believed in the idea of the earth and the cosmos as created by a benevolent God as a suitable habitat for man. Paradoxically, as the century drew to a close, and well into the next, a favourite argument for the existence of God, especially in Protestant countries, continued to be the 'order and contrivance' of nature. In this, as in much else, science sent contradictory messages into Enlightenment religious development.

Nor was this confusion unique to this particular area of the religious thought of the Enlightenment. Older, orthodox beliefs and Enlightenment speculation sat uneasily side by side in the minds of many. Throughout the century, while *philosophes* preached the natural goodness and perfectibility of man, orthodox theologians continued to emphasise his innate sinfulness, due to the sin of Adam, and to thunder about the Divine retribution which would surely follow sinners after death.[14] The problem raised here was a deeper one than that of maintaining clarity in the mind of the average believer. It returned to a central tenet of the Christian religion, the divine nature of Christ, and the necessity for his sacrifice on the Cross to redeem man from the sinful condition into which

[13] P. Gay, *Deism: An Anthology* (Princeton, NJ, 1968).

[14] John McManners, *Death and the Enlightenment: Changing Attitudes to Death among Christians and Unbelievers in Eighteenth-Century France* (Oxford, 1981); C. McDonnell and B. Long, *Heaven: A History* (New Haven, CT, 1988).

Adam's disobedience had thrown him. If man was not in fact innately sinful, what need to believe in Christ?

At the same time, belief in Christ's divinity was coming under attack from another quarter. Proof of his divinity was held to be the miracles which Christ performed, and which were attested to in the Gospels. Such miracles, such as the raising of Lazarus from the dead, or the changing of water into wine at the wedding at Cana, or the very Resurrection itself, all involved an overthrow of the laws of nature, those very laws of nature which many in the Enlightenment were so eager totally to identify with God. David Hume's 1748 *Essay on Miracles*, published six years after Dublin audiences flocked to the first performance of Handel's *Messiah* which celebrated the miraculous birth and resurrection of Christ, laid much of the ground-work for subsequent controversy, together with Voltaire's 1765 *Questions sur les Miracles*. A Newtonian view of the laws of nature brought into doubt the likelihood of miracles actually occurring. Hume also pointed out that the 'evidence' for the miracles of Christ having occurred lay with the allegedly eyewitness accounts in the Gospels and that eyewitness accounts were often the least reliable of all forms of evidence. How could the reliability of the Gospel witnesses be assessed, he asked, if there are no contemporary analogues to the events they relate? Certainly there was no contemporary analogue for the most important miracle of all, the Resurrection. Hume also pointed out that while human testimony might be a necessary part of establishing the credibility of miracles (otherwise we would not even know of their existence), human eyewitness testimony was not sufficient to lend credibility to accounts of events that were contradicted both by the laws of nature, and by present-day human experience.

Debates on the nature of historical knowledge and its relationship to religion also entered the fray. German *philosophes* such as Gotthold Ephraim Lessing (1729–81) and, most famously, Johann Gottlieb Fichte (1762–1814) pointed out that historical study could only show 'what happened', not the ethical meaning or rational status of events. Because of this, they argued, the historical data in the New Testament were insufficient to establish its status as revelation. At the same time, historians in the eighteenth century increasingly abandoned the medieval and Renaissance view of history as by definition the story of the working out of divine intentions in the 'theatre of the world' inhabited by sinful humans. They came much closer to the view of history espoused by the Neapolitan historian Giambattista Vico (1668–1744) that history should be seen as the story of man's own capacity for progress. Edward Gibbon (1737–94), for example, was to provide in his *Decline and Fall of the Roman*

Empire (1776, Chapter 15), a famous account of the rise of early Christianity as a purely human organisation, whose development could be understood in exactly the same terms as those of the Roman Empire itself.

Miracles thus became an increasing target for anti-religious thinkers like d'Holbach. The miracle stories were easily attacked as belonging to a long line of priestly confidence tricks on an ignorant and credulous people. For those influenced by the work of Newton, or who wished to construct a 'reasonable' religion, miracles were also a problem: why should God have wished to disrupt his own natural and rational laws? None of this made the status of central Christian beliefs any more secure among those of the educated classes who were aware of these debates, though they probably had little impact on the mass of ordinary believers, particularly in Catholic countries; nor was it the intention of the *philosophes* to destroy what they saw as the simple (and socially necessary) faith of their social inferiors, by diffusing their own rational enquiries too far down the social scale.

Nor was all Enlightenment questioning of religious teaching based on simple logical enquiry. At times, events focussed minds on particular issues which had always been problematical in Christian teaching. One such 'focusing moment' occurred in 1755, when an earthquake, followed by a tidal wave, killed more than 10,000 people in the city of Lisbon and reduced most of the city to ruins. How, asked Voltaire and many others, could this event be reconciled with a conception of God as a loving or omnipotent creator? How could God have permitted such a misfortune to occur to so many people? The problem of the existence of evil was hardly new in the eighteenth century. But what the Lisbon earthquake did was to focus minds on the discrepancy between the existence of evil and of unmerited misfortune, and the increasing optimism taught by many Enlightenment thinkers. This 'optimism' had become so prevalent that the philosopher Leibniz had coined the new term, 'theodicy', to describe the repeated attempts to 'solve' the problem of evil, or provide an explanation of its existence consistent with the possibility of a 'reasonable' religion and of a benevolent and omnipotent creator. By 1759, Voltaire, in his significantly entitled *Candide or Optimism*, was able mercilessly to satirise Leibniz in his character of Dr Pangloss, who believes that this is the 'best of all possible worlds'.[15] Such a change from optimism could only destabilise Christian belief even further.

There were many different responses to these problems. One way out was Deism, with its total hostility to revelation. Another was to reject

[15] François-Marie Arouet de Voltaire, *Candide ou l'optimisme* (Paris, 1759).

the attempt to make Christianity 'reasonable', and return to a view of religion which emphasised faith, trust in revelation, and personal witness to religious experience. In this way came much impetus for the new 'enthusiastic' religious sects, such as Methodism, which broke away from Anglicanism in England, and the religious revival known as the 'Great Awakening' in the North American British colonies. Much the same original impulse lay behind the movement known as Pietism in North Germany.[16]

In looking at Pietism, we are looking at the way in which religious issues could move far beyond the polite discussions of elites, and have dramatic effects on society and government. Pietism was a movement of religious revival which swept through the Protestant states of Germany in the aftermath of the Thirty Years' War, which Pietists saw as a terrible punishment for sin inflicted by God on Germany. Its founders emphasised an idea of personal religious experience far removed from contemporary attempts to create a 'reasonable Christianity'. The early Pietists were concerned to work within the Lutheran church for its reform. For them, the struggles over religion since the early sixteenth century had resulted in Lutheranism paying too much attention to the reform of the church, and too little to the issue of how the church might reform the world. While many German princes viewed the movement with hostility because of its capacity to create religious disturbance in society, and to upset their *modus vivendi* with the Lutheran church, the ruler of Prussia, Frederick William I (1688–1740), welcomed the movement with open arms. The Prussian Elector saw how to use Pietism's enthusiasm for the reform of the world, which was channelled in Prussia into dedication to serving the poor and serving the state. In Prussia at least, Pietism was not merely a vehicle for ecstatic religious witness and the awaiting of the Second Coming of Christ, but an active social and political force. Frederick William used Pietism to drive a wedge into the formerly strong links binding the Lutheran church in Prussia to the Estates, or representative bodies of the nobility, many of which were opposed to his plans for centralisation and reform. The Elector handed over the control of education and of other institutions formerly dominated by orthodox Lutherans to known Pietists. Pietism, as Fulbrooke has argued, thus became a powerful force enhancing the power of the ruler over the social elites and the Lutheran church, and providing a powerful impetus for cultural unity in Prussia's divided lands. The spread of Pietism's ideas of service to others and

[16] The following discussion of Pietism owes much to M. Fulbrooke, *Piety and Politics: Religion and the Rise of Absolutism in England, Württemburg and Prussia* (Cambridge, 1983).

to the state was crucial to the conversion of the Prussian nobility into a court-orientated service bureaucracy, without which Prussian absolutism could not have emerged or functioned.

This also means that even for a new and active sect such as the Pietists, the impact of their religious beliefs cannot be read off from their dogma alone, but was altered by the social and political context in which they operated. What was an ecstatic, emotional, socially disruptive, sect in Württemburg, was an organised force in the service of the state in Prussia.

It is also important to note that in the Enlightenment almost all major faiths developed internally generated reforming movements. Where Lutheranism had Pietism, Catholicism had Jansenism, and Anglicanism had Methodism. Just as the Elector Frederick William used Pietism to further his own reform plans, so did the Grand-Duke Peter Leopold of Tuscany use the Jansenist faction to further his own plans for church reform, despite the opposition of much of the Catholic hierarchy. In Austria too, Jansenism was a powerful factor behind demands to reform. In spite of the fact that in many of the states, such as France, Jansenism was interpreted as a threat to monarchal powers, rather than its support, all this shows, nonetheless, how aware were Enlightenment rulers of the social function of religion. It is arguable that the success of Prussian Pietism in the years before 1740 in bolstering the power of the ruler was what made it possible for Frederick the Great to have enough power to enforce his policy of tolerance after 1740.

Additional tensions were present in many Catholic states, where the rulers' allegiance to the Church, and their reliance on its ritual to legitimise their authority as rulers, did not prevent renewed conflict between monarchy and the church hierarchy. In the Austrian lands too, it was strongly believed, especially by Joseph II, that control of education should be transferred from the Catholic Church to the state; and that the allegiance of his subjects to their duties could be better inculcated by the teaching of a 'rational' Christianity. All sought for more independence from Rome and increasing control over religious observance and church appointments in their own lands. The expulsion of the Jesuit order, sworn to uphold Papal power, from all Catholic countries between 1759 and 1771 is only the most dramatic example of this tension. Spurred on too, especially in the Italian states and in Josephian Austria, by economic advisors who believed that the land market was underdeveloped and agricultural productivity held back by the Church's role as predominant landlord, and that monastic orders were detaining many potential recruits to the labour force and the army, many Catholic monarchs, such as Joseph II and Charles III of Spain, launched attacks on the church.

The picture which emerges of religion in the Enlightenment is thus complex. In terms of belief, traditional theology competed with new religious sects such as Pietism, and more fundamentally with religious enquiries such as Deism, which seemed bent on nothing so much as removing religion from religious belief. Attempts to construct a 'reasonable' or 'rational' Christianity caused as many problems as they solved. Some historians have argued, and Hegel would probably have agreed, that Deists and 'reasonable' Christians alike ran the risk of erecting human reason itself as the focus of a new religion, while social movements such as the Masonic Lodges could easily be seen as the outward sign of new, secular, substitute cults, and were so especially in Catholic countries.[17]

Religious change and debate also had profound consequences in the political sphere. It is a truism that the central metaphor of political thought in the seventeenth century was religious, whereas the eighteenth century sees the slow breakdown of the idea that political and religious communities must be co-terminous. This was the logic involved in the debate on religious toleration which took place all over Europe, and which involved those rulers and communities which supported it in a conscious effort to change the basis of legitimate power. This is the major reason why the implementation of freely debated ideas of religious toleration, so obvious to us, took such a long time, and involved such hard debate in the eighteenth century. For those rulers who implemented toleration would have to base their legitimation on something other than religious sanction. Debating toleration was thus ultimately debating the nature of kingship itself (see Chapter 3). The issue was thus an intrinsic part of what some historians have described as the 'desacralisation' of kingship in this period. In this sense, as in others, Hegel was surely right to see Enlightenment as a continuation of the Reformation. Whether it also thereby opened the gates to revolution is another matter, to be discussed in Chapter 10.

[17] See the argument of Carl Becker, *The Heavenly City of the Eighteenth-Century Philosophers* (New Haven, CT, 1932).

10 The end of the Enlightenment: conspiracy and revolution?

> The empire of ignorance and superstition was moving closer and closer towards its collapse, the light of Aufklärung made more and more progress, and the convulsive gestures with which the creatures of the night howled at the dawning day showed clearly enough that they themselves despaired of victory, and were only summoning up their reserves for one final demented counter-attack. Then the disorders in France erupted: and now they again reared their empty heads and screeched at the top of their voices, 'Look there at the shocking results of the Aufklärung! Look there at the philosophers, the preachers of sedition!' Everyone seized this magnificent opportunity to spray their poison at the supporters of the Aufklärung.[1]

In 1789, France entered a period of revolutionary change which was to see the complete restructuring of the state, the collapse of the monarchy, and its replacement by a republic. By 1793, France was riven by civil war and factional struggles and had also opened hostilities upon several neighbouring states. At home, political dissent and economic collapse were repressed by the use of political terror. For many contemporaries, as for later historians, the connection between these events and the Enlightenment was highly problematic. How could an era which had seen so much struggle for the rational reform of society, government and the individual have ended with such turmoil and violence? Was the Revolution caused by the Enlightenment, or was it a repudiation of it? Did it happen because Enlightenment had been pursued too strongly or not strongly enough? Was Revolution always implicit in Enlightenment, or had the Revolution in France only occurred because of much more contingent, short-term factors? In particular, was the violence of the Revolution, which traumatised contemporaries, an inevitable outcome of the intense political stresses of a revolutionary situation after 1789, or was it generated by the ideas of the Enlightenment, ideas in which the men of the Revolution

[1] Quoted from the *Oberdeutsche Allgemeine Literaturzeitung* of August 1793, in T. C. W. Blanning, 'The Enlightenment in Catholic Germany', in R. Porter and M. Teich (eds), *The Enlightenment in National Context* (Cambridge, 1981), 126.

were thoroughly steeped? The answers to these questions were to be of decisive importance in assessing the importance of both Enlightenment and the Revolution itself in the nineteenth century. In turn, this Revolution did much to shape public attitudes towards social change and revolutionary movements ever since. Conservative writers such as the influential French historian Henri Taine, for example, interpreted the impact of the Enlightenment on the Revolution in very negative ways, ways which are therefore very different from the insistence upon Enlightenment as an uncompleted project of immensely liberating force, which is characteristic of the writings of some twentieth-century theorists such as Jürgen Habermas.

Possibly the best known of the conservative interpreters of the Enlightenment and its impact upon the French Revolution was the Abbé Barruel (1741–1820), a former Jesuit, whose 1797 *Mémoires pour servir à l'histoire du jacobinisme* was of great importance in determining many of the attitudes of the nineteenth century towards the Enlightenment and its links with the French Revolution. Barruel published his book in an atmosphere of political instability only to be ended with Bonaparte's seizure of power in 1799. As an ex-Jesuit he had also well-founded personal reasons for disliking the Enlightenment principles which had contributed to the downfall of his order, and his own consequent exile in Russia. Barruel believed that the Revolution in France, with all its attendant violence, and the sacrilege of its attack upon the French monarchy and the Catholic Church in France, had been caused by a conspiracy of Enlightenment *philosophes*, banded together in secret organisations such as the Illuminati in Germany, or the Masonic lodges which had spread through many parts of Europe. While the writings of the *philosophes* undermined the traditional values on which state and society depended, members of the Illuminati or the habitués of the Masonic lodges infiltrated government. For Barruel it was clear that the French revolutionary political faction known as the Jacobins, during whose period of dominance the use of terror in the Revolution had peaked, were nothing more than the continuation of this conspiracy to destroy civil society. Barruel thus saw the Revolution not as a radically new form of politics, or a dramatic break with the past, as did many of the revolutionaries themselves, but much more as the unmasking of very long-term previous developments within the Enlightenment.

The detail of these arguments may seem absurd to us: conspiracy theories to explain grand historical developments have had a bad press in the past century. Benefiting from more than two century's work on the origins and course of the Revolution, his thesis now seems unable to account for the diversity of factors which went into the making of the

Revolution in France, let alone to reflect the diversity of the Enlightenment itself. Some of Barruel's contemporaries, even those opposed to the Revolution in France, found his arguments unconvincing. But it is worth remembering that others did not. Barruel's arguments were for example foreshadowed in Edmund Burke's famous 1790 *Reflections on the Revolution in France*.[2] Barruel's work became a bestseller and had a widespread impact not simply on expert appraisals of the relationship between Enlightenment and Revolution, but also on much wider public perceptions of these issues. The reasons for this are twofold. Firstly, at the time of its publication, Barruel's *Mémoires* fitted into a thesis about Enlightenment which had already been consistently argued in other quarters during the eighteenth century itself, in a whole sub-species of novels and contemporary comment. For example the very popular novel *Le comte de Valmont*, which went into seven editions between 1774 and 1785, described a conspiracy of *philosophes* to gain control of Europe.[3] The conservative journal the *Année Littéraire* had consistently argued for the idea of a *philosophe* conspiracy as early as the 1770s. Part of the impetus for this viewpoint came from the fact that the editor of the *Année Littéraire*, Elie-Catherine Fréron, and many of its contributors, who included Barruel himself for a time, were Jesuits dispossessed by the abolition of their order in 1773. Fréron and his team played cleverly on contemporary concerns, by making direct parallels between the alleged *philosophe* 'conspiracy' against throne and altar, and Protestant 'heresy' associated in the minds of their readers with the period of religious civil war in France in the sixteenth and seventeenth centuries, a period which had seen not only chaos and civil strife, but also a great weakening of the authority of the monarchy in France. As one recent historian puts it, the concept of conspiracy emerges as 'a secularized form of the idea of heresy' in the *Année Littéraire*, which was probably the most widely read journal in eighteenth-century France.[4]

These arguments played to renewed religious intolerance in France, which peaked in the famous case of the Protestant Jean Calas, convicted

2 Compare Edmund Burke, *Reflections on the Revolution in France*, ed. Conor Cruise O'Brien (London, 1986), 211: 'The literary cabal had some years ago formed something like a regular plan for the destruction of the Christian religion. This object they pursued with a degree of zeal which hitherto had been discovered only in the propagators of some system of piety.' For an opposing view see the royalist Mallet du Pin, 'Of the Degree of Influence which the French Philosophy has had upon the Revolution', *The British Mercury*, 14 (15 March 1799).

3 Philippe-Louis Gérard, *Le comte de Valmont, ou les égarements de la raison* (Paris, 1774), which achieved twelve editions by 1807.

4 Amos Hoffman, 'The Origins of the Theory of the *Philosophe* Conspiracy', *French History*, 2 (1988), 152–72.

in 1762 on flimsy evidence of the murder of his son. Calas's rehabilitation was the subject of a famous campaign by the atheist Voltaire. The success with which Fréron's band of writers played to such concerns should remind us of the extent to which religious issues still organised the thought of educated elites in Enlightenment France. It should also remind us that 'marginal' or 'dispossessed' men, as were Jesuits after 1773, making a living by the pen, did not always, as Robert Darnton would have us believe, devote their talents to attacking the powers that be. 'Grub Street' and the *Année Littéraire* were not ideological equivalents, and did not put out the same message.

Thus, by describing the Enlightenment as a form of heresy which wished to weaken throne and altar in the same way that Protestant theological 'heresy' had allegedly done in previous centuries, the *Année Littéraire* picked up on a whole series of concerns still vibrant in France in the eighteenth century. Such concerns were undoubtedly strong enough to raise support for Barruel's thesis by the 1790s and 1800s. By the 1820s, renewed evidence seemed to be on hand to support his arguments. The wave of revolutionary movements which swept through Europe in the 1820s and 1830s, and which were in fact, especially in southern European states such as Naples, influenced by secret societies of political activists, seemed to provide vivid empirical evidence of the link between conspiracy, revolution, and mutant forms of 'Jacobinism'.[5]

However, Barruel's was far from being the only attempt to ponder on the connection between Enlightenment and Revolution. In 1856, Alexis de Tocqueville published his *The Ancien Régime and the French Revolution*. De Tocqueville, a liberal politician worried by increasingly authoritarian trends in France after Louis Napoleon's seizure of power in 1852, was no conservative figure looking back with regret to a time when throne and altar stood unchallenged. He was strongly concerned to argue that there was a continuity between the eighteenth century and the Revolution, but he saw that continuity not as lying, as Barruel had argued, in a successful *philosophe* conspiracy, but rather in the increasing power of the centralised state, which had, he believed, continued unabated between Old Regime and Revolution, and which had a capacity to extinguish true liberty, as much as had the excesses of mob rule. He argued that once catapulted into practical politics after 1789, the *philosophes*, whom he viewed as inexperienced utopian thinkers, had been unable to provide any ideological bulwark against the progress of political terror which had carried on the progress of centralisation. In fact their utopian idealism both before and

[5] See J. M. Roberts, *The Mythology of the Secret Societies* (Oxford, 1972); 'The French Origins of the "Right"', *Transactions of the Royal Historical Society*, 23 (1973), 27–53.

4 Voltaire and the Calas Affair.
Voltaire's intervention in this well-known scandal (1762) is shown here in a composite picture with a portrait of Voltaire in the top panel, and a scene from its history on the bottom. It was this case which established him as a well-known fighter against religious intolerance and judicial torture.

after 1789 had created a situation where debate and legitimate differences could not be contained, and terror became therefore the only way to exercise power, leading to a vast increase in dictatorial central government. For our purposes, de Tocqueville's influential history emerges as a negative version of Barruel's thesis.

Much of de Tocqueville's thesis has found echoes, some more distant than others, in current historical scholarship. Robert Darnton's emphasis on the oppositional writings of 'Grub Street' as a factor undermining authority at the end of the eighteenth century, is one example. So, in a different direction, is Keith Baker's thesis that the Republic of Letters served not only as a substitute for true political debate before the Revolution, but also as the prototype for the politics of the revolutionary public sphere.[6] Baker would agree with de Tocqueville that under the Old Regime

> the philosophe's cloak provided safe cover for the passions of the day, and political ferment was canalised into literature, the result being that our writers now became leaders of public opinion, and played for a while the part which normally in free countries, falls to the professional politician.[7]

This opinion also converges with that in Habermas' arguments on the Enlightenment public sphere, which we examined in Chapter 1. François Furet's recent re-interpretation of the Revolution also picks up this 'benign version' of de Tocqueville's thesis, by emphasising the importance of pre-revolutionary informal intellectual gatherings, the *sociétés de pensée*, as foreshadowing many of the forms of revolutionary organisation and mobilisation.[8] All these modern interpretations, however, differ from that of de Tocqueville in one important respect. They are far more concerned with the *form* of association amongst *hommes de lettres*, *philosophes*, or amateur intellectuals, than in the actual *content* of the criticism of the Old Regime. In other words, they do not directly engage either with Barruel's accusations that the anti-regime *content* of their thought also damaged church and monarchy, or with de Tocqueville's accusations of

[6] K. M. Baker, 'Enlightenment and Revolution in France: Old Problems, Renewed Approaches', *Journal of Modern History*, 53 (1981), 281–303; 'In a critical conceptual shift, "opinion" became an imaginary substitute for "power" as symbolically constituted under the Old Regime, and took on some of its fundamental characteristics' (285).

[7] Alexis de Tocqueville, *The Old Regime and the French Revolution*, ed. H. Brogan (London, 1966), 163–4.

[8] François Furet, *Interpreting the French Revolution* (Cambridge, 1981) first published as *Penser la Révolution française* (Paris, 1978). Particularly relevant here is Furet's analysis of work by that 'most misunderstood among the historians of the French Revolution' (p. 212), Augustin Cochin, on what he calls the *sociétés de pensée* of the Old Regime, the heterogeneous group of intellectual associations, ranging from provincial academies to Masonic Lodges and clubs.

impracticality or 'utopianism'. François Furet in particular makes little attempt to link his account of the specific nature of revolutionary, especially Jacobin, thought and language, with that of the Enlightenment. Thus, emphasis on the continuity between the social forms of the Republic of Letters, and the political forms of the Revolution leaves unanswered the question of the impact of the actual writings of the *philosophes*.

In part, this is a deliberate turning away from the style of analysis of, for example, Louis Blanc, who in his 1847 *Histoire de la Révolution française* makes a sustained attempt to trace the ideas of the *Encyclopédie* throughout the Revolution. It also reflects the fact that it is extremely difficult to assess the impact of Enlightenment writers on the Revolution, especially since the *philosophes* hardly produced a unified body of thought. While the revolutionaries themselves often alluded especially to Voltaire and Rousseau, their own thinking often proceeded in directions which would have horrified those whose names they used in order to legitimate their actions. It is debatable for example, whether Rousseau would have appreciated the uses to which his *Contrat Social* was put to justify the use of terror by reference to the General Will. While much use was made of appeals to Enlightenment ideals such as 'progress' or 'reason', few could foresee in 1789 the extent of the changes that were to occur by 1792. If the Enlightenment was not a unity, neither was the Revolution. To many it seemed that 1792 marked the opening of far greater changes than could have been thought of in 1789, and many subsequent historians have asked whether the years 1789–99 saw one Revolution or many separate ones, each with a different relationship to the eighteenth century and its own complex debates.

We are thus left with many unanswered problems in our understanding of the relationship between Enlightenment and Revolution. Part of the problem stems from the great redefinition which has taken place in our understanding of the Enlightenment itself. It is no longer possible to see it, even within France itself, as a movement uniquely dedicated to the ideological undermining of throne and altar. Outside France, as we have seen (Chapter 3), such an interpretation would have even less justification. At the same time, our understanding of the character of the Revolution itself has also greatly changed. Thanks to the work of François Furet and others, the French Revolution has ceased to be viewed, as Marxist orthodoxy would have it, as an episode of class struggle, and has increasingly been seen as a political phenomenon, driven by a particular political culture and discourse, whose origins in the Enlightenment are still unclear. Problems of chronology are also largely unresolved. Some historians, such as Dale Van Kley, have pointed out that the key words of the political discourse of the French Revolution, such as 'nation' or 'representation', had already been used as early as the 1760s by the French Parlements, not in support of Enlightenment, but in their *opposition* to attempts by the Crown itself to change political and economic structures underpinned by tax inequality and privilege.[9] If the key terms of the Revolution's political discourse were in place so early, and if the Revolution can be understood as a phenomenon primarily of political culture, why did it take more than thirty years from the emergence of the key words of the Revolution, to the beginning of the collapse of the Old Regime? François Furet, on the other hand, seems to argue that the particular political culture of the Revolution crystallised very late, maybe as late as the election campaign for the Estates-General in 1788. Though we know a great deal more than we did before, therefore, on the nature of political culture in the Enlightenment, especially in France, it seems that, as each field is redefined, answers seem to be further away than ever.

Part of the problem might, however, lie in the linear approach which has been adopted in the debate. 'The Revolution' has been seen as the terminus of 'The Enlightenment'. This was particularly so during the historiographical era which defined the Enlightenment as a peculiarly French phenomenon. Yet, anyone who looks at the course of the eighteenth century as a whole can easily see that this is a misleading view. A peaceful period called 'Enlightenment' was *not* ended by a sudden upheaval called 'Revolution'. For most of Europe it is far truer to say that Enlightenment and Revolution proceeded side by side for much of the century. One could even say that the Enlightenment *began* with Revolution, that which occurred in England in 1688, which created the conditions for the emergence of the philosophy with which John Locke discussed new thinking about the relationship between ruler and ruled. Revolts against established authority, especially in the second half of the century, were widespread. From the 1760s onwards, the century saw revolts in places as far apart as Geneva (1764), Corsica, for which Rousseau produced a new draft Constitution (1720s and 1760s), the British colonies in North America (1775–83), and the Austrian Netherlands (1789). To these revolts Palmer has applied the term 'democratic'.[10] However this typology has aroused great controversy over *how* 'revolutionary' or democratic were the upheavals he chronicles. The Austrian Netherlands, for example, were as much concerned to restore the historical relationship

[9] Dale Van Kley, *The Damiens Affair and the Unravelling of the Ancien Regime, 1750–1770* (Princeton, NJ, 1984) and 'The Jansenist Constitutional Legacy in the French Revolution', in K. M. Baker (ed.), *The French Revolution and the Creation of Modern Political Culture* (Oxford, 1987), I, 169–201.

[10] R. R. Palmer, *The Age of the Democratic Revolution* (2 vols, Princeton, NJ, 1956).

of the province to Vienna which they saw as threatened by Joseph II, as they were to create a slight extension of political participation.

In this context, the American Revolution has often been seen as the place where Enlightenment ideas and a violent change of government can best be seen in conjunction. Certainly, the Americans did seem to want to create a *novus ordo saeculorum*, a new order in the new world, not a return to a superior past. But how far can in fact the American colonists be seen as inspired by purely Enlightenment ideas in their struggle against British rule? It is certain that there are plenty of reasons for resentment between colony and home government even without any input from the Enlightenment. After 1763 London attempted to transfer the rising costs of empire, and the colossal war debt accumulated since 1754, to the colonies. This meant that the political relationship between the thirteen colonies and London came under increasing pressure, as the colonies questioned their lack of representation in the London Parliament which was laying such heavy new burdens upon them.

But the ideology that filled this conflict had many different sources. Puritan religious ideas of man's essential sinfulness sat uneasily with Enlightenment ideas of progress, optimism and faith in man's rationality and were strongly present in the colonies due to the religious revivals or 'Great Awakening' of the 1730s and 1740s. Other elements in American ideology also antedated the Enlightenment, especially the Republicanism which originated with classical models and was strengthened by the influence of the civic humanists of the Renaissance. The American interpretation of Republicanism emphasised the virtue of a simple society of autonomous citizens committed to the common good and the independence of each individual. While there was much here that would have appealed also to Rousseau, American ideals antedated those of the Genevan by many years. However Americans also believed that citizen and government should be united by contract, an idea very strong in John Locke's *Two Treatises of Civil Government*, which many have seen as the true opening of the Enlightenment itself. This idea of contract itself however ran into several difficulties in the American situation. Locke's idea of contract presupposed a society whose members were equal. Could it really be applied in the American colonies, which were underpinned by the labour of slaves? This is one of the central conflicts in the Enlightenment, and we have seen how difficult it was for the men of the Enlightenment, even for those not living in slave societies, to extend the logical implications of equality and natural rights to all those they classified as 'other' (see Chapters 5, 6 and 7). Perhaps just because the American revolutionaries did try and create a *novus ordo*, they were bound to exemplify the ultimate problems of Enlightenment ideas in relation to change. Maybe in the end the American revolutionaries found themselves faced with the same problem as was to face the French twenty years later, which was the impossibility of constructing a political order based on equality of rights without recasting the entire unequal social order. What the American Revolution perhaps teaches us is that some strands of the Enlightenment were powerful in allowing certain groups to think of change; but also that they could not overcome the limits to change which they envisaged as possible for the social order. This contradiction between support for supposedly universal rights, and the actual exclusion of large numbers of human beings from the enjoyment of those rights, is central to, and characteristic of Enlightenment thought.[11]

It is clear from our reflections on the American example that we obscure more problems than we solve if we think of the connection between 'Enlightenment' and 'Revolution' as meaning the French Revolution alone. It must also not be forgotten that not only did the eighteenth century before 1789 see many attempts to change governments, but that it was also the case that the 1790s saw many other violent attempts in other countries outside France to change either the direction of government policy, or the actual holders of power. Many of these revolts were concerned quite explicitly with conflicts over Enlightenment programmes in government and they could be led by either opponents *or* supporters of Enlightenment. In Tuscany for example, a whole series of revolts broke out after the departure to Vienna of the Grand-Duke Peter Leopold, who succeeded his brother Joseph as Austrian Emperor. These so-called *Viva Maria* riots, as their slogan indicates, were triggered by opposition to religious reforms instituted by Peter Leopold and 'Jansenist' bishops in Tuscany, with the objective of reducing the splendour and extravagance of worship, the number of religious holidays, and the wealth of the religious orders, especially those who did no socially useful work.[12] In Hungary rebellion threatened over Emperor Joseph's own efforts to change relations between serf and landlord and to alter the relationship between Vienna and Budapest. Many rulers themselves backtracked away from Enlightenment reforming programmes in the 1790s, leaving isolated those elements in the elites and in the state service who had supported such reforms before. Such groups were the basis of French support in many areas when the armies of the French

[11] Henry F. May, *Enlightenment in America* (New York, 1976); Colin Bonwick, *The American Revolution* (London, 1991); J. G. A. Pocock, *The Machiavellian Moment: Florentine Political Thought and the Atlantic Republican Tradition* (Princeton, NJ, 1975).

[12] These riots soon also became linked to hostility to Peter Leopold's economic reforms, especially the deregulation of the grain trade. See Gabriele Turi, '*Viva Maria*': *La reazione alle riforme leopoldine 1790–1799* (Florence, 1969).

Revolution began to create satellite republics in the Netherlands, Switzerland, Naples, and northern Italy after 1792; many in these areas managed to convince themselves that annexation by France was the only way to preserve Enlightenment programmes of reform. These contemporaries at least saw no break between Enlightenment and Revolution in France. That their hopes in the French were often partly or totally misplaced does not alter this fact. All this means that once we abandon the linear model of an older historiography, of an enlightened century ending catastrophically in revolution, we can thus see that the relationship between the two was far more complex. Revolt and revolution occurred throughout the Enlightenment. Some of it was accepted into the heart of the Enlightenment itself, which was evidenced by the lionising of Pasquale Paoli, the leader of the movement for Corsican independence from the Genoese Republic, who appeared as a heroic fighter against despotism to such diverse thinkers as David Hume and Jean Jacques Rousseau. Others, like the *Viva Maria* uprisings in Tuscany, were in outright opposition to Enlightenment programmes.

Nor was the Enlightenment entirely at ease itself with the concept of 'revolution'. It is clear, for example, that it was only gradually in the eighteenth century that the word came to take on its twentieth-century connotations; thus, in asking about the link between Enlightenment and revolution, one is in danger of imposing anachronistic terminology, and thus defining a problem in a way unrecognisable to contemporaries. For much of the eighteenth century, it would seem from the evidence of dictionaries, and surveys of current usage, that 'revolution' derived its original meaning from mechanics and astronomy, and simply meant 'turning full circle' or 'a completed orbit', as in the phrase 'the earth's revolution around the sun'. In the context of political commentary 'revolution', especially in the early part of the century, meant a 'change bringing back a former state of affairs'. This fits in very well with the stated aim of the majority of 'revolutions' before 1776, which was to restore an original, and better, state of affairs, rather than to create a radically new one. As the century progressed, 'revolution' came to mean any upset of established order, any set of crises or changes. This is the way the term was used in the many history books published in the eighteenth century which had titles like 'The Revolutions of Poland' or the 'Revolutions of France'. The term 'revolution' only started to approach its modern meaning after the revolt of the American colonies against British rule which began in 1775. This successful revolt seemed to demonstrate to many contemporaries that it was possible to establish a new sort of state, a secular republic. This impression was enhanced when the thirteen colonies took as the motto of their federal seal the words *Novus ordo saeculorum*, 'a new order of the centuries'. These words signified that this Revolution, far from restoring a former state of affairs, in fact, had created something completely new, a break in the passage of history, and a 'new order'. This was the sense of 'revolution' which was to be picked up by the French in 1789, and by all subsequent movements for change.[13]

It may be that historians have taken on board only the late-Enlightenment meaning of 'revolution', which makes problematic the links between Enlightenment and revolution by its assertion of the possibility of producing a political order radically different from that which has gone before, and have engaged too little with the problem of *how much* and what sort of change Enlightenment thinkers themselves saw as coming within the scope of their idea of revolution. Certainly, as the century progressed, an idea that human affairs manifested 'progress', rather than a series of reconstitutions of past affairs, began to come to the fore. The dominant metaphor for historical change, in other words, became 'time's arrow', rather than 'fortune's wheel'; the metaphor so beloved by the Middle Ages and the Renaissance, became directional rather than cyclical. Thus at least some of the pre-conditions for being able to visualise radical distancing from the past were certainly present by the end of the Enlightenment, and due to classically Enlightenment ideas, such as that of 'progress'. That this process was far from complete, however, is shown by the way in which the Revolution in France, particularly in its Jacobin phase, produced a rhetoric which described itself *both* as a *return* to a Golden Age, and as a new order of being, a total *break* with the preceding historical process.

However, Enlightenment thinkers were never far from the problem which, as we have seen, was at the heart of Kant's *Answer to the Question: What is Enlightenment?*: how far, and with what consequences, should ideas be allowed to achieve their full potential to effect change in the world? Most thinkers in France, as we have already seen, were clear that they did not want Enlightenment to percolate too far down the social scale, for fear of causing social upheaval. Those areas of central Europe which saw Enlightenment consciously used to foster and legitimate social change, did so in the context of the overall aim of the long-term stabilisation of society and monarchy. Educational policy in the Austrian lands, for example, was a matter of producing a less superstitious, more 'rational', hence more stable, acceptance by individuals of the duties attached to the social status in which they were born, rather than aiding their social mobility.

13 For fuller discussion of the word see K. M. Baker, *Inventing the French Revolution: Essays on French Political Culture in the Eighteenth Century* (Cambridge, 1990), 203–23.

It would thus seem that the dossier on the relationship between Enlightenment and revolution is still open. It is no longer possible to see Enlightenment simply as a movement of ideas located in France which produced a violent revolution there, either by reforming too much, or questioning too much, or, alternatively, by substituting opinion for politics to such an extent that needed reforms could only be carried out by revolutionary and violent means. Nor, in spite of the work of Darnton and others, is it possible to endorse fully arguments also common in the nineteenth century, that reading the works of the *philosophes* must necessarily have undermined the social and ideological consensus on which monarchy rested. It is difficult to argue about any given book that its readers would be instantly mobilised to rise up against the powers that be. It is also right to stress that readers do not pick up a single unequivocal message from what they read. Every written message may be interpreted in many different ways by readers, some, if not many of them, unintended by the author. It is also probable that the growing circulation of books and pamphlets of a critical tendency, ranging from the pornographic attacks on the royal family, currently attracting notice in feminist scholarship,[14] to serious commentary by Voltaire, Rousseau or Raynal, may partly only be the register or *result* of a pre-existing state of affairs, rather than its *cause*. The actual political and financial problems of the monarchy in France, its declining power to impress and mobilise elites, the attrition of the power of court life and royal patronage to mobilise the symbols of a powerful Christian monarchy, may have been the pre-conditions for the rise of Enlightenment critiques, rather than their result. All of which having been said, it is impossible to doubt that a rising tide of criticism of monarchy could hardly have failed to weaken its hold on the hearts and minds of subjects. Especially important here, at least in France, were the continual attacks on religious belief, belief on which the ideological foundations of the monarchy rested, and of which Louis XVI's own actions after 1789 show him to have been well aware. It is, however, quite another question as to whether, if Enlightenment contributed to revolution in France by weakening attachment, especially among the elites, for throne and altar, its influence necessarily caused the violence of the Jacobin phase of the Revolution, a phase which the majority of nineteenth-century commentators saw as the heart of the revolutionary experience. Beyond that question lies yet another which is still far from resolved: was the French Revolution a single movement, or several distinct revolutionary phases? That dossier too is still open.

[14] E.g., Lynn Hunt, *The Family Romance of the French Revolution* (Berkeley, Los Angeles and London, 1992); *The Invention of Pornography* (New York, 1993).

Reinhard Kosselleck has argued in his *Critique and Crisis* that it was the internal contradictions of Enlightenment in central Europe and particularly in Prussia, which led to the creation of a revolutionary situation.[15] Whilst attempting reform, as we have seen, in accordance with some specifically Enlightenment ideals, such as rationality and uniformity (Chapters 3 and 9), monarchs had still continued to insist on their positions guaranteed by dynastic right, and religious sanction. At the same time, many monarchs, especially Joseph II and Frederick the Great, dismantled a great deal of the court ceremonial which had been built up by their forebears with the objective of creating a symbolic order focussed upon the royal person. Tradition and innovation, rationality, universalism and the personal interventions of the monarch, uneasily combined, and, Kosselleck argues, produced a situation where contradiction had become so great as to paralyse the development of monarchy, so that further change and reform could not be achieved except by dismantling the basis of monarchy itself. This thesis also receives support from some contemporary comments. On the other hand, this case is also not proven. Who knows what would have happened had the outbreak of Revolution in France not led to a feeling of general instability in Europe which undermined reform programmes? It is also not impossible that monarchies themselves could have continued to evolve in the same direction, gradually bridging the contradiction between their traditional and sacral basis and their rationalist reform programmes. Kosselleck's argument, in other words, is posed in terms that make it impossible to answer. Nor should the extent of social opposition to Enlightenment reforms be forgotten. The *Viva Maria* risings in Tuscany, the urban revolts in the Austrian Netherlands in 1789, and landlord resistance, coming very close to armed rebellion, in Hungary, all show that far from ending in revolution because it was the only way out for Enlightenment policies at an *impasse* with the traditional basis of the old regime, it might be more that Enlightenment in central Europe ended in very much more traditional revolts aimed *against* enlightened policies and *for* the restoration of a previous state of affairs.

To sum up, much of the argument about the relationship between Enlightenment and revolution grew out of a historiography mesmerised by the Revolution in France, and in particular by its most violent, 'Jacobin' phase between 1792 and 1794. It failed to take account of the concurrency of Enlightenment and revolution in Europe and in the North American colonies of Britain. The limits of change and critique

[15] Reinhard Kosselleck, *Critique and Crisis: Enlightenment and the Pathogenesis of Modern Society* (Oxford, New York and Hamburg, 1988).

were constantly being tested within the Enlightenment itself. It also failed sufficiently to emphasise the difference in the practice and direction of Enlightenment in different regions of Europe, and played down the number of revolts at the end of the century which were not 'frustrated Enlightenments', as Kosselleck argues, or 'Enlightenments turning into revolutionary terror' as right-wing historians would have argued, but were actual movements *against* Enlightenment policies by significant sections of society.

A new twist to these arguments has however, recently been given by the American historian Jonathan Israel. His trilogy (*Radical Enlightenment: Philosophy and the Making of Modernity*, (Oxford, 2001), *Enlightenment Contested: Philosophy. Modernity and the Emancipation of Man, 1670–1752* (Oxford, 2006), and *Democratic Enlightenment: Philosophy, Revolution, and Human Rights* (Oxford 2011)), has sparked considerable controversy, controversy important because it has raised so many fundamental questions about the nature of the Enlightenment, and the problem of its relationship to the French Revolution. Basing my interpretation of Israel on the polemical Introduction to *Democratic Enlightenment*, we see that Israel is in no doubt that the Enlightenment is the '. . . single most important topic, internationally, in modern historical studies, and one of crucial significance also in our politics, cultural studies, and philosophy' (*DE*, p.1). Nonetheless, he argues, there is a crisis in Enlightenment studies caused by the work of post-modern theorists, and by the work of Michel Foucault. Post-modernism, in Israel's account, sees the Enlightenment's abstract universalism as ultimately destructive. It has the project of 'replacing the intellectual foundations forged by the Enlightenment with a fresh set of criteria framing a post-modern world built on multiculturalism, moral relativism, and the indeterminacy of truth' (*DE*, p.2). Foucault, Israel argues, sees the Enlightenment insistence on the primacy of reason as a mask for the exercise of power: the Enlightenment is not about liberation, but about new forms of constraint (*DE*, p.2).

Israel's own definition of Enlightenment, however, has itself been hotly contested. He argues that the Enlightenment in fact contained two entirely separate and incompatible currents of thought, the 'moderate' Enlightenment, and the 'radical' Enlightenment, which after a long period of semi-underground existence, came to the fore in the 1770s, and was ultimately responsible for the French Revolution of 1789–92 (*DE*, p.22). Israel thus reverses the trend towards the study of national Enlightenments (*DE*, p.6), as well as questioning the study of social spaces and reading habits long attached to the names of Robert Darnton and Roger Chartier (*DE*, pp.23–5). On the contrary, he maintains that the 'radical' Enlightenment is grounded in the work of one great thinker, the

Dutch Jewish philosopher Baruch Spinoza (1632–77). 'Spinoza was crucial because he went further in undermining belief in revelation, divine providence and miracles and hence ecclesiastical authority'. Spinozism, furthermore is a well-defined movement (*DE*, p.11) supporting ideas like a 'one-substance metaphysics, ruling out all teleology, divine providence, miracles and revelation, along with spirits separate from bodies and immortality of the soul, and denying that moral values are divinely delivered, (with the corollary that therefore they have to be devised by men using terms relative to what is good or bad for society)' (*DE*, p.11). Opposing Spinoza was the moderate Enlightenment, with its refusal of the exclusive privileging of reason, and claiming two distinct sources of truth: reason and tradition. While the moderate Enlightenment remained often socially conservative, the radical Enlightenment, Israel argues, unreservedly endorsed freedom of expression, thought and of the press (*DE*, p.19). All this was connected with 'radicality', as is demonstrable in the history of the French Revolution down to 1792 (*DE*, p.22).

But the argument is doubtful. Israel states that the 'primary task of the historian of the French Revolution today is to define, clarify and deepen the late eighteenth-century insight that *la philosophie* was the primary cause of the Revolution' (*DE*, p.17). This is a point that Israel's critics have seized upon, denying any necessary homology between philosophical outlooks and political ideas (*DE*, p.22). It is true that many of Israel's interpretations of the Revolution are questionable. He does acknowledge, for example that the Revolution contained great violence. But he denies any relation between violence, the Terror and 'philosophy'. By seeing ordinary people as merely providing the 'muscle' for the Revolution, he is able to discount the ideological bases of sans-culotte militancy, and their support for political and economic equality, state support for the poor, public education, and Terror. And by bringing his account to a close in 1792, he is able to neglect the Great Terror of 1793–94. To that, the 'radical' Enlightenment certainly set up no convincing or lasting barrier.

Israel makes clear his larger ideological programme, which travels beyond the histories of his two Enlightenments. Debating with Foucault, he states, 'Anyone believing truth is universal, and that human rights imply a common code that it is the duty of everyone to defend, cannot avoid taking up cudgels not just against Foucault and post-modernist philosophy, but also against the exponents of historiographical theories and approaches focusing attention on sociability, ambiguities and opinion' (*DE*, pp.23–4). It is unclear why these last are not to be counted as part of general history.

There are thus major problems with Israel's account, and his critics have not been slow to point them out. Most notable of these critiques are that by Antoine Lilti in *Annales ESC* for 2009, and that by Anthony La Vopa in the *Historical Journal* also for 2009. But their critiques also point to problems common to the history of any intellectual project, and with the Enlightenment in particular, which has been seen so frequently, rightly or wrongly, as the origin of all that is most characteristic of the modern era.

In the end, we may argue that Enlightenment posed no significant barrier in France, and in other states, to a mounting tide of criticism of the *status quo*, much of it from within the ruling class itself. Criticism of the powers that be of course was no new experience in European history. But what the Enlightenment had contributed was not only a great number of new, non-traditional ways of defining and legitimating power, through ideas such as 'natural law', 'reason' and so on; it had also mobilised sections of society into 'public opinion', which Kant had earlier identified as requiring tight control if it were not to disrupt social and political order. As remarked in Chapter 2, the Enlightenment was much better at creating new relationships amongst elites, and bringing sections of elites together in the new forms of sociability centring on ideas, than it was in reaching out to lower social classes. Perhaps it was in this redefinition and remobilisation of elites, and their relationship with traditional sources of power, as well as in the specific nature of the ideas it discussed, that the Enlightenment in creating 'public opinion' also created conditions which given the right factors or political stress allowed revolution to occur. In the end, Kant's concerns about the disruptive impact of Enlightenment, a problem which has been at the heart of the concerns of this book, were probably justified.

Brief biographies

Alembert, Jean le Rond dit d' (1717–83). Illegitimate son of the writer and *salon* hostess Claudine de Tencin (1682–1749) and rapidly famous as a mathematician. He was a member of the *salons* of Mme Geoffrin and Madame du Deffand, where he encountered his life-long passion, Julie de Lespinasse. With Diderot, he co-edited the *Encyclopédie*, and wrote its *Preliminary Discourse*, an important reflection on the nature and organisation of knowledge. He wrote about 1,400 articles for the *Encyclopédie*, which led him into controversy with Rousseau and the musician Rameau. After 1758, he allowed Diderot to take over the *Encyclopédie*, and began to write musical and literary criticism. In 1779 he became Perpetual Secretary of the Royal Academy of Sciences in Paris. D'Alembert has often been seen as one of the last thinkers capable of contributing over the whole range of knowledge.

Beccaria, Cesare (1738–94), is best known as the author of the treatise *Dei Delitti e dei Pene* (1764). Had a huge impact on Enlightenment thinking on law, crime and capital punishment, which is denounced in his work, along with judicial torture and arbitrary justice. His book secularised the idea of punishment, which he argued was a necessary self-defence mechanism by the social structure, rather than an infliction legitimated by Divine sanctions against sin. His work left little indication as to how governments were to be persuaded to alter systems of criminal law; however, it was widely translated and did have a major impact on practice especially in the smaller states, such as Tuscany, and even in France, where judicial torture began to be dismantled in the 1780s.

Buffon, Georges-Louis Leclerc, Comte de (1707–88), was born at Montbard, of a family of high-ranking legal officeholders. After an important tour of Italy, he took up residence in Paris, and was a member of both the *Académie française* and the Academy of Sciences. His impact on the Enlightenment stemmed primarily from his writings on natural history (*Histoire naturelle, générale et particulière*, 15 vols, 1749–67). Buffon saw nature as having a history far older than that suggested by Biblical chronology, and came close to supporting the idea that species could change over time. These views, and his implicit support for the idea that man was intrinsically *within* the natural order led to condemnations by the theology faculty of Paris in 1749. As Director of the Jardin Royal or royal botanical gardens, Buffon also played an important role in increasing the accessibility of natural history to the general public.

Catherine II (1729–96) Empress of Russia (1762–96), was influenced by Voltaire, Montesquieu and the *Encyclopédie*, and corresponded with Voltaire, Diderot, and with the *salon* hostess Mme Geoffrin. Tried to Europeanise Russia, but her relationship with the Enlightenment has often been questioned, as she systematically advantaged the nobility, and steadily increased the numbers of serfs. Her territorial conquests at the expense of Turkey and Poland also seemed to have had little to do with the general Enlightenment support for peaceful international relations. Nonetheless, her reputation was high amongst the *philosophes*, and Catherine was probably most influenced by Enlightenment thinkers in her project for a general law code for Russia.

Diderot, Denis (1713–84) achieved fame in his lifetime largely as the co-editor of the *Encyclopédie*, and to a lesser extent as a playwright, art critic and commentator on current issues – and of course none of these functions was wholly distinct. Many other works were known only posthumously, such as the *Supplément au Voyage de Bougainville*, published in 1796. Diderot came from a family of provincial artisans and workshop owners, orthodox believers who saw their son take minor orders in 1726. Rejecting the religious life he earned a living as a lawyer's clerk, writer and private tutor, until his marriage in 1743. Diderot quickly rejected belief in the existence of a personal God, and instead saw nature itself and matter as full of energies, constantly in transformation. In apparent contradiction to this implicit determinism, Diderot also preached a secular morality of benevolence and civic virtue, as well as satirising what he regarded as social prejudices against adultery, and sexual repression. In 1773–4 he visited Russia at the invitation of the Empress Catherine, but left disillusioned. Many of Diderot's ideas were also discussed in his extensive correspondence.

Franke, August Hermann (1663–1727). After attending the University of Leipzig, Franke was attracted to Dresden to become the disciple of the famed religious reformer Philip Spener. Franke, with Spener behind him, went on to preach as well as educate. In the process he converted many to the way of thinking of the Pietists, as his group of reformed Christians came to be known. His success earned him persecution from orthodox Catholics however, and his enemies succeeded in prohibiting his Bible study classes and, later, getting him removed from the church in Erfurt where he was preaching. Spener then sent Franke to Halle, promising him a position as a professor of Greek and Oriental languages at the university that would soon be founded at the city. Franke became the pastor at Glaucha, one of Halle's poorest suburbs. As Halle became the Pietist headquarters, Franke utilised the movement to help the poor there. He laboured to get them food, jobs and, most famously, free education. He established several free schools, as well as his well-known Orphan-house. The Orphan-house not only cared for orphaned children, but also fed and educated thousands of poor students free of charge. Franke's establishments became the model for similar institutions throughout Germany, providing the poor with greater access to organised relief and schooling.

Franklin, Ben (1706–1790). Franklin trained as a printer in Philadelphia. He published the *Pennsylvania Gazette* from 1730 to 1748, and *Poor Richard's Almanac*, a collection of moral precepts and information, from 1732 to 1757. He formed the discussion club called the 'Junto' about 1727. It is usually regarded as the origin of the American Philosophical Society, chartered in 1743, and still today one of the most important institutions in American cultural life. Franklin was also involved with the foundation of Philadelphia Public Library in 1742. From 1746, he experimented with electricity, though whether the famous experiment with a kite was ever performed is now disputed. So far his life had been an exemplification of Enlightenment manipulation of the power of print and discussion. The eminence he thus gained translated into positions of political power. He spent the years 1766 to 1770 attempting to build conciliation between London and the American colonists. He was a member of the committee that drafted the Declaration of Independence, and spent 1776–1785 in Paris negotiating a treaty of commerce and a defensive military alliance. In 1790, he presented several memorials to Congress demanding the abolition of slavery. His direct actions here contrast with Jefferson's equivocal opinions on the same issues.

Frederick II, King of Prussia (1712–86). After a difficult early life, he succeeded his father as King in 1740; in this year he seized the rich province of Silesia from Austria, and thus plunged Europe into the War of the Austrian Succession. In 1756, his aggression again triggered the international conflict known as the Seven Years' War. He played a leading role in the partition of Poland in 1773. During his reign, the Prussian economy was modernised, while the powers of the aristocratic class increased, and serfdom remained. Frederick surrounded himself with *philosophes* such as La Mettrie, the Marquis d'Argens and Maupertuis, whom he engaged to head the new Academy of Sciences in Berlin. Voltaire visited him in 1750. Frederick himself wrote extensively on his own life and times, and more generally on politics and kingship, pieces which were admired by the *philosophe* Grimm, and condemned by Diderot, in his 1771 *Pages contre un tyran.*

Goethe, Johann Wolfgang (1749–1832). Goethe is widely regarded as the most influential writer of the German Romantic period, and also by many as Germany's single greatest literary figure. Despite an early desire to devote his energies to the study of the classics, at sixteen Goethe was sent to Leipzig University at the urging of his father to study law (1765–68). This did not stifle Goethe's literary ambitions, however, and he wrote lyric poetry, plays and fiction, in addition to practising law. Several of his works served to fuel the *Sturm und Drang* (Storm and Stress) movement, which combated Enlightenment rationality. His wildly popular novel *The Sorrows of Young Werther* (1774), for example, provided the outline for the romantic hero. In 1775, Goethe became a court official at Weimar, where he came to be in charge of mines, roads, finance and war. He was also the president of the Treasury beginning in 1782. He continued to grow as a writer, and also busied himself with scientific pursuits. These included alchemy and the formulation of a theory of light in opposition to Newton's. He also proved the existence of the intermaxillary bone in man, evidence he used to demonstrate the continuous nature of anatomy across species, human and animal (although the bone had previously been discovered in Paris in 1780). In 1791 he was freed from most of his court duties to devote himself more fully to his art. He continued, though, to function as the court's general supervisor for arts and sciences and as director of the court theatres for many years. In addition to numerous other writings, Goethe published what most believe is his masterpiece, his drama in two parts, *Faust*, in 1808 and 1832. During his later years, Goethe was revered as a living German cultural icon, and artists and statesmen from around the world made the pilgrimage to Weimar to meet with him.

Herder, Johann Gottfried von (1744–1803), was born in East Prussia, of a strongly Pietist family, and became a pupil of Immanuel Kant at the University at Königsberg. Ordained in 1767, he took up a living in Riga, and published his *Fragments on a New German Literature*, where he argued for an independent German literature. In 1769, he travelled to France and, returning to Germany, met Lessing in Hamburg, and became court preacher to Count Schaumburg-Lippe. In 1774 he published *Another Philosophy of History*, which combated cosmopolitanism and rationalism.

In 1776, he left for Weimar where he met Goethe, and published on Hebrew poetry, and his *Ideas on the Philosophy of Human History* (1784–91). Some of these ideas were reconsidered, under the impact of the French Revolution, in his 1793 *Letters on the Progress of Humanity*.

Holbach, Paul-Henri Thiry, Baron d' (1723–89), was of Swiss origin, and made a fortune as a financier in Paris. He gathered round him a group which included d'Alembert, Diderot, Buffon, Raynal and Rousseau. He attacked organised religion and argued for the sole reality of the material world. Much of his work was clandestinely published to avoid censorship, but he also wrote articles for the *Encyclopédie* on religion and on earth sciences. His 1770 *Système de la Nature* was his most famous work, and was attacked by Voltaire and by Frederick II of Prussia.

Jefferson, Thomas (1743–1826), third President of the United States (1801–1809), was born into Virginia planter society. He involved himself in natural history, exploration (especially the expeditions of Zebulon Pike, and Lewis and Clark (1804–1806)), and founded the University of Virginia. Elected to the Virginia House of Burgesses (1769–1776), he served as Chairman of the Committee that composed the Declaration of Independence. He inserted anti-slavery passages into the Declaration which were removed at the insistence of delegations from Georgia and South Carolina. Governor of Virginia between 1779 and 1781, he was US Minister in France 1785–1789. His presidency saw the expansion of the USA through the 'Louisiana Purchase', a vast territory of unknown borders westwards of the Mississippi river. A life-long slave-holder, he prohibited the importation of slaves, but not slave holding or the slave-trade internal to the US. His only published work, *Notes on the State of Virginia*, a compilation of information about the geology and natural history of the state, as well as remarks on the problem of slavery, was published in 1787.

Jones, Sir William (1746–1795). Born in England, Jones had already demonstrated a keen interest in languages by the time he was a young man. His interest persisted throughout his time at Oxford, where he studied oriental literature, and emerged with a knowledge of languages such as Persian, Arabic, Hebrew, Italian, Spanish, Chinese and Portuguese (by his death, he knew thirteen languages in all). After gaining some standing as an Orientalist, Jones decided to pursue a more profitable occupation. He passed the bar in 1774 and went on to become a supreme court judge in Bengal, India, in 1783. He was knighted soon after. Thankfully, his interests in oriental studies did not end with his success in the field of law. He studied Sanskrit, founded the Bengal Asiatic Society, translated many key Indian texts, and in general advocated the importance of looking to the east for wisdom. He also gave birth to the field of comparative philology when he noted the similarity of Sanskrit with Latin and Greek.

Kant, Immanuel (1724–1804), came from a strongly Pietist background in Prussia. After studying at the University at Königsburg, he became professor of mathematics and philosophy there in 1756. Kant was influenced by d'Alembert and by Rousseau, as well as by the Scots philosopher David Hume. His most famous work, the *Critique of Pure Reason*, appeared in 1783. In 1784 he wrote an essay to answer the question 'What is Enlightenment?', and in 1795 published a *Project for Perpetual Peace*. Though Kant's reflections on the basis of rationality proceeded from Locke's rejection of innate ideas, he asked whether reason or the soul could be autonomous or independent of sense impressions.

La Mettrie, Julien Offroy de (1709–51), was born in Caen, and educated by Jesuits. He studied medicine at Leiden, where he was a student of Boerhave. These medical interests led him to a materialist position affirmed in his 1747 *L'Homme Machine* (*Man the Machine*) and the 1748 *Discourse on Happiness*. La Mettrie was much influenced by Epicurian philosophy of which he published an analysis in 1750. These views attracted hostility from Catholics and Protestants alike, and La Mettrie was forced to leave Leiden for Berlin, where he was welcomed by Frederick II. Nor was much *philosophe* opinion in his favour, as his thinking ran counter to much optimism, and to the idea that morality was somehow 'natural' and therefore innate.

Lavater, Johann Caspar (1741–1801). Lavater was born in Zurich, the thirteenth child of a doctor, who also held important positions in city government. In 1763, he made a one-year journey to Pomerania in northern Germany, one of the 'education journeys' often undertaken by aspiring middle-class intellectuals. The objective of such journeys was to make contacts, and accumulate information of all kinds. Lavater's journey brought him the friendship of Moses Mendelssohn and the poet Klopstock. In 1774, he made a similar trip along the Rhine, and met Goethe, who initially supported his physiognomic theories, but later argued against them. In 1772 he published his most famous work, the *Physiognomische Fragmente*. The book was highly controversial, and in the end received little support from the intellectual community. Its theory, that qualities of character (e.g. 'contentiousness' or 'affection') might be localised on features on the exterior of the skull was important for later researchers of brain localisation. Contemporaries, however, pointed out the arbitrary nature of Lavater's definitions of character qualities, and queried the idea that the exterior formations of the skull had any relationship to the configuration of the brain itself. Lavater was strongly opposed to the French Revolution, and was fatally injured during the French siege of Zurich in 1799.

Lichtenberg, Georg Christoph (1742–1799). After studying mathematics, astronomy and natural science at Göttingen, Lichtenberg became a philosophy professor there in 1770. From there his career evolved into one in which he functioned as a writer, mathematician, inventor, and as the first experimental physicist in Germany. As a critic and wit he became very well regarded. Among countless others, he took many of the *Sturm und Drang* writers and Sentimentalist poets in his sights. His *Waste Book*, a collection of random thoughts that he had recorded over the years, was published after his death, and has been enjoyed by many as an intriguing portrait of a fertile mind. Lichtenberg also became a staunch anglophile in the course of his lifetime, and he promoted England as the greatest country in existence until his death. His studies of electricity led him to invent 'Lichtenberg Figures', which were an ancestor of modern xerography. He also did much to contribute to the development of scientific methodology.

Linnaeus, Carl (1707–1778). Although Linnaeus harboured a lifelong love of plants, he began his higher education by studying medicine at both the University of Lund and Uppsala University. His knowledge about the sexuality of plants, however, gained him a position as a lecturer in botany at Uppsala. He eventually gained his degree in medicine at the University of Hardewijk in 1735, but continued to write essays on botany and mingle with the top naturalists of the day. After several years away from his native Sweden, Linnaeus returned to establish a prominent medical practice in Stockholm. He became a botany professor at Uppsala in 1741. Linnaeus' most famous contribution to science was his systematic method for identifying plants and animals using the hierarchy of genus, class and order. He also conceptualised ecology as a specific field of scientific research. Linnaeus was appointed chief royal physician in 1747 and was made a knight in 1758.

Locke, John (1637–1704), was author of the *Essay Concerning Human Understanding* (1690), and one of the key figures of the early Enlightenment. This work was of fundamental importance because it criticised Descartes's doctrine of innate ideas, and thus opened the way for much subsequent thinking by Hume, Condillac, Kant and others, on the meaning of human intelligence. Locke was also seen as a pioneer of the struggle for religious tolerance, after his 1689 *Letters on Toleration*, as well as his *The*

Reasonableness of Christianity of 1695. Locke's influence on Voltaire was very strong, as it was on Rousseau, whose *Emile ou de l'éducation* (1762) was affected by his 1693 *Thoughts Concerning Education*. The Enlightenment also gained from Locke's *Second Treatise on Civil Government* the basis of its thinking on the idea of the contractual nature of society and government.

L'Ouverture, Toussaint (1743–1803). Leader of the only successful slave revolt in the Caribbean, Toussaint was born near Cap François on the French possession of St Domingue (now Haiti), of slave parents. His life was defined by resistance to slavery. He took part in the slave insurrection of 1791, which resulted in the collapse of the system of slavery on the island by 1793. He led forces against the British occupation of the island in 1798, and defeated a mulatto (mixed race) revolt in 1799. By 1801, he and his forces controlled the whole island, and resisted Napoleon's attempts to re-establish slavery. In 1802, he was overcome by a French military force under General Leclerc. He was captured and died in prison in France.

Mendelssohn, Moses (1729–86), grandfather of the composer, was the first major Jewish figure to intervene in the Enlightenment. He profited by the climate of religious toleration enforced by Frederick II to form an intellectual circle and publish widely, while at the same time composing in Hebrew, including a valuable commentary on Maimonides. Mendelssohn contributed to contemporary debates on religious toleration and Jewish emancipation, though insisting on the necessity for cultural diversity and avoiding uniformity. He contributed to the 1784 debate on the definition of 'Enlightenment', and wrote widely on aesthetics. Mendelssohn's work demonstrates the capacity of Enlightenment debates to mobilise thinkers right across ethnic and religious lines.

Montesquieu, Charles-Louis de Secondat, Baron de la Brède (1689–1755), was a member of a prominent family among the legal nobility of France, and he himself was President of the *Parlement* or sovereign appeal court of Bordeaux from 1726. The year 1721 saw the appearance of his first major work, the *Persian Letters*, a satire on the institutions of France, as well as presenting a less idealised view of the Orient than was usual. *The Spirit of the Laws* (*Esprit des lois*) (1748) was equally a bestseller widely translated, and one of the most widely diffused works of the Enlightenment, especially after it attracted the hostility of the church and was placed on the Index in 1751. Montesquieu argues for the inevitability of different systems of government, because of the way in which states are moulded by climate, geography, history, extent and by the *morale* of inhabitants.

Newton, Isaac (1642–1727), has often been seen as the founder of modern cosmology, after his theory of universal attraction, or gravitation, was set forward in his *Philosophiae Naturalis Principia Mathematica* (1687). Newton, who was a Fellow of Trinity College, Cambridge and Master of the Royal Mint, pursued fundamental research in optics, and was often seen, especially in Europe, as an exemplar of empirical, rationalist research. However, Newton also worked on alchemical problems and on numerical interpretations of Biblical prophecy.

Quesnay, François (1694–1774). After an eventful early life, Quesnay became a surgeon employed first by the Duc de Villeroi, then by Louis XV. His quarters at Versailles became a meeting place for Diderot, Turgot and Mirabeau. He is most associated with the new economic theory called Physiocracy which was discussed in Quesnay's articles for the *Encyclopédie*. Physiocracy sees land as the sole source of wealth, and advocates strong monarchy to guarantee the operation of a free market, in land and agricultural products. Quesnay's major works were his *Droit naturel* of 1765 and his *Maximes générales du gouvernement économique d'un royaume agricole* of the same year. His theories also influenced Karl Marx.

Raynal, Guillaume-Thomas, Abbé (1713–96), was a priest in minor orders who until 1750 earned a living tutoring and through journalism. The publication of his *Anecdotes littéraires* in 1750 secured Raynal a rising place among Paris intelligentsia. In 1770 he produced the work on which his modern reputation rests, the *Histoire philosophique et politique des établissements et du commerce des Européens dans les deux Indes*, one of the first major histories of European colonialism, a vast compendium of geographical and economic knowledge, as well as an argument for the morality of commerce, and the immorality of slavery. This book, produced with the help of Diderot, produced such fame for Raynal that he left Paris for the provinces to try to reduce the inconvenience of publicity. He was an opponent of the French Revolution.

Rousseau, Jean Jacques (1712–78), was born in Geneva, where he was raised by his father, a watchmaker. Leaving Geneva, he entered a vagabond existence, converted to Catholicism in Turin, and became linked to Mme de Warens at Chambéry from 1736 to 1738. Focussed at this period on music, he arrived in Paris in 1742, and became friendly with Diderot. The 1740s saw him moving increasingly to writing, beginning with articles for the *Encyclopédie*. In 1750, Rousseau's *Discours sur les* *sciences et les arts* won a prize competition at the Academy of Dijon, which was followed in 1755 by the *Discours sur l'origine de l'inégalité parmi les hommes*. Disputes with Voltaire and Diderot followed. Other major works were his novel *Julie ou la Nouvelle Héloïse* (1761); *Emile ou de l'éducation* and *Du contrat social* (1762). His autobiography, the *Confessions*, appeared posthumously between 1782 and 1788. His influence, particularly that of the *Social Contract*, actually increased during the French Revolution.

Smith, Adam (1723–1790). Probably the most famous economic thinker of the Enlightenment, Smith's work is still used to justify modern economic ideologies. From 1748, he was a member of an intellectual circle including David Hume, Hugh Blair the philosopher of 'common sense', and the historian of the Spanish Empire William Robertson. Smith's first book, the 1759 *Theory of Moral Sentiments*, made him famous. He spent 1763–5 in France, and came to know not only Voltaire, but also physiocrat thinkers such as Turgot. Physiocrat thinkers believed that land was the basis of wealth. From 1767 to 1776, Smith concentrated on producing theories of the division of labour, of money, and on the liberty of trade and commerce. These studies were the basis of his most famous work, the 1776 *The Nature and Causes of the Wealth of Nations*.

Turgot, Anne-Robert-Jacques (1727–81), began his career as an office-holder in the Paris *Parlement* and collaborated on the *Encyclopédie*, with articles mainly on economics. He became *Intendant*, or royal civil governor of the province of the Limousin in 1761, and Finance Minister from 1774 to 1776. One of the few Enlightenment thinkers to have held high office in France, his economic ideas closely resembled those of the Physiocrats such as Quesnay, though he was also influenced by Adam Smith. His career in government was undermined by his support for a free market in wheat, which led to high prices, and riots all over the Île de France, the *Guerre des Farines*, in 1775. He was also opposed to the existence of the artisan guilds, which he saw as a restriction on free trade.

Voltaire, François-Marie Arouet, dit (1694–1778), was one of the dominant figures of the Enlightenment, due to his longevity, his enormous output, his capacity to mobilise public opinion, and his relations with the great. Born into a legal family and educated by Jesuits, he was quickly introduced at court, began his literary career as a dramatist, made an important stay in England (1726–29), and turned to history with his *Charles XII* (1731) and to political comment with the *Lettres anglaises* (1734). The favour of Mme de Pompadour made him court historian, and he was invited to Berlin by Frederick II in 1750–3. He used his prestige to save the lives and reputations of the Calas and Sirvin families, and produced in 1763 his *Treatise on Toleration.*

Wedgwood, Josiah (1730–1795). Born in England, Wedgwood helped transform pottery production into a major industry and also devised some new forms of pottery himself. After establishing himself by working in the family pottery business and later becoming a partner of the prominent potter Thomas Whieldon, he opened his own factory in Burslem in 1759. Ten years later he opened another which he named 'Eturia', where he notably built his employees their own village as a contribution to society. Also, with the help of partner Thomas Bentley, he applied modern marketing techniques to his business, which successfully expanded its influence. By looking to antiquity as a model, Wedgwood invented unglazed black basalt ware and blue jasper ware with white raised designs.

Wesley, John (1703–91). Wesley is best known as a great evangelist and as the founder of Methodism. He also wrote a great deal during his lifetime, including hymn collections, histories, biographies and his journals. After studying at Oxford, Wesley was ordained first as a deacon (1725), and then himself became a fellow at Oxford (1726), teaching Greek. He was ordained as a priest in 1728. After a failed mission to Georgia (1735–8), Wesley had a revelation while reading *Luther's Preface to the Epistle of the Romans* at a meeting in London. He felt strongly that his salvation was a certainty, and was moved to transmit that certainty to others. Most regular clergy were unnerved by his extreme passion, however, and shut him out. He went on to found the first Methodist chapel (1739) and the Moorfields Foundry, the Methodist headquarters.

Winckelmann, Johann Joachim (1717–68). Born in Germany, Winckelmann began his career with an education in theology and medicine at both Halle and Jena universities. However, he decided that art history was his true path in 1748, and travelled to Rome to become librarian to a cardinal there. He would also find a calling as an archaeologist, and in 1763 he was appointed the superintendent of Roman Antiquities. Perhaps the most influential work among many that he produced was *History of the Art of Antiquity* (1764). He finally met his end by murder in Trieste.

Wollstonecraft, Mary (1759–1797). Born in London, England, Wollstonecraft began her career as a teacher and headmistress of a school in Newington. There, along with her sister Eliza, she first came to grips with the realisation that the girls that she was trying to educate had been forcibly put in an inferior position to men by their society. She expressed her concerns in *Thoughts on the Education of Daughters* in 1787, in which she proclaimed that Enlightenment ideals demanded that women be given a decent education. She went on to become the governess to Lord Kingsborough and, following that, went to France for a number of years to observe and write about the political and social upheaval there. When she returned home, she joined a radical group, whose membership included William Godwin, Tom Paine, Fuseli and Priestley. Among her many writings, undoubtedly her most famous is *A Vindication of the Rights of Woman* (1792), a feminist classic. She eventually married Godwin and died while giving birth to her daughter Mary, who would gain fame for writing *Frankenstein*.

Zinzendorf, Nikolaus Ludwig, Graf von (1700–1760). Born in Dresden, Germany, Zinzendorf's religious sensibilities were shaped by the Pietism of his godfather Spener and of Franke's Paedagogium in Halle. He went on to become educated as a jurist at Wittenberg, also studying theology. He worked as a public official from 1721 to 1727, before abandoning that path to become the leader of a group of Moravians who were exiled because of their religious beliefs. He allowed the group to stay at his estate, where they founded a community called *Herrnhut* (the Lord's keeping). He became the founder of the Moravian church, and its bishop when he was ordained in Tübingen in 1734. He considered the Moravians to be part of the Lutheran church and focussed on 'Jesus mysticism' and the importance of 'religious community'. His actions put him at odds with more orthodox Christians, and he was exiled from Saxony in 1736. He continued to labour to expand the influence of Moravianism, founding congregations all over the world. He was also a prolific writer, producing more than 100 books and numerous Moravian hymns.

Suggestions for further reading

This bibliography does not aim at comprehensiveness. It is conceived as a guide to future reading and research, beyond the works mentioned in the text.

The topic of the Enlightenment has never been short of major general surveys. Besides those mentioned in the text, the reader might consult still valuable examples of an older style of interpretation well represented by the lively writing of Paul Hazard, *The European Mind 1680–1715* (first published in French in 1935, English translation 1963), and his *European Thought in the Eighteenth Century: From Montesquieu to Lessing* (1946 and 1963). Norman Hampson, *The Enlightenment* (London, 1968) is valuable for its extended treatment of science in this period. Lucien Goldmann, *The Philosophy of the Enlightenment: The Christian Burgess and the Enlightenment* (Cambridge, MA, 1973) examines this period from a Marxist perspective. Radical reinterpretations of the Enlightenment are well represented by Margaret C. Jacob, *The Radical Enlightenment: Pantheists, Freemasons and Republicans* (London, 1981). More recently, Jonathan Israel's trilogy, *Enlightenment Contested: Philosophy, Modernity and the Emancipation of Man 1670–1752* (Oxford, 2006), *The Radical Enlightenment: Philosophy and the Making of Modernity 1650–1750* (Oxford, 2001), and *Democratic Enlightenment: Philosophy, Revolution and Human Rights, 1750–1790* (Oxford, 2011) has been hotly debated. See also Anthony J. La Vopa, 'A New Intellectual History? Jonathan Israel's Enlightenment', *Historical Journal*, 52 (2009), 717–38; Antoine Lilti, 'Comment écrit-on l'histoire intellèctuelle des Lumières?', *Annales ESC* 64 (2009), 171–206. See also Keith Michael Baker and Peter Hans Reill, eds, *What's Left of the Enlightenment? A Post-Modern Question* (Stanford, CA, 2001); Daniel Gordon, ed., *Postmodernism and the Enlightenment: New Perspectives in Eighteenth-Century French Intellectual History* (New York, 2001). Conflicts over the meaning of the Enlightenment may be further explored in E. Behr, 'In Defence of Enlightenment: Foucault and Habermas', *German Studies Review*, 2 (1988), 97–109, and in Michel Foucault, 'What is Enlightenment?' in *The Foucault Reader*, ed. P. Rabinow (New York,

1984). See also Craig Calhoun, ed., *Habermas and the Public Sphere* (Cambridge MA, 1992).

National studies include Jonathan I. Israel, *The Dutch Republic: Its Rise, Greatness and Fall, 1477–1806* (Oxford, 1998), and Daniel Roche, *La France des Lumières* (Paris, 1993); Derek Beales, *Joseph II* (2 vols, Cambridge, 1987 and 2009); Linda Colley, *Britons: Forging the Nation, 1707–1837* (London, 1992). The reader might also like to consult James Buchan, *Crowded with Genius: The Scottish Enlightenment: Edinburgh's Moment of the Mind* (New York, 2003), Roy Porter, *The Creation of the Modern World: the Untold Story of the British Enlightenment* (New York, 2000); Elizabeth Badinter, *Les passions intéllectuelles*, (2 vols, Paris, 1999 and 2002). On the counter-Enlightenment see Isaiah Berlin, *Three Critics of the Enlightenment: Vico, Hamann, Herder* (Princeton, NJ, 2000), and Darrin M. McMahon, *Enemies of the Enlightenment: The French Counter-Enlightenment and the Making of Modernity* (Oxford and New York, 2002).

There is a limited number of comprehensive anthologies of Enlightenment writing. S. Eliot and Beverley Stern, eds, *The Age of Enlightenment* (2 vols, New York, 1979) is very full, but inexplicably omits Rousseau. Peter Gay, *The Enlightenment* (New York, 1973), is almost equally comprehensive, though paying less attention to science and the arts, and more to political writing. Jane Rendall, ed., *The Origins of the Scottish Enlightenment, 1707–1776* (London, 1978) is still the unique anthology on this topic.

Biographical coverage of Enlightenment figures is patchy. See however, John Hope Mason, *Irresistible Diderot* (London and New York, 1982); Arthur Wilson, *Diderot* (Oxford and New York, 1972); Peter France, *Diderot* (Oxford, 1983); Christopher Kelly, *Rousseau's Exemplary Life* (Ithaca, NY, 1987); Lester G. Crocker, *Jean-Jacques Rousseau* (2 vols, New York, 1968 and 1973); Robert Wokler, *Rousseau* (Oxford and New York, 1995); Maurice Cranston, *Rousseau* (2 vols, London, 1983 and 1991); Haydn Mason, *Voltaire: A Biography* (London, 1981); Richard Westfall, *Never at Rest: A Biography of Isaac Newton* (Cambridge, 1980). On Montesquieu, the classic biography is R. Shackleton, *Montesquieu: A Critical Biography* (Oxford, 1960). For Locke see John Yolton, *John Locke and the Way of Ideas* (New York, 1956), and Roger Woolhouse, *Locke: A Biography* (Oxford, 2007). Ronald Grimsley, *Jean D'Alembert 1717–1783* (Oxford, 1963) is still useful. For Hume see E. C. Mossner, *The Life of David Hume* (2nd edn, Oxford, 1980). Kant can be approached via Stefan Korner's readable *Kant* (London, 1955), Herder in F. M. Barnard, *Herder's Social and Political Thought* (Oxford, 1965). For more extreme thinkers, see A. C. Kors, *D'Holbach's Circle: An Enlightenment in Paris* (Princeton, NJ, 1977), and D. W. Smith, *Helvétius: A Study of Persecution*

(Oxford, 1965). Newton has been subjected to increasing examination in recent times, especially since the publication of the corpus of Newton's manuscripts by Richard Westfall, whose *Never at Rest: A Biography of Isaac Newton* (Cambridge, 1980), should be supplemented by Betty Jo Teeter Dobbs, *The Foundations of Newton's Alchemy: Or the 'Hunting of the Greene Lyon'* (Cambridge, 1975), and Margaret C. Jacob, *The Newtonians and the English Revolution, 1689–1720* (Hassocks, Sussex, 1976).

The ideas of the Enlightenment are difficult to assess without their social and political background. The American wars of this period which did so much to stretch the resources of Enlightenment monarchies are discussed in Paul W. Mapp, *The Elusive West and the Contest for Empire 1713–1763* (Chapel Hill, NC, 2011), and Walter R. Borneman, *The French and Indian Wars: Deciding the Fate of North America* (London, 2006). For the American Revolution and its relationship with the Enlightenment, see Garry Wills' much-debated *Inventing America: Jefferson's Declaration of Independence* (New York, 1978); Henry F. May, *The Enlightenment in America* (New York, 1976); and N. E. Cunningham, *The Pursuit of Reason* (Baton Rouge, LA, 1981). Enlightenment governments struggled to implement reforms often based on Enlightenment thinking. Here see Isabel V. Hull, *Sexuality, State and Civil Society in Germany, 1700–1815* (Ithaca, NY, 1996); Harvey Chisick, *The Limits of Reform in the Enlightenment: Attitudes Towards the Education of the Lower Classes in Eighteenth Century France* (Princeton, NJ, 1981); Marc Raeff, *The Well-Ordered Police State: Social and Institutional Change through Law in the Germanies and Russia, 1600–1800* (New Haven, CT, and London, 1984) remains one of the best studies in this field. The vital creation of new bureaucracies to carry out Enlightenment policies is examined in one national case by Anthony La Vopa, *Grace, Talent and Merit: Poor Students, Clerical Careers and Professional Ideology in Eighteenth-Century Germany* (Cambridge, 1988); state creation of universities in which these bureaucrats were trained is examined in William C. Clark, *Academic Charisma and the Origins of the Research University* (Chicago, 2006). More general studies include T. C. W. Blanning, *The Pursuit of Glory: The Five Revolutions That Made Modern Europe, 1648–1815* (London, 2007). Blanning has also written the short survey *The Eighteenth Century* (Oxford, 2000). Franco Venturi, *The End of the Old Regime in Europe 1768–1776: The First Crisis* (Princeton, NJ, 1989) should be read with Bernard Bailyn, *Atlantic History: Concept and Contours* (Cambridge, MA, 2005), and Thomas Benjamin, *The Atlantic World: Europeans, Africans, Indians and Their Shared History, 1400–1900* (Cambridge, 2009).

The growth of political economy centered on state, society and economics in ways that fed into Enlightenment debates on government. See

Richard Herr, *The Eighteenth-Century Revolution in Spain* (Princeton, NJ, 1958); S. L. Kaplan, *Bread, Politics and Political Economy in the Reign of Louis XV* (The Hague, 1976); I. Hont and M. Ignatieff, eds, *Wealth and Virtue: The Shaping of Political Economy in the Scottish Enlightenment* (Cambridge, 1983); I. Hont, ed., *Jealousy of Trade: International Competition and the Nation State in Historical Perspective* (Cambridge, MA, 2005); Ronald Meek, ed., *The Economics of Physiocracy* (Cambridge, MA, 1962); A. O. Hirschman, *The Passions and the Interests: Political Arguments for Capitalism before Its Triumph* (Princeton, NJ, 1977); Emma Rothschild, *Economic Sentiments: Adam Smith, Condorcet and the Enlightenment* (Cambridge, MA, 2001), and J. G. A. Pocock, *Virtue, Commerce and History: Essays on Political Thought and History, Chiefly in the Eighteenth Century* (Cambridge and New York, 1985); Catherine Larrère, *L'invention de l'économie au dix-huitième siècle: du droit naturel à la physiocratie* (Paris, 1992); see also Jean-Pierre Poirier, *Turgot: laissez-faire et progrès social* (Paris, 1999), Michael Sonnenscher, *Before the Deluge: Public Debt, Inequality and the Intellectual Origins of the French Revolution* (Princeton, NJ, 2007), and the classic Robert J. Shafer, *Economic Societies in the Spanish World, 1763–1826* (Syracuse, NY, 1958).

The slave trade was constitutive of the Enlightenment Atlantic world. R. B. Davis, *The Problem of Slavery in the Age of Revolution 1770–1823* (Ithaca, NY, 1995) remains the classic treatment, to be read alongside Sue Peabody, *There Are No Slaves in France: The Political Culture of Race and Slavery in the Ancien Regime* (New York, 1996); Philip D. Curtin, *The Rise and Fall of the Plantation Complex: Essays in Atlantic History* (Cambridge, 1990); Herbert Klein, *The Atlantic Slave Trade* (Cambridge, 1999); Michael Mullin, *Africa in America: Slave Acculturation and Resistance in the American South and the British Caribbean, 1736–1831* (Urbana, IL, 1992); David Eltis and David Richardson, eds., *Direction, Ethnicity and Mortality in the Transatlantic Slave Trade* (London, 1997); Mervyn C. Alleyne, *Roots of Jamaican Culture* (London, 1988); Gwendolyn M. Hall, *Africans in Colonial Louisiana: The Development of Afro-Creole Culture in the Eighteenth Century* (Baton Rouge, LA, 1992); Jon F. Sensbach, *A Separate Canaan: The Making of an Afro-Moravian World in North Carolina, 1763–1840* (Chapel Hill, NC, 1998). For Enlightenment abolitionism, see Thomas P. Slaughter, *The Beautiful Soul of John Woolman, Apostle of Abolition* (New York, 2008); Yves Benoit, *Diderot: De l'athéisme à l'anticolonialisme* (Paris, 1970); Sankar Muthu, *Enlightenment against Empire* (Princeton, NJ, 2003); and Robin Blackburn, *The Overthrow of Colonial Slavery 1776–1848* (London, 1988).

Recent scholarship argues that the Enlightenment would have been impossible without the rise of printing and reading cultures, the development of public opinion and a 'public sphere'. Habermas' major work is mentioned in the text. See Craig Calhoun, ed., *Habermas and the Public Sphere* (Cambridge, MA, 1992); E. Behr, 'In Defense of Enlightenment: Foucault and Habermas', *German Studies Review*, 2 (1988), 97–109; James van Horne Melton, *The Rise of the Public in Enlightenment Europe* (Cambridge, 2001); Jeffrey Ravel, *The Contested Parterre* (Ithaca, NY, 1999); Mona Ozouf, 'Public Opinion at the End of the Old Regime', *Journal of Modern History*, 60 (1988), 1–21; Dena Goodman, *The Republic of Letters: A Cultural History of the French Enlightenment* (Ithaca, NY, 1994); Anne Goldgar, *Impolite Learning: Conduct and Community in the Republic of Letters 1680–1750* (New Haven, CT, and London, 1995); Arlette Farge, *Subversive Words: Public Opinion in Eighteenth Century France* (University Park, PA, 1995); Sara Maza, *Private Lives and Public Affairs: The Causes Célèbres of Pre-Revolutionary France* (Berkeley, CA, 1993); Benjamin W. Redekop, *Enlightenment and Community: Lessing, Abbt, Herder, and the Quest for a German Public* (Montreal, 2000); John Brewer, *The Pleasures of the Imagination: English Culture in the Eighteenth Century* (Chicago, 1997). Work on print culture is well represented in Adrian Johns, *The Nature of the Book: Print and Knowledge in the Making* (Chicago, 1998). The legal and economic pre-conditions for writing are explored in Martha Woodmansee, 'The Genius and the Copyright: Economic and Legal Conditions of the Emergence of the "Author"', *Eighteenth Century Studies*, 17 (1984) as well as in Robert Darnton's classic *The Business of Enlightenment: A Publishing History of the Encyclopédie* (Cambridge, MA, 1979) and his *Great Cat Massacre and Other Episodes in French Cultural History* (New York, 1984). The underside of Enlightenment writing is examined in his *The Forbidden Best-Sellers of Pre-Revolutionary France* (London, 1996); see also his *The Literary Underground of the Old Régime* (Cambridge, MA, 1982); see also Richard B. Sher, *The Enlightenment and the Book: Scottish Authors and their Publishers in Eighteenth Century Britain, Ireland and America* (Chicago, 2006), and Hugh Amory and David D. Hall, eds, *The Colonial Book in the Atlantic World* (Cambridge and New York, 2000).

Recent work has also focussed on the idea of science as an Enlightenment public spectacle. See Jan Golinski, *Science as Public Culture: Chemistry and Enlightenment in Britain 1760–1820* (Cambridge, 1992); Jessica Riskin, *Science in the Age of Sensibility: The Sentimental Empiricists of the French Enlightenment* (Chicago, 2002); Julia V. Douthwaite, *The Wild Girl, Natural Man, and the Monster: Dangerous Experiments in the Age of Enlightenment* (Chicago, 2002); Simon Schaffer, 'Natural Philosophy and Public Spectacle in the Eighteenth Century', *History of Science* 21 (1983), 1–43; Robert Darnton, *Mesmerism and the End of the Enlightenment in France*

(Cambridge, MA, 1968); and the essays in William Clark, Jan Golinski, and Simon Schaffer, eds, *The Sciences in Enlightened Europe* (Chicago, 1999). For women in science, see Londa Schiebinger, *Nature's Body; Gender in the Making of Modern Science* (Boston, MA, 1993); Geoffrey V. Sutton, *Science for a Polite Society: Gender, Culture and the Demonstration of Enlightenment* (Boulder, CO, 1995).

For more highly organised institutional settings of science, see Daniel Roche, *Le siècle des lumières en province: Académies et académiciens provinciaux* (2 vols, Paris, 1978); Roger Hahn, *Anatomy of a Scientific Institution: The Paris Academy of Sciences 1666–1803* (Berkeley, CA, 1971); James E. McClellan III, *Science Reorganised: Scientific Societies in the Eighteenth Century* (New York, 1985); for colonial science see James E. McClellan III, *Saint Domingue and the Old Regime* (Chicago, 1992); I. Bernard Cohen, *Benjamin Franklin's Science* (Cambridge, MA, 1990); Lee Alan Dugatkin, *Mr. Jefferson and the Giant Moose: Natural History in Early America* (Chicago, 2009), and Thomas P. Slaughter, *The Natures of John and William Bartram* (University Park, PA, 2005). The run-up to the French Revolution is ably treated by Ken Alder, *Engineering the Revolution: Arms and Enlightenment in France 1763–1815* (Chicago, 1997) and Emma C. Spary, *Utopia's Garden: French Natural History from Old Regime to Revolution* (Chicago, 2000). More general treatment of Enlightenment science may be found in J. L. Heilbron, *Electricity in the Seventeenth and Eighteenth Centuries: A Study of Early Modern Physics* (Berkeley, CA, 1979); Lester G. Crocker, *Nature and Culture: Ethical Thought in the French Enlightenment* (Baltimore, MD, 1963); C. Glacken, *Traces on the Rhodian Shore: Nature and Culture in Western Thought* (Berkeley, CA, 1967); Mary Terrall, *The Man Who Flattened the Earth: Maupertuis and the Sciences in the Enlightenment* (Chicago, 2002); Richard Holmes, *The Age of Wonder: How the Romantic Generation Discovered the Beauty and Terror of Science* (New York, 2011); K. M. Baker, *Condorcet: From Natural Philosophy to Social Mathematics* (Chicago, 1975). For the mid-century life-sciences, there is still no substitute for Jacques Roger, *Les sciences de la vie dans la pensée francaise au XVIIIe siècle* (Paris, 1963), and his *Buffon: un philosophe au Jardin du Roi* (Paris, 1992). The emergence of global sciences is discussed in Richard Grove, *Green Imperialism: Colonial Expansion, Tropical Island Edens, and the Origins of Environmentalism 1600–1860* (Cambridge, 1997), and Richard Drayton, *Nature's Government: Science, Imperial Britain and the 'Improvement' of the World* (New Haven, CT, 2000); David Phillip Miller and Peter Hans Reill, eds, *Visions of Empire: Voyages, Botany and Representations of Nature* (Cambridge, 1996); David N. Livingstone and Charles W. J. Withers, eds,

Geography and Enlightenment (Chicago, 1999). Simon Schaffer, Lissa Roberts, Kapil Raj, James Delbourgo, eds, *The Brokered World: Go-Betweens and Global Intelligence 1770–1820* (Sagamore Beach, MA, 2009) has much to say about the history of science. R. E. Schofield, *The Lunar Society of Birmingham* (Oxford, 1963), is a classic account of an informal group of natural philosophers, and Lisbet Koerner, *Linnaeus: Nature and Nation* (Cambridge, MA, 1999) places natural history squarely in the context of political economy. More generally, see Barbara M. Benedict, *Curiosity: A Cultural History of Early Modern Enquiry* (Chicago, 2001); and Margaret C. Jacob, *Scientific Culture and the Making of the Industrial West* (Oxford and New York, 1997).

There are many recent accounts of the Enlightenment 'science of man'. See R. Fox, ed., *Inventing Human Science: Eighteenth-Century Domains* (Berkeley, 1995); John H. Zammito, *Kant, Herder, and the Birth of Anthropology* (Chicago, 2002); Larry Wolff and Marco Cipolloni, eds, *The Anthropology of the Enlightenment* (Stanford, CA, 2007); David Livingstone and Charles Withers, eds, *Geography and Enlightenment* (Chicago, 1999). The voyages of exploration profoundly changed the self-consciousness of the Enlightenment. See the pioneering work of Bernard Smith, *European Imagination and the South Pacific* (New Haven, CT, and London, 1982); Jonathan Lamb, *Preserving the Self in the South Seas, 1680–1840* (Chicago, 2001); Neil Rennie, *Far Fetched Facts: The Literature of Travel and the Idea of the South Seas* (Oxford, 1995); D. Outram, 'On Being Perseus: New Knowledge, Dislocation and Enlightenment Exploration', in Livingstone and Withers, eds, *Geography and Enlightenment*, 281–94; Greg Dening, *Mr. Bligh's Bad Language: Passion, Power and Theatre on the Bounty* (Cambridge, 1992); P. J. Marshall and Glyndwr Lewis, *The Great Map of Mankind: British Perceptions of the World in the Age of the Enlightenment*; Anne Salmond, *The Trial of the Cannibal Dog: Captain Cook in the South Seas* (London, 2001); for an account of two of Captain Cook's companions, see John Gascoigne, *Science in the Service of Empire: Joseph Banks, the British State and the Rise of Science* (Cambridge, 1998) and his *Joseph Banks and the English Enlightenment* (Cambridge, 1994); and N. Thomas, H. Guest and M. Dettelbach, eds, *Johann Reinhold Forster: Observations Made during a Voyage Round the World* (Honolulu, 1996). James Axtell, *Natives and Newcomers: The Cultural Origins of North America* (Oxford, 2001) discusses cross-cultural encounters between white settlers and Indian nations. Still valuable is the classic work by Robert F. Berkhofer, *Salvation and the Savage: An Analysis of Protestant Missions and American Indian Response* (Lexington, KY, 1965). Complex interactions between whites and Indians are described in Jorge

Canizares-Esguerra, *How to Write the History of the New World: Historiographies, Epistemologies and Identities in the Eighteenth-Century Atlantic World* (Stanford, CA, 2001).

The changing material culture of Enlightenment Europe and its colonies sparked debate on the moral and economic consequences of 'luxury'. See J. P. Sekora, *Luxury: The Concept in Western Thought*, (London, 1977); Maxine Berg and Elizabeth Eger, eds, *Luxury in the Eighteenth Century: Debates, Desires and Delectable Goods* (London, 2003) and Daniel Roche, *The History of Everyday Things: The Birth of Consumption in France 1600–1800* (Cambridge, 2000); John Brewer and Roy Porter, *Consumption and the World of Goods* (London, 1993); John Brewer, N. MacKendrick and J. H. Plumb, *The Birth of a Consumer Society: The Commercialisation of Eighteenth-Century England* (London, 1982) are the classics in the field. See also John E. Crowley, *The Invention of Comfort: Sensibility and Design in Early Modern Britain and Early America* (Baltimore, MD, and London, 2001).

Religious change was a major theme in the Enlightenment. Gordon Cragg, *The Church in the Age of Reason* (Oxford, 1960); W. R. Ward, *Christianity under the Ancien Regime 1648–1789* (Cambridge, 1999); Ward, *The Protestant Evangelical Awakening* (Cambridge and New York, 1992) remain the best general studies. See also the *Cambridge History of Christianity*, vol. VII: *Enlightenment, Revolution and Reawakening, 1660–1815*, ed. Timothy Tackett (Cambridge, 2006). Religious conflict within the Catholic Church is studied in Dale Van Kley, *The Jansenists and the Expulsion of the Jesuits from France 1757–1765* (New Haven, CT, 1975), while Carl Becker, *The Heavenly City of the Eighteenth-Century Philosophers* (New Haven, CT, 1932) points to the alternative Enlightenment 'religion' of reason. The classic account by Frank Manuel, *The Eighteenth Century Confronts the Gods* (New York, 1967), shows attempts to demystify religion by many of the *philosophes*, Hans Frei, *The Eclipse of Biblical Narrative* (New Haven, CT, 1977) discusses a different aspect of the same story. The classic study by John McManners, *Death and the Enlightenment: Changing Attitudes to Death among Christians and Unbelievers in Eighteenth-Century France* (Oxford, 1981) is still valuable. On Catholicism see R. Po-Chia Hsia, *The World of Catholic Renewal 1540–1770* (Cambridge and New York, 1998). On the missionary churches see Colin Podmore, *The Moravian Church in England 1728–1760* (New York, 1998); Frank Lambert, *'Pedlar in Divinity': George Whitefield and the Transatlantic Revivals, 1737–1770* (Princeton, NJ, 1994). Religious tolerance was still highly problematic for the Enlightenment: Perez Zagorin, *How the Idea of Religious Toleration Came to the West* (Princeton, NJ, 2003); Benjamin S. Kaplan, *Divided by Faith: Religious Conflict and the Practice of Toleration in Early Modern Europe* (Cambridge, MA, 2007); John Marshall, *John Locke, Toleration and Early Enlightenment Culture* (Cambridge, 2006); Roy Porter and Ole Grell, eds, *Toleration in Enlightenment Europe* (Oxford, 2000); Lynn Hunt, Margaret C. Jacob and Wijnand Mijnhardt, *The Book that Changed Europe: Picart's and Bernard's Religious Ceremonies of the World* (Cambridge, MA, 2010); Geoffrey Adams, *The Huguenots and French Opinion 1685–1787: The Enlightenment Debate on Toleration* (Waterloo, ON, 1991). See also Michael Heyd, *Be Sober and Reasonable: The Critique of Enthusiasm in the Late Seventeenth and Early Eighteenth Centuries* (Leiden, 1995), and Robert E. Sullivan, *John Toland and the Deist Controversy: A Study in Adaptations* (Cambridge, MA, 1982). For two other major religions, Frederick Quinn, *The Sum of All Heresies: The Image of Islam in Western Thought* (Oxford, 2008), and Lionel Kochan, *The Making of Western Jewry 1600–1819* (New York, 2004); Jonathan I. Israel, *European Jewry in the Age of Mercantilism 1550–1750* (Oxford and New York, 1989), and Shmuel Feiner, *The Jewish Enlightenment* (Philadelphia, 2002). For a comparative study, see David Sorkin, *The Religious Enlightenment: Protestants, Jews and Catholics from London to Vienna* (Princeton, NJ, 2008).

Finally, there has been much recent work on the Enlightenment role of women. See Florence Mauro, *Emilie du Châtelet* (Paris, 2006); Linda Timmermans, *L'accès des femmes à la culture sous l'ancien régime* (Paris, 2005); Carla Hesse, *The Other Enlightenment: How French Women Became Modern* (Princeton, NJ, 2001); Catherine Rabinger, ed., *Femmes savantes et femmes d'esprit: Women Intellectuals of the French Eighteenth Century* (New York, 1994); S. Knott and B. Taylor, *Women, Gender and Enlightenment* (New York, 2005); Steven D. Kale, *French Salons, High Society and Political Sociability from the Old Régime to the Revolution of 1848* (Baltimore, MD, 2004); Antoine Lilti, *Le monde des salons: sociabilité et mondanité à Paris au dix-huitième siècle* (Paris, 2005).

Electronic sources for further research

Today's historian has been blessed by the production of a large number of electronic search engines for Enlightenment materials, search engines which can often obviate the need for travel to distant libraries and archives. Undoubtedly the premier of these search engines is ECCO (Eighteenth-Century Collections Online), a research database that includes every significant English- and foreign-language title printed in the United Kingdom, along with many works from North America. (Searches for North American materials should be supplemented by Evans Early American Imprint.) ECCO is scanned rather than transcribed, which can lead to problems reading faint or broken type. But the extent of its reach makes it an invaluable research tool. It holds more than 32 million pages of text and over 205,000 individual volumes, all fully searchable. However, ECCO is not without its problems. Students should consult Patrick Spedding, '"The New Machine": Discovering the Limits of ECCO', *Eighteenth-Century Studies*, 44 (2011), 437–53. ECCO is also discussed on http://earlymodernonlinebib.wordpress.com/category/ecco.

Some leading research libraries host similar if inevitably smaller projects. The Bibliothèque Nationale in Paris offers a large searchable range of scanned original editions for free download at http://gallica.bnf.fr. The Bodleian Library, Oxford, hosts a project known as Electronic Enlightenment. This is primarily concerned with correspondence and related documentation, and is also a unique community project 'continually building new research into its database and encouraging external users to participate in its evolution'. The project also runs an annual colloquium on the sociology of the letter. It can be accessed at www.e-enlightenment.com. At the British Library in London, a digitisation project will make available online out-of-copyright books published between 1700 and 1870, the majority from continental Europe.

For Enlightenment periodical literature, there is a valuable database hosted by the Bergische Universität, at Wuppertal in Germany, the 'Repertorium deutscher wissenschaftlicher Periodike des 18. Jahrhunderts' (Repertory of German learned periodicals of the eighteenth century) which can be accessed at www.izwt.uni-wuppertal.de/repertorium/MS Main.html. It contains contents and tables of most eighteenth-century periodicals that published scientific articles (a large and poorly defined category in the Enlightenment), as well as reviews. There is a similar website at the University of Bielefeld in Germany for literary journals and review periodicals of the German Enlightenment (1750–1815). See www.ub.uni-bielefeld.de/diglib/aufklaerung/index.htm.

Another major research resource, a searchable electronic search engine for the *Encyclopédie*, is also available. This project has gone through several incarnations, which means that it is not immune from inaccuracy. It includes not only the four-volume *Supplément* to the *Encyclopédie*, but also the proofs of censored articles and related legal documents bound together in the so-called 'Eighteenth Volume'. Researchers should try to compare entries with images of the relevant pages.

Many historical figures from the Enlightenment have digitised archives of their own papers and authored books. For example the poet Thomas Gray at www.thomasgray.org. The poet, playwright and spy Aphra Behn may be researched through the online journal www.aphrabehn.org/aphraonline/Aphra_Online_vol_1_cpp.pdf.

Maps have also been digitised. Eighteenth-century Paris can be revisited with the aid of http://pds.lib.harvard.edu/pds/view/7289023. This site has the capability of zooming into the building level. The Turgot plan for Paris, and a variety of other maps of Paris between 1540 and 1800 are available on http://perso.numericable.fr/parisbal/plans/Plansanciens.html.

Electronic sources make invaluable teaching tools. See Alison Muri, 'Teaching the Eighteenth Century Online from Ctrl-7 to Digital Editions', at http://english.illinoisstate.edu/digitaldefoe/teaching/muri1.html.

It is to be hoped that this small selection of electronic resources available to the student, researcher and teacher, will encourage all their efforts by making accessible more material than could previously have been dreamed of. What use this material is put to, however, remains as usual up to individual judgement.

Index